Advance Praise for *Space*

'India's space programme, founded in 1963, is an outstanding success. It has faced many odds but has always overcome them, going from strength to strength. Dinesh Sharma narrates this voyage wonderfully well. The book is both very educative and engaging.'

Jairam Ramesh
Member of Parliament, former minister,
and author of *The Light of Asia*

'This excellent book is a comprehensive story of one of India's great success stories. *Space* will inspire generations to come.'

Nandan Nilekani
Co-founder and Chairman, Infosys; and
Founding Chairman, UIDAI (Aadhaar)

'The Indian space programme is an engineering success story closely followed in the country and abroad. India now routinely launches satellites with fewer resources than most other space-faring countries. Dinesh Sharma tells us how this became possible through two sets of stories – India in space and Indians in space – to unfold individual and statist ambitions that have made this possible. Written in lucid prose, the book will appeal to readers across age and professions for an interesting overview on the people, the institutions and the projects that made this history.'

Jahnavi Phalkey
Founding Director, Science Gallery Bengaluru

SPACE

SPACE

The India Story

DINESH C. SHARMA

B L O O M S B U R Y
NEW DELHI • LONDON • OXFORD • NEW YORK • SYDNEY

BLOOMSBURY INDIA
Bloomsbury Publishing India Pvt. Ltd
Second Floor, LSC Building No. 4, DDA Complex, Pocket C – 6 & 7,
Vasant Kunj, New Delhi, 110070

First published in India 2025
This edition published 2025

ISBN: PB: 978-93-61315-45-9; eBook: 978-93-61318-30-6
2 4 6 8 10 9 7 5 3 1

Typeset in Bembo by Manipal Technologies Limited
Printed and bound in India by Gopsons Papers Pvt. Ltd., Noida

FSC
www.fsc.org
100%
Paper from well-managed forests
FSC® C191020

To find out more about our authors and books visit www.bloomsbury.com
and sign up for our newsletters

Contents

Abbreviations

AEC	Atomic Energy Commission
APPLE	Ariane Passenger Payload Experiment
ASLV	Augmented Satellite Launch Vehicle
ASTE	Aircraft Systems Testing Establishment
ATS	Applications Technology Satellite
BAS	Bharatiya Antariksha Station
BJP	Bharatiya Janata Party
BSIR	Board of Scientific and Industrial Research
CARE	Crew Module Atmospheric Re-entry Experiment
CME	Coronal Mass Ejection
CNES	Centre National d'Etudes Spatiales
COSPAR	Committee on Space Research
CSIR	Council of Scientific and Industrial Research
DAE	Department of Atomic Energy
DFRL	Defence Food Research Laboratory
DoS	Department of Space
DRDO	Defence Research and Development Organisation
DTH	Direct-to-Home
ECLSS	Environmental Control and Life Support System
ESA	European Space Agency
FAA	Federal Aviation Authority
GSLV	Geosynchronous Satellite Launch Vehicle
GTO	Geosynchronous Transfer Orbit
HAL	Hindustan Aeronautics Limited
HSFC	Human Space Flight Centre

IAF	Indian Air Force
IAM	Institute of Aerospace Medicine
ICSU	International Council of Scientific Unions
ICBM	Intercontinental Ballistic Missile
IGY	International Geophysical Year
IISc	Indian Institute of Science
IMD	India Meteorological Department
INCOSPAR	Indian National Committee for Space Research
Insat	Indian National Satellite
IN-SPACe	Indian National Space Promotion and Authorisation Centre
IRS	Indian Remote Sensing Satellite
ISAC	ISRO Satellite Centre
ISRO	Indian Space Research Organisation
ISS	International Space Station
ISSP	Indian Scientific Satellite Project
JSC	Johnson Space Centre
LAM	Liquid Apogee Motor
LEO	Low Earth Orbit
LPP	Liquid Propulsion Project
LPSC	Liquid Propulsion Systems Centre
MAVEN	Mars Atmosphere and Volatile Evolution Mission
MIP	Moon Impact Probe
MiST	Water-Mist Fire Suppression Experiment
MIT	Massachusetts Institute of Technology
MOM	Mars Orbiter Mission
MTCR	Missile Technology Control Regime
NAL	National Aerospace Laboratories
NASA	National Aeronautics and Space Administration
NDA	National Defence Academy

NEEMO	NASA Extreme Environment Mission Operations
NGLV	Next Generation Launch Vehicle
NPC	National Planning Committee
NPL	National Physical Laboratory
NRSA	National Remote Sensing Agency
PAM	Payload Assist Module
PAT	Pad Abort Test
PEC	Punjab Engineering College
PMO	Prime Minister's Office
PRL	Physical Research Laboratory
PSLV	Polar Satellite Launch Vehicle
PTI	Press Trust of India
PUC	Pre-university Course
SAC	Space Applications Centre
SEP	Societe Europeenne de Propulsion
SAR	Synthetic Aperture Radar
SHAR	Sriharikota High Altitude Range
SITE	Satellite Instructional Television Experiment
SOHO	Solar and Heliospheric Observatory
SSPO	Sun-Synchronous Polar Orbit
SSTC	Space Science and Technology Centre
STS	Space Transportation System
SRE	Space Capsule Recovery Experiment
TIFR	Tata Institute of Fundamental Research
TERLS	Thumba Equatorial Rocket Launching Station
UN	United Nations
USSR	Union of Soviet Socialist Republics
VOM	Venus Orbiter Mission
VSSC	Vikram Sarabhai Space Centre

Introduction

THE EXPLORATION OF OUTER space and the application of space technology for the benefit of humanity is one of the greatest scientific achievements of the 20th century. It is on a par with other momentous turning points in human history such as the development of nuclear energy and the nuclear bomb as well as the discovery of antibiotics. Each such scientific landmark heralded a so-called new age – the nuclear age, the space age, the golden age of antibiotics and so on. Among all such endeavours, the space age stands out for its continuing and wide-ranging impacts on the everyday lives of billions of people around the globe. It has also kept a sense of curiosity and adventure alive through grand exploratory projects and discoveries related to our universe and beyond. We know more about the Earth and its atmosphere, celestial neighbours like the Moon, the planetary system and the universe than ever before.

The benefits of the space age are for all to use – better communications, direct-to-home broadcasting, navigation and rescue systems, weather forecasting, disaster warning, telemedicine, distance education, natural resources monitoring, urban planning and so on. Space technology and its spin-offs have touched our lives in multiple ways, making them comfortable and enjoyable. At the same time, space technology has promoted adventure, courage and imagination through human space travel. Among the space-faring nations, a new race began at the turn of the century to reach the moon and send humans to outer space for longer stays. From the time when space travel was the exclusive domain of fighter jet pilots trained as astronauts, we are about to enter the era of space tourism. Tickets for space travel are available for sums between US$200,000 and US$450,000. Virgin Galactic, a pioneering space tourism company, has a waiting list of 800 passengers. The new edition of the space age is going to be as exciting as it was when it all began.

Fortunately, India has not been a mere bystander in the space age. Our scientists were active participants in international processes, which led to the birth of the space age in 1957. Within five years of the space era beginning with the launch of Sputnik, India took baby steps in the space age. The Indian space programme stands out as one of the best success stories of independent India. From its humble beginnings with sounding rockets fired from the Kerala coast to launching landmark interplanetary missions such as Chandrayaan and Mars Orbiter Mission (MOM), India has firmly established itself as a significant player in the global space arena. Now, it enters a new phase with its most ambitious mission ever – the human space flight, Gaganyaan.

India put together the technological building blocks of this magnificent edifice one by one. There are very few developing countries that have deployed home-grown space technology for applications ranging from communication and remote sensing to national security. We stumbled on the way but never lost sight of the goal. In the 1960s, when the space programme started, people wondered how a country steeped in poverty, hunger and illiteracy could think of developing a space programme and use it for the welfare of the masses. A country that did not have telephone lines, terrestrial television networks or electricity in villages leapfrogged to satellite communication, direct broadcasting and remote sensing within two decades. It is a remarkable – and fascinating –

story. This book is an attempt to provide a concise overview of this journey with all its twists and turns, heroes and villains.

The book is divided into two sections, one about the journey of the Indian space programme (with chapters on early years, launch vehicles, satellites and applications, interplanetary missions) and the other about Indian astronauts, past and future. It is not a chronological or technological history of the Indian Space Research Organisation (ISRO) or the space programme, but I have tried to emphasise the context and the processes relating to important pit stops in India's space journey. Sometimes there is criticism about celebrating the lives and contributions of Indian-origin astronauts like Sunita Williams, Kalpana Chawla or Raja Chari because they are not Indian citizens. To me, they represent extraordinary tales of determination, hard work, courage and perseverance, and they need to be celebrated for this reason. As explorers, they are global citizens, and their Indian roots are secondary. Our young minds have a lot to learn from them.

I consider myself a child of the space age, having been born in the same year as the historic space flight of Yuri Gagarin. It was an interesting time to grow up. Science was seen as the promise of the future and a solution to all our problems. Yuri Gagarin, Valentina Tereshkova and Neil Armstrong were household names in India in the 1960s, occupying large spaces in newspapers and magazines. Every space mission of the Soviet Union and its space heroes kindled the public imagination, given the large sway held by the Soviet propaganda juggernaut in India. Closer to home, the direct broadcasting experiment, called the Satellite Instructional Television Experiment (SITE), was the first time Indian people realised the potential of space technology. The image of India's first satellite, Aryabhata, printed on currency notes and postal stamps is still fresh in my mind.

For several generations of Indians like me, Rakesh Sharma's 1984 space journey onboard a Soviet spaceship remains ingrained in their memories. It was an iconic moment when the then prime minister, Indira Gandhi, asked Sharma in a televised interaction, 'How does India look from outer space?', and a smiling Sharma instantly replied, '*Sare Jahan Se Achcha.*' As a budding science reporter at the news wire service Press Trust of India (PTI), I was part of the teams in Delhi and Bangalore that covered different facets of Sharma's space journey while seniors reported from Moscow and Baikonur. I covered several public events of Rakesh Sharma and Ravish Malhotra that followed Sharma's flight as well as press conferences of visiting NASA and Soviet scientists and astronauts. In this period, the most exciting of all was the opportunity I got to cover launches of Indian space missions from the Sriharikota range, which I have described in the book.

As a science reporter, I have benefited immensely from my interactions over the decades with several pioneering scientists and policymakers connected with the ISRO and related scientific bodies – Prof. M.G.K. Menon, Dr Vasant Gowarikar, Prof. Satish Dhawan, Dr A.P.J. Abdul Kalam, Prof. Yashpal, Dr Y.S. Rajan, Dr N. Seshagiri, Prof. Roddam Narasimha, Dr A.P. Mitra and Dr Ashok Parthasarathi. It is only later in my career as a book writer that I could fully appreciate the larger context and significance of their contributions to the space programme and science and technology, in general. While I bring this personal experience of covering major scientific events in the past four decades, this book is not an impressionistic account of the space programme. I dug into the archives, historical material and the work of other scholars and interviewed experts to put together this book. I express my gratitude to all the experts, writers and archivists who helped me.

I am particularly indebted to S.P.K. Gupta, PTI's Moscow correspondent in the 1980s who extensively covered the India–USSR joint space flight and diligently kept notes and copies of his despatches from Moscow. He was generous in sharing the material, including pictures, with me a few months before he passed away in January 2023. This apart, I have learned a great deal about science writing from him. I must thank Chirag Thakkar, associate publisher at Bloomsbury India, for seeing the potential in this idea and putting the book through fast-track. The editorial, design and marketing teams of Bloomsbury India deserve a big thanks for putting in a great deal of effort in this project. Annu Anand has been a doting companion through all my book projects, and this one is no exception.

Hope you enjoy reading it as much as I enjoyed writing it.

A note about city names and web links: The names of several cities mentioned in the book have changed over time. To retain the historical flavour, old names have been retained until the time new names were adopted. Given the dynamic nature of the Internet, some web links cited in this book may have changed since their first publication or may no longer be valid.

I

India in Space

1

The Space Age Comes to Thumba

On 27 February 2024, the Indian Space Research Organisation (ISRO) presented to the nation four astronaut designates at a simple ceremony at the Vikram Sarabhai Space Centre (VSSC), considered to be the mother organisation of the Indian space programme. It was befitting that the space agency formally launched its most ambitious project ever, human space flight, at a place where its journey started sixty years ago. Not far from VSSC is Thumba, India's first window to outer space. The selection of Thumba, a tiny fishing village on the scenic Kerala coast, to establish India's pioneering rocket launching pad was not a mere historic coincidence as is often the case with the location of ventures of likely national significance. In the case of Thumba, it was the result of a curious mix of geography, science and great ambition.

An ideal site had to fulfil two major criteria: it should be on a coast for safety reasons, and it should be in the vicinity of Earth's equatorial line because scientists wished to study meteorological and atmospheric problems along the magnetic equator. This narrowed the search to a part of India's west coast where the equatorial line passed through the Indian land mass. Kanyakumari, on India's southernmost tip, is closest to the geographic equator, while the stretch from Trivandrum to Alleppey on the Kerala coast is close to the magnetic equator.

The earth's magnetic field does not coincide with its spin axis, making the geographic and magnetic equator distinct. The magnetic equator passes across only a few regions that could afford accessible sites for firing rockets to study the earth's magnetic field as well as the physics and the chemistry of the upper atmosphere.

The coast near Quilon town appeared to meet the scientific criteria but posed logistic problems: the area was highly populated, and the sea had substantial fishing activity. Rocket launches need sparse areas since burnt-out parts could fall on the ground or the sea. Locating a rocket launch pad near Quilon would have involved a sizeable human displacement and intermittent loss of livelihood for fishing communities. Another factor that went against the site was its rather peculiar name – Vellana Thuruthu (Malayalam for 'island of white elephant'). Scientists wanted to steer clear of such a place that could potentially make it a national joke.[1] So, Thumba, 32 km south of Quilon, was selected. It was relatively less populated and had a lower density of fishing crafts.

Through the 1960s, Thumba became India's gateway to enter the space age and the site of India's first international scientific facility that attracted scientists from countries in the Western as well as the Soviet blocs at the height of the Cold War. Before embarking upon this fascinating story, let us get the big picture of the organisation of scientific research in a newly independent nation beset with widespread poverty, illiteracy and hunger.

In the decades leading to the end of colonial rule in August 1947, a distinct vision of guiding India to the path of industrialisation and development through natural resources planning and the application of science and technology emerged from the Indian National Congress (INC), which led the political movement against the British. The exercise to prepare a blueprint was initiated by INC president Subhas Chandra Bose, who, in 1938, formed the National Planning Committee (NPC) with Jawaharlal Nehru as the chairperson. It was a unique collaborative venture involving political leaders, scientists, industrialists and businesspeople.

On the other hand, the British, fighting a bitter Second World War, enlisted their colonies to supply men and materials by promoting industrial research in the colonies. This gave birth to a string of research laboratories in India, Australia and Canada modelled after the ones working under the Board of Scientific and Industrial Research (BSIR) in Britain. It eventually inaugurated the era of State-funded organised science in the form of a string of laboratories under the umbrella body, Council of Scientific and Industrial Research (CSIR).

Another important third stream of scientific research, a prominent one and often referred to by historians as the nationalist science as opposed to the colonial science, consisted of independent research centres founded by individual scientists: Indian Statistical Institute of Prasanta Chandra Mahalanobis, Bose Institute of Jagadish Chandra Bose, Saha Institute of Nuclear Physics of Meghnad Saha, Tata Institute of Fundamental Research (TIFR) of Homi Jehangir Bhabha, Raman Research Institute of C.V. Raman and Physical Research Laboratory (PRL) of Vikram Sarabhai.

In addition, large organisations like the India Meteorological Department (IMD), Geological Survey of India, university departments and research stations, too, were engaged in scientific research at the time of India's independence in 1947.

Theoretical and experimental physics was a common thread that tied top scientists in the 1930s and 1940s – Raman, Saha, K.S. Krishnan, S.N. Bose, J.C. Bose, Ruchi Ram Sahni, Bhabha and several others. The community of Indian physicists had all the right credentials. One was a Nobel laureate; several of them were fellows of the Royal Society; they worked with leading physicists like Albert Einstein, Niels Bohr and Ernest Rutherford; they were well connected with their Western peers; and many had discoveries named after them (Raman Effect, Bhabha–Heitler Cascade, Bose–Einstein Statistics, Mahalanobis Distance and the like). Path-breaking discoveries in particle physics such as the discovery of the neutron, the splitting of the nucleus and the release of energy through fission evoked great interest among Indian experimental physicists, and they decided to pursue nuclear research. Some of them saw the possibility of producing electric power by harnessing nuclear energy. The use of nuclear bombs in Hiroshima and Nagasaki brought out the horrors of nuclear weapons but did not deflect Indian scientists from pursuing nuclear research. A clutch of Indian physicists, according to historian Robert S. Anderson, had 'an advanced grasp of the potential power of the nucleus of the uranium atom', even before the bombings in Japan in 1945.[2]

After Independence, Prime Minister Nehru wanted to translate into practice his vision of applying science to solve basic problems of hunger, poverty and lack of infrastructure like electricity, roads, health and so on. He had a tough task at hand – organising scientific research to optimally use scarce resources available so that it could deliver results quickly. Advising him was a set of elite scientists: Homi Jehangir Bhabha, Shanti Swarup Bhatnagar (head of CSIR) and P.C. Mahalanobis, among others. Nehru also had the British scientist Patrick Blackett – who was familiar with the work of Indian scientists – as his scientific and military adviser.

Bhabha was born in an elite Parsi family in Bombay and educated in Cambridge. Forced to return to India during the Second World War years, he joined the Indian Institute of Science at the insistence of C.V. Raman and continued his research on cosmic rays. He was closely networked with contemporary physicists such as Paul Dirac, Niels Bohr, Bernard Peters, John Cockroft and Cecil Frank Powell, and was nominated thrice for the Nobel Prize for Physics for his work on cosmic rays. Later, he founded TIFR with financial help from the Tata Trusts.

As per the NPC blueprint, the Planning Commission (it had the same abbreviation NPC as it was called National Planning Commission initially) was established, and Mahalanobis was tasked with the formulation of national plans. The expansion of the network of laboratories under CSIR got top priority after 1947, while TIFR and Indian Statistical Institute (ISI) were accorded the legal status of 'institutes of national importance' and received funding from the central government. Nehru acceded to Bhabha's request to establish a separate Department of Atomic Energy (DAE) to work on nuclear energy and keep it under the administrative control of the prime minister.

The Advisory Committee for Coordinating Scientific Work was formed in 1949 under the Ministry of Education to handle cross-cutting issues in research, training and India's participation in international science projects and conferences. The idea was to utilise available resources optimally while exploring new areas of research of relevance to India. One of the major international projects in which Indian scientists participated was the International Geophysical Year (IGY) initiated by the International Council of Scientific Unions (ICSU). It was a landmark project that eventually led the world into the space age and unwittingly triggered the space race between the two superpowers.

Artificial Moons and the Space Age

The IGY was observed for eighteen months, from July 1957 to December 1958, coinciding with the period when solar activity would be at its high point. This would have enabled many geophysical studies throughout the world. In the preparatory scientific meetings held since 1952, ICSU proposed that Earth-orbiting satellites could be a novel way to study Earth and its atmosphere. In response to this call, both America and the Union of Soviet Socialist Republics (USSR) announced plans to develop satellites, which were referred to as 'artificial moons' since till then the only Earth-orbiting satellite was the Moon. The Naval Research Laboratory in America started working on its Vanguard satellite in 1955, while the USSR worked on an IGY satellite. This was seen as an extension of the expertise the two blocs had acquired for making intercontinental ballistic missiles (ICBMs) during the Second World War and the years that followed. It was widely believed that the launchers used to fire missiles could be repurposed to inject a satellite into an orbit around the Earth.

India was an active participant in the IGY preparations. The effort was led by a sub-committee of CSIR's Radio Research Committee, which was housed in the National Physical Laboratory (NPL). The sub-committee formed in March 1953 had five members: NPL director K.S. Krishnan (chairperson), S.K. Mitra, H.J. Bhabha, K.R. Ramanathan and the director of the Solar Physics Laboratory at Kodaikanal Observatory as an ex-officio member.[3] The committee was officially notified by the government to represent India in IGY and coordinate related projects domestically.

In June 1953, Bhabha expressed his inability to serve on the committee 'owing to pressure of work'.[4] Instead, he suggested the name of PRL director Vikram Sarabhai. Krishnan forwarded the suggestion to the government, and it was accepted. Subsequently, more members were added to the panel. Ashesh Prosad Mitra of the Institute of Radio Physics and Electronics at the University of Calcutta, who was a visiting assistant professor at Pennsylvania State College in 1953, attended the meetings of the International Union of Scientific Radio in America. He later joined NPL and actively participated in IGY activities.

Like Bhabha, Sarabhai was engaged in the study of cosmic rays, fast-moving particles from outer space produced by the Sun and other exploding stars that travel all over the universe. Cosmic ray research was a fascinating subject in the first half of the 20th century since a study of cosmic rays could help unravel the mysteries of outer space and the universe. Scientists launched high-altitude balloons carrying detectors and set up ground-based observatories to track secondary cosmic rays. Bhabha started a balloon programme at TIFR, while Sarabhai initiated experimental work at PRL to study variations in cosmic ray intensity concerning solar activity. This was one of the scientific topics to be investigated during the IGY.

The Cambridge-educated Sarabhai was a multifaceted personality. He belonged to a prominent industrial family of Ahmedabad whose members were close to Mahatma Gandhi and participated in the freedom movement. Besides his scientific pursuits, Sarabhai managed several industrial units of the family concerning textiles, chemicals and pharmaceuticals. He also founded new ventures like the Ahmedabad Textile Industry Research Association (ATIRA) and Operations Research Group (ORG). However, PRL remained closest to his heart, and he devoted much of his energies to this institution.

Under the national committee of IGY, fourteen sub-committees were formed to look after various disciplines like geomagnetism, ionosphere and meteorology. New astrophysical observatories were set up, and old ones got new equipment. Lloyd Berkner, an American physicist who was behind the idea of IGY, met Prime Minister Nehru in January 1957, reflecting the importance IGY attached to India's participation.[5]

While IGY was underway, the USSR surprised the world by launching the first-ever satellite, Sputnik I (Russian for 'travelling companion'), on 4 October 1957 from Baikonur Cosmodrome. It was a spherical ball made of aluminium alloy with four antennas jetting out, weighing about 80 kg. It became the first artificial object to reach outer space and orbit around the Earth. The satellite was active for ninety-two days and orbited the Earth 1400 times. Radio signals it sent in two frequencies were monitored around the world, and the satellite could be seen with the naked eye at several locations. Sputnik was not just a technological achievement but a political statement in a world bitterly divided by the Cold War. The satellite sent shock waves throughout the Western world and created a sense of euphoria in the Soviet bloc.

With Sputnik I, the world entered the space age – just as it entered the atomic age with the bombing of Hiroshima and Nagasaki in 1945. The Soviets followed up by launching Sputnik II within a month, with the first live cargo, a dog named Laika, and Sputnik III with an array of scientific instruments in May 1958.

The USSR scored another first by sending a human being, Yuri Gagarin, into an orbit around Earth on 12 April 1961. The mission took place under a cloak of secrecy. Even Gagarin's wife did not know about it. Secrecy was necessitated due to the dangers involved in this unique mission. Twenty of the forty-eight dogs flown before Gagarin's flight had perished. Ten of them were flown to test the Vostok capsule, which was to fly Gagarin, and four of the canines did not survive. The Soviets were in a hurry following news reports about a possible human space mission from America.

Gagarin was a twenty-seven-year-old fighter pilot (with the rank of second lieutenant) in the Soviet air force. He became the first human being to leave the Earth's atmosphere and enter outer space. His short flight (total duration from the launch to landing was 108 minutes), during which the spacecraft orbited the Earth once, made Gagarin a national hero and an international icon. He survived the space flight but died mysteriously during a routine training flight in 1968. Gagarin was followed by Gherman Titov, who became the first human to spend a full day in orbit. After a few more successful flights with male cosmonauts, the USSR launched the first woman to outer space: Valentina Tereshkova on 19 June 1963.

America launched its first satellite, Explorer I, on 31 January 1958. The same year, a dedicated civilian space agency, the National Aeronautics and Space Administration (NASA), was founded. America started training astronauts much before the formation of NASA under Project Mercury. Space capsules with animals – chimpanzees and rhesus monkeys – were launched and recovered after short flights.[6] Yuri Gagarin's flight upstaged NASA. It hurriedly launched its first human mission on 5 May 1961 by hurtling into space Alan Shepard, a thirty-seven-year-old Navy commander, in a small space capsule atop a Redstone rocket. It was a suborbital flight. Unlike Gagarin, Shepard did not orbit Earth during his 15-minute journey to space.

The emerging field of space became a tool for political supremacy and whipping up nationalist feelings. America was humiliated in the Bay of Pigs in Cuba, and then came Gagarin's successful fight. Against this backdrop, Shepard's short space sojourn came as a morale booster for the

American public and the political leadership. NASA's first orbital flight came in February 1962 with John Glenn.

In 1962, President Kennedy challenged American scientists to put an American on the Moon before the end of the decade. This sent NASA into a frenzy. The space race heated up with several human flights from the Soviets and Americans – multi-cosmonaut flights, space flights involving spacewalks, space docking and an orbiting crewed mission around the Moon. The race saw many mishaps and serious accidents killing cosmonauts and astronauts who were then idolised as national heroes in their respective homelands. Finally, the space race reached its peak, which also proved to be a landmark in human history, on 16 July 1969 when American astronauts Neil Armstrong and Edwin 'Buzz' Aldrin became the first humans to walk on the Moon. It was a momentous step for humanity. With this, America successfully won the space race, at least in the first round.

In comparison to Americans and the Soviets, India's participation in IGY was modest as it was a newly independent country with a meagre budget for scientific research and weak technological and engineering capabilities. Scientific results of studies conducted by Indians during IGY were incremental, but it opened new vistas for Indian scientists and introduced them to a new field of science and engineering – satellites – according to historian Rajesh Kochhar.[7] In the meetings of IGY and ICSU, Indian scientists could interact with peers from America, the USSR and other countries, and forge new networks. As a part of an IGY project, the Smithsonian Astrophysical Observatory established a powerful camera at the Nainital Observatory to track artificial earth satellites. The event was considered important enough for the *New York Times* to publish a Nainital-datelined story about the camera.

A Space Programme for India

The IGY experience was vital for the nascent space research community in India. It 'paved the way for the Indian space programme under Sarabhai. He had already been interested in observational studies of the impact of solar activity on cosmic rays. The IGY exposure helped Sarabhai expand his horizons,' notes Kochhar.[8] While it is true that IGY helped Sarabhai and other Indian scientists expand their horizons and make contacts with international peers, the question of which Indian laboratory should lead post-IGY activities was a vital one. The IGY-related research was coordinated by NPL, and so, logically, it should have led the follow-up activities like a coordinated space research programme.

Because of the enthusiasm IGY generated in space research, particularly the potential of satellites, ICSU formed the Committee on Space Research (COSPAR) in 1958 and decided to hold a space science symposium annually. The conference was conceived as a platform for scientists from different countries to present their research and exchange notes. Soon it became a cradle for many collaborative projects and helped catalyse the birth of national space programmes in many countries. Around the same time as COSPAR, the United Nations (UN) established the Committee on the Peaceful Uses of Outer Space, with India as one of its eighteen founding members, and NASA launched a programme for international cooperation.

The NPL was invited to represent India in COSPAR, and accordingly, A.P. Mitra of NPL was deputed to attend the meeting at Florence in April 1961 where he presented a report on space research activities in India. In this report, the NPL director Krishnan was listed as chairperson of the National Space Committee of India reporting to COSPAR. 'Although NPL had essentially inherited India's space activities from its role in the IGY, within a year, Sarabhai fully established himself as the focal node for all space-related activities in India, often at the expense of others who might have aspired to do so,' points out historian Asif A. Siddiqi.[9] Sarabhai could do so 'by leveraging his large international network of elite scientists' and by steering the subject of space research away from CSIR and bringing it under DAE, which was emerging as a centre of scientific power rivalling CSIR.[10] Though PRL received government funds, it was not a government entity. Bhabha, who declined the membership of the IGY preparatory committee in 1953, readily agreed to host the post-IGY space committee in DAE.

Despite having helmed IGY work, NPL could not stake its claim to the space committee. One of the main reasons was the death of its founder, Krishnan, a powerful voice in India's scientific community and CSIR, in 1961. Consequently, DAE became the home for the national space research efforts – Indian National Committee for Space Research (INCOSPAR) – and Bhabha nominated Sarabhai as its chair in February 1962. For all practical purposes, PRL in Ahmedabad was the headquarters of the committee, making the laboratory the birthplace of India's space endeavours. Justifying the need to invest in space research, Bhabha said in 1963, 'If we do not do so now, we will have to depend later on buying know-how from other countries at much greater cost.'[11]

The prime objective of INCOSPAR was 'to advise the government in the promotion of research in and exploration of space and its utilization for peaceful purposes'. The official note on the justification of setting up INCOSPAR mentioned 'favourable geographical factors' like the geomagnetic latitude passing through the southern tip of the Indian peninsula and a range of geomagnetic latitudes available for studies.[12] The note mentioned a proposal to 'establish a rocket launching site on the west coast of India at the geomagnetic equator' with initial facilities for launching meteorological sounding rockets that could carry payloads of 30 to 50 kg to altitudes of 150 to 200 km. This was in line with the suggestion made by COSPAR for the establishment of sounding rocket launch facilities on the magnetic equator under the UN to fill the gaps in the coverage of sounding rocket facilities.

With a formal mechanism and funding from DAE, Sarabhai began identifying a suitable place for the rocket launching facility and gathering necessary technologies and equipment for rockets, ground station and other facilities. The plan was to launch sounding rockets to study the atmosphere, particularly the equatorial electrojet – a kind of intense east–west current flowing in the ionosphere. The atmospheric region between altitudes of 40 km and 200 km, where the electrojet occurs, is not accessible to high-altitude balloons and is below the operational altitude of satellites. Sounding rockets are considered ideal to study this part of the atmosphere. These rockets are relatively low-cost, can be quickly developed and do not need elaborate launch infrastructure. They take their name from the nautical term 'to sound', meaning to take measurements. It was felt that a sounding rocket programme could be run with a modest budget, and the scientific results would have a direct bearing on a better understanding of meteorology, particularly the Indian monsoons, which had a great practical significance to the Indian economy.

The first challenge was to zero in on a location on the Kerala coast where the magnetic equator passed over the peninsula. The PRL, still a fledgling laboratory, had an enthusiastic bunch of researchers, most of them with post-graduate and doctoral degrees in space-related subjects from top American universities like Massachusetts Institute of Technology (MIT), Harvard and University of California, Los Angeles. Sarabhai, during his frequent visits to America, persuaded most of them to come back and join PRL. E.V. Chitnis and P.R. Pisharoty were among the early recruits. Sarabhai despatched them to Kerala to select a site in July 1962. The search continued for some time. A team from the Wallops Island sounding rocket facility of NASA was with Chitnis, and it helped determine the exact location of the magnetic equator.

This is Chitnis's account of the final stage of the site selection operation in November 1962: 'We stayed with the Governor at his Guest House, and a fleet of 15 cars was available to for site inspection. Bhabha, Sarabhai, Goveas, chief architect R. B. Patel and I – all five of us stayed at the Guest House of Governor V.V. Giri and he hosted a dinner for us. We had no difficulty in approaching anybody.'[13]

After flying over the shortlisted locations, the team decided in favour of Thumba. However, there were other difficulties on the ground. Though the place was less populated than other options, still it required displacing several people, many of whom prayed at an old church: St Mary Magdalene Church. Local officials found it difficult to convince people in this regard and suggested that Sarabhai seek the help of the archbishop of Trivandrum, Dr Peter Bernard Pereira.

When Sarabhai met the archbishop, he asked him to see him on the next day, a Sunday. According to one account recounted by Sarabhai's son Kartikeya, the archbishop introduced Sarabhai in the morning service as 'a famous scientist who wants our church and the place I live for the work of space science research'. He told the congregation, 'Science seeks truth by reasoning. In one way, science and spiritualism seek the same divine blessings for doing good for the people. My children, can we give God's abode for a scientific mission?' There was a chorus of 'Amen', and the way was cleared to the rocket launching facility, officially named Thumba Equatorial Rocket Launching Station (TERLS) with the church building used for rocket assembly.[14] TERLS became a new facility under DAE.

Concurrently, work started for setting up a space technology laboratory at Trivandrum for payload design, fabrication and testing. It was later renamed the Space Science and Technology Centre (SSTC) and had Sarabhai as the director. After his untimely death in 1971, it was renamed the Vikram Sarabhai Space Centre (VSSC).

Help came readily from NASA, which was looking to expand its sphere of influence through cooperation in space science. Sarabhai had proposed way back in 1961 to the international cooperation division of NASA to develop a 'joint' sounding rocket facility at a magnetic equatorial site in India. Eventually, NASA helped develop thirteen such facilities globally. In India, it signed a memorandum of understanding with DAE. Under this, it agreed to provide four Nike-Cajun (or equivalent) scientific sounding rockets with nose cones, an appropriate launching device on a loan basis, training for Indian personnel responsible for conducting launch operations, and necessary advisory personnel to assist in launching operations. The six engineers of TERLS went on a year-long training at the Goddard Space Flight Centre soon after their recruitment in December 1962. They were H.G.S. Murthy (director, TERLS), D. Easwara Das (head, Rocket Integration Division), A.P.J. Abdul Kalam (head, Range Engineering Division), B.Ramakrishna Rao (head,Electronics Division-Rockets), R. Aravamudan (head, Ground Support Division, Test and Evaluation Division) and Pramod Kale (head, Electronics Division-Satellites).

In January 1963, INCOSPAR hosted a space physics seminar at PRL. Those present were Dr R.E. Bourdeau, Dr Upendra Desai, Dr Wendell Smith of NASA and Dr G.V. Groves of the British Space Science Organisation. Desai, who was working at the Goddard Space Flight Centre, also helped Sarabhai recruit Indian scientists and engineers working in NASA, MIT and other institutions. Contacts were made with the Academy of Science of the USSR and the newly formed French space agency, Centre National d'Etudes Spatiales (CNES). Sarabhai had met Jacques Blamont, the scientific and technical director of the fledgling CNES, at one of the COSPAR meetings. Blamont was introduced to Sarabhai by Praful Bhavsar, a cosmic ray researcher at PRL, who earlier collaborated with Blamont while the two were at the University of Minnesota.

NASA provided Nike-Apache rockets to be fired from TERLS, along with a launcher. These were two-stage solid-propellant unguided sounding rocket systems, which could go up to 160 to 210 km altitudes with scientific payloads. (Nike and Apache represent the two stages of the rocket.) Later, the United States gave a US$2-million Doppler radar trailer as well. The USSR science academy was also generous. It provided an MI-4 helicopter for payload recovery and surveillance, a Minsk computer (which could execute 5000 operations per second, considered high-speed output then) and data processing equipment, and a 'shake table' for environmental testing of payloads. Also, TERLS acquired an IBM computer, while CNES gave tracking radar, photographic equipment and a launcher.

The date fixed for the first Nike-Apache firing from Thumba was 21 November 1963. 'I provided the payload – a sodium ejector fabricated in my laboratory – to be placed in the nose cone of the Nike-Apache provided by NASA,' recalled Blamont.[15] A.P.J. Abdul Kalam, who was in charge of rocket integration and safety, experienced some tense moments before the launch recalled, in 2010: 'The rocket was assembled in the church building at Thumba. The only equipment available to transport the rocket was a truck and a manually operated hydraulic crane. When the rocket was lifted by the crane and was about to be placed on the launcher, it started tilting indicating a leak in the hydraulic system of the crane.... We managed to lift the rocket manually using our collective muscle power and finally placing it on the launcher.'[16] The moment has been somewhat dramatically captured in the 2022 web series *Rocket Boys*.

The maiden launch from Thumba was a success, marking India's formal entry into the space age. As the sodium vapour ejected from the rocket left a trail of orange-coloured cloud that was visible to the naked eye in places up to 250 km away, it became a spectacle for people along the rocket's trajectory. The Kerala State Assembly suspended its proceedings for 20 minutes to enable legislators to watch the rocket trail.

It was a modest effort but a significant one as it opened a new vista for Indian science. Over the next five years, TERLS saw hectic activity: the launch of over 200 sounding rockets (Nike-Apache, Judi-Dart and Centaure); visits of scientists from America, USSR, France, Japan, Germany, Sri Lanka and so on; development of telemetry and tracking facilities; and recognition of TERLS as an international facility under the UN. For manufacturing Centaure rockets in India, DAE obtained licensed technology from Sud-Aviation of France in 1964. As the Rocket Fabrication Facility at SSTC was still getting ready, the manufacturing was taken up at the Atomic Energy Establishment, Trombay, while the Rocket Propellant Plant came up at Thumba. The first indigenously built sounding rocket, Rohini-75 (RH-75), was fired on 20 November 1967. It was a tiny, single-stage rocket weighing just 7 kg.

As more rockets were fired, Thumba attracted a variety of visitors, besides international scientists, including the Dalai Lama, Malayalam superstar Prem Nazir, industrialist J.R.D. Tata and French photographer Henri Cartier-Bresson. Two of Cartier-Bresson's photographs acquired iconic status over time, one showing a scientist, C.R. Sathyu, carrying a rocket nose cone on the carrier of his cycle and the other showing two young scientists sitting on the floor and preparing a payload in the Thumba church (one of them was A.P.J. Abdul Kalam, the future president of India). R. Aravamudan, who was featured in the picture with Kalam, recalled in his memoir: 'Kalam and I were fixing a timer unit to a sodium vapour cloud payload. Those were still our makeshift days and both of us were crouched on the floor of the church building in front of the altar. We had no fans, let alone air conditioning. It was so unbearably hot that I had removed my shirt.'[17]

In a short time, and under difficult circumstances such as the national emergency due to the wars, TERLS could make a start in all segments of space technology – development of rockets, payloads, ground facilities, tracking, data computing and conducting scientific experiments. As a UN facility, it helped raise India's profile as an emerging contender in the space sector. India already had a robust nuclear energy programme under Bhabha. Both Bhabha and Sarabhai were recognised as leaders of Indian science, holding important positions in global bodies: the International Atomic Energy Agency and the UN Committee for Peaceful Uses of Outer Space respectively.

Bhabha's sudden death in the tragic crash of Bombay–Geneva Air India flight 101 over Mont Blanc on 24 January 1966 was a jolt to the Indian scientific community and Sarabhai personally. TERLS functioned under DAE, and

Sarabhai was a member of the Atomic Energy Commission. So the government decided to appoint Sarabhai to head DAE. This put him in charge of two strategically important national scientific endeavours – atomic energy and space. To give the space programme a separate institutional framework, INCOSPAR was replaced by a new entity named Indian Space Research Organisation (ISRO) on 15 August 1969 but still working under DAE. It was only after Sarabhai's sudden demise on 30 December 1971 that the government decided to move ISRO out of DAE and give it a new independent identity in September 1972.

ISRO Takes Shape

In the winter of January 1972, the vast campus of Caltech was embraced by a crisp, cool breeze. Satish Dhawan was in a lecture room, surrounded by graduate students of the Guggenheim Aeronautical Laboratory, taking a class on experimental fluid dynamics. From the windows of the classroom, the view stretched out over the sprawling campus where vibrant greenery contrasted with laboratory buildings and academic blocks. Dhawan was on his first sabbatical to his alma mater since becoming the director of one of India's most prestigious scientific centres, the Indian Institute of Science (IISc) in Bangalore. It was at Caltech that Dhawan got his double PhD in aeronautics and mathematics two decades ago.

A gentle knock on the hall's door drew Dhawan's attention momentarily. An administrative assistant informed him that there was a call from Washington and the caller wished to speak with Dhawan urgently. As he rushed out of the lecture hall, his mind shifted gears from fluid dynamics to the unexpected news awaiting him. 'Hello Prof. Dhawan, L.K. Jha this side,' the caller said. Dhawan was familiar with Jha. He was India's ambassador in Washington. Jha said he had two pieces of news. The first one shocked Dhawan. Vikram Sarabhai, the head of India's atomic energy and space programmes, had passed away suddenly. Jha paused for a few seconds and let the bad news sink in. Then he said, in an official tone, 'I have a message from Mrs Gandhi for you.' What the ambassador said next stumped fifty-one-year-old Dhawan. The prime minister, Indira Gandhi, wanted him to lead the space programme.[18] Jha also informed him that a new department of space was being planned so that ISRO could be transferred from DAE to it.

A multitude of thoughts and emotions crossed Dhawan's mind – the loss of a dear contemporary scientist and an offer to succeed him. Heading an emerging national programme was a daunting responsibility and a tough one, given the infamous Indian bureaucracy. Having been a member of the Atomic Energy Commission (AEC) and the Scientific Advisory Committee to the Cabinet in the 1960s, Dhawan was conversant with the difficulties and intricacies of running large science projects in the government.

A few moments later, Dhawan responded in a composed tone, requesting Jha to convey his gratitude to the prime minister for making the offer but said he would let her know his decision only after he returned home. Dhawan said later while recalling the momentous telephonic conversation that was to steer his placid academic career in a new direction: 'I told him [Jha] that I was in the middle of a class. I had been pulled out to attend the telephone call. I will complete my assignment here which was another couple of months. And I will come and see the Prime Minister. I also had to take the advice of the Governing Council of IISc since I am employed there as a professor.'[19]

He returned to India after his sabbatical ended a month later. He went to Bombay to consult J.R.D. Tata, chairperson of the board of governors of IISc, and J.D. Choksi, a member of the board. Both advised him to accept the government's offer. Back in Bangalore, he wrote a lengthy letter to the prime minister, detailing his ideas on how ISRO should be organised to take up in an integrated manner the development of satellites, launch vehicles, ground facilities and applications.[20] It was implied that he would accept the offer if the government shared his vision. In addition, he had two 'conditions': he wanted the proposed Department of Space (DoS) and the Space Commission to be run on the same lines as DAE and the AEC, with autonomy and at a distance from the bureaucracy of the national capital. Unlike other government departments, DAE and AEC functioned from Bombay and not New Delhi. Second, he wanted to continue as the director of IISc.

The prime minister approved the reorganisation of scientific departments. The creation of the Department of Space and the Space Commission was notified on 12 May 1972, and Dhawan was appointed to head the new entities as well as ISRO on 2 June 1972. As desired by Dhawan, he continued to work out of his office at IISc. The support staff operated from the old Gymkhana building on the campus, making it the first headquarters of ISRO and DoS. On his frequent visits to Delhi, Dhawan used the office of H.N. Sethna, the chairperson of AEC.

Sarabhai envisioned a robust national space programme to use space technology for applications like education, broadcasting, communications, remote sensing, weather forecasting, and the like as detailed in the Ten-Year Profile (1970–1980) published by AEC in 1970. It envisaged the development of India's first rocket capable of launching satellites, SLV-3; a communication satellite system called Indian National Satellite (Insat); and a remote sensing satellite, Indian Remote Sensing Satellite (IRS).[21] The challenge before Dhawan was to translate this vision into reality.

Technically, ISRO had been in existence for a little over two years when Dhawan took it over after Sarabhai's death. It did not have a separate budget or a fully organised infrastructure. TERLS was built through international help, and it was unsuitable for launching orbiting satellites. A site had been identified to build a spaceport at Sriharikota on the east coast. There was no industrial capability to build rocket parts and propellants. The Space Science and Technology Centre in Trivandrum was still in its early days though preliminary work had been initiated in a range of areas. The ground facilities for telemetry and tracking were rudimentary, and India had little expertise in the fabrication of satellites or associated electronics and instrumentation.

Dhawan decided to organise ISRO with clearly identifiable teams and centres to handle different space technologies: rockets and propellants, design and fabrication of satellites, payload development, launch stations, ground testing facilities, tracking stations and applications. To begin with, the Space Science and Technology Centre in Trivandrum was renamed VSSC and tasked with building rockets. The Space Applications Centre (SAC) was built in Ahmedabad where the Experimental Earth Station was already operational. The space station, Sriharikota High Altitude Range (SHAR), was developed on a vast tract of the Bay of Bengal coast. Hyderabad got the National Remote Sensing Agency (NRSA) for processing remote sensing data. By the mid-1970s, the space programme was bubbling with activity at multiple centres – Trivandrum, Hyderabad, Sriharikota and Ahmedabad.

The satellite group was shifted from Trivandrum to Bangalore when the Indo-Soviet Satellite Project (ISSP) got started, and it eventually took the shape of the ISRO Satellite Centre or ISAC (now known as U.R. Rao Satellite Centre) where all Indian satellites are built. Bangalore was chosen as it had the advantage of electronics and aerospace industries. The shifting of ISSP to Bangalore became a political issue with the Kerala chief minister Achutha Menon taking it up with Indira Gandhi, and Kerala members of Parliament like Vayalar Ravi expressing their fears in the Parliament about the possible job loss. The ISSP started its operations from industrial sheds allocated by the Karnataka government in the Peenya Industrial Estate, which was just coming up.

2

Soaring High with Dream Rockets

On the morning of 18 July 1980, the mission control room at the Sriharikota spaceport on the east coast was filled with anticipation and tension as engineers, scientists and officials gathered for India's most important space mission yet. The room buzzed with a mixture of nervous energy and quiet determination, as memories of what happened a year ago were still fresh in the minds of everyone in the room. The morning newspapers published a vivid recall of the failure of the maiden flight of SLV-3, India's first rocket designed to launch Earth-orbiting satellites in space, in August 1979. The SLV was often caricatured in the media as the 'Sea Loving Vehicle'.

One newspaper had reported that the 'Project Director is missing and could not be contacted', referring to the media-shy forty-nine-year-old aerospace engineer A.P.J. Abdul Kalam.[1] Unmindful of what was happening in the outside world, Kalam sat at his designated seat amidst the rows of computer consoles occupied by team members, each one monitoring a crucial parameter as the countdown proceeded. Screens flickered with technical data and simulations, displaying intricate diagrams of the rocket's trajectory and readings of vital functions. Engineers double-checked systems, running through final checks and ensuring every rocket stage was ready for the historic launch.

Outside, the morning sun cast a golden hue over the sprawling spaceport, highlighting the towering silhouette of the rocket on the launch pad with coconut trees in the distance providing a perfect backdrop. All eyes were fixed on the 22-m-tall slender rocket – with the Rohini satellite, RH-1, in its uppermost cone and the Indian tricolour logo embossed on the top – standing impressively against the vast coastal landscape. Every second seemed to stretch, filled with the weight of expectations and hope of success.

Tension and anxiety gripped everyone as, for the first time, the country was going to watch the big moment live. The state-run Doordarshan was permitted to arrange a live telecast through a special arrangement. A high-altitude balloon from TIFR was flown at a point between Sriharikota and Madras, 100 km away, to relay the signals to the transmission tower in Madras. Senior scientists Yashpal and Aravamudan were the commentators. The arrangement came to naught as strong coastal winds wrenched the balloon off its tether and the experiment of live telecast failed. At the launch pad, there was a more serious problem. One of the remote-controlled umbilical cords of the rocket refused to detach as planned. The countdown was paused. A technician climbed up the launch tower, flouting safety norms, and detached the cable in time.[2]

At 08:03 hours, SLV-3 ignited and took off with a powerful roar at the end of the tense countdown. The rocket surged upwards, leaving behind a streak of blazing fire against the sky, embarking on its journey into space. There was a mild cheer and applause in the room as the rocket followed its trajectory and its different stages separated as planned. As the computer displayed data about SLV's fourth stage gaining the required velocity and pushing the satellite into its orbit, it brought a mild smile to Kalam's face. He swiftly took the mike to his table to deliver the most important lines of his life as a rocket scientist: 'Mission Director calling all stations, stand by for an important announcement, all stages performed to mission requirements, the fourth-stage Apogee motor has given the required velocity to put the Rohini satellite into orbit.'[3]

The room erupted in thunderous applause. Smiles of relief and pride crossed the faces of dozens of engineers and technicians who had worked tirelessly to make this moment possible. India finally became a space-faring nation, next only to the United States, USSR, France, China and Japan. The Western media, however, remained sarcastic. The launch was remarkable 'for a country that still used bullock carts as a prime mode of transportation', the *Washington Post* commented, typifying the Western media response to India's space ambitions.[4]

The first experimental flight of SLV-3 was followed by two developmental flights on 31 May 1981 and 17 April 1983. Three successful flights in a row helped Indian scientists test and validate several critical technologies. Sounding rockets to SLV-3 was an impressive jump, but it could only be the first step, a stepping stone to larger rockets. The SLV-3 could launch scientific payloads or satellites weighing just about 35 to 40 kg in a low earth orbit (LEO). A LEO can range from 160 km to 1000 km altitude. Operational satellites weigh much more and need heavier rockets, as they need to be placed in much higher orbits. For instance, the Ariane Passenger Payload Experiment (APPLE) satellite developed by ISRO teams – placed by an Ariane rocket in the geosynchronous transfer orbit at an altitude of 35,000 km – weighed 670 kg. Remote sensing and communication satellites are in the range of 1000 to 4000 kg.

The job of a launch vehicle (this differentiates it from sounding rockets) is to pilot a satellite along a predetermined trajectory and altitude and impart orbiting velocity to the satellite so that it gets injected into a pre-decided orbit. All this should work with precision for the satellite to reach its desired orbit. The design of a launch vehicle, therefore, needs several technologies: propulsion; avionics for navigation, guidance and control; separation mechanism; onboard mission management; advanced materials and thermal systems. The vehicle system should be able to withstand extreme temperatures, vibration and hostile flight environments and keep the satellite in its belly safe and stable till it is injected into its orbit. All this required multidisciplinary teams to work together with a meticulous project management plan and a project manager.

The propulsion system is one of the most important technologies for a launch vehicle as it helps it attain targeted altitude and velocity for the satellite. Usually, launch vehicles use three types of propellants – solid, liquid and cryogenic. Solid propellants are relatively simpler to use. A basic solid propellant is a mixture of an oxidiser and fuel that reacts chemically in the combustion chamber of an engine when ignited to propel the rocket. Liquid and cryogenic propellants are more complex and expensive, but they are more efficient than solid propellants. Multi-stage large launch vehicles have solid propellants in boosters while using liquid and cryogenic propellants in the upper stages of the rocket.

Sounding rockets fired from TERLS used solid propellants, giving ISRO engineers an opportunity to gain experience in handling such propellants. The facilities at TERLS were rudimentary in the initial phase. To make ammonium perchlorate, for instance, ingredients were ground using a porcelain mortar and pestle, sieved with a kitchen sieve, mixed in a beaker and cured in a laboratory oven, which once exploded. Over the years, scientists mastered the technique of making different types of complex solid propellants and established a full facility for propellant production at Thumba. An early polyester-based propellant, which powered the first locally made sounding rocket, RH-75, was named Mrinal after Sarabhai's wife, Mrinalini.[5]

Vasant Gowarikar, a chemical engineer who had worked on tactical missiles at the Summerfield Research Station in the United Kingdom, was recruited by Sarabhai to head the Propulsion Engineering Division at TERLS. Abraham E. Muthunayagam was working on a NASA project at FluiDyne Engineering Corporation, an aerospace company in Minneapolis, when he was appointed to TERLS in 1966. Over the years, they built formidable propulsion teams that developed solid and liquid propulsion systems for generations of ISRO rockets. Subsequently, both Gowarikar and Muthunayagam left ISRO prematurely and took up other government assignments.

Given all the experience with solid propellants, it was decided to launch SLV-3 with solid propulsion. Another reason for this technology decision was the fact that SLV-3 was modelled after the American Scout rocket (solid controlled orbital utility system), which was a solid propellant rocket. The decision was also in line with the ISRO strategy of step-by-step development of increasingly more sophisticated technologies needed to launch heavier satellites with higher injection accuracies. The development teams drew important lessons from failures, using an elaborate failure analysis mechanism. Already developed rocket stages and technologies were incorporated into next-generation vehicles, reducing overall development costs and time. SLV-3 stages were used in the next launch vehicle – the Augmented Satellite Launch Vehicle (ASLV) that followed.

In addition, Dhawan decided to involve the industry right from the conceptual stage of SLV-3 to develop its capacity to make space-grade components, electronics, composite materials and the like for SLV-3 as well as future vehicles. He deputed Kalam on a nationwide tour to sensitise the industry on the special requirements of the space programme.[6] Some 250 large, medium and small industrial units across different sectors worked with ISRO to develop and deliver parts for satellite, rocket and ground facilities.

A Witness to Failures

The SLV-3 design was augmented to develop ASLV with a higher payload capacity (150 kg). This was achieved by two new technologies: two motors were strapped on to the first stage of the four-stage rocket, and the heat shield was made bulbous to accommodate larger satellites. Strap-on motors were a difficult technology because both motors should ignite simultaneously. If there was a difference in the thrust of the two, it could jeopardise the vehicle's stability. Several other new features were added – a closed-loop guidance system, new digital avionics, a new type of heat shield, vertical integration and so on. In the 'open guidance system' (used in SLV), the rocket attitude (angular orientation) and propulsion burn programmes are pre-fed, and no change is possible once the vehicle is in flight. In the 'closed-loop guidance system', corrections are made using onboard systems depending on the flight conditions. The navigation, guidance and control systems of launch vehicles constitute an important technological challenge in rocketry, requiring special hardware like gyros, sensors and thrusters as well as sophisticated algorithms.[7]

Four years after the last successful launch of SLV-3, the stage was set for the first launch of ASLV-D1. A lot had changed since then in ISRO. Satish Dhawan had retired and was succeeded by Udupi Ramachandra Rao, a satellite pioneer who led the Aryabhata and APPLE projects. Kalam had moved to the Defence Research and Development Organisation (DRDO) to lead its fledgling integrated guided missile programme at Hyderabad. The Missile Technology Control Regime (MTCR) had kicked in, affecting the supply of components and sub-systems. The prime minister, Rajiv Gandhi, in the middle of his first term, was facing some rough political weather and unrest in many parts of the country.

In my memory, 24 March 1987 is firmly fixed. For a budding science reporter working in the national wire service, PTI, it was an exciting opportunity to cover the first launch of ASLV from Sriharikota. I reached Madras from Bangalore by state road transport corporation bus the previous night to join the press party that was to leave from the ISRO guest house for SHAR early morning to witness the launch. The last few kilometres of the 100-km-long journey took the minibus carrying the press party through a picturesque landscape, a narrow road almost cutting through the vast Pulicat Lake. The press group was taken to a moderate conference room with a mid-sized television screen that showed a live feed from the mission control room situated a couple of kilometres away. It was the first time Rajiv Gandhi was at SHAR to witness a rocket launch. There were also officials from the German Aerospace Research Establishment as the Rohini series satellite that ASLV was carrying had a remote sensing payload from Germany.

The launch countdown that began the previous day proceeded as planned. All eyes were glued to the screen, and some of us were leafing through the flight sequence of the mission brochure handed out to us. The giant mobile service structure crawled away on rails 2 hours before the launch, with the 25-m-tall rocket with two shiny strap-on motors standing high in the afternoon sun. The final few minutes of the launch operation sequence command was automated and run by the mission computer. Some 7 minutes before the launch, an improper pressure pump reading was noticed. The countdown was stopped and resumed after attending to this. At 12:09 hours, the computer control issued the command for ignition. The two strap-on motors ignited simultaneously, and the rocket zoomed into the sky.

Everybody in the conference room rushed to the terrace of the double-storeyed building to watch the rocket rising with the naked eye. By the time we reached the rooftop, the two strap-on motors separated after 52 seconds of the lift-off as per the flight sequence. But 2 seconds before they separated, the first stage of the rocket should have ignited. This did not happen. We could see the rocket going down. It was an unbelievable sight. We knew the mission had failed as we rushed back to the conference room. The live feed in the conference room was on, but there was deathly silence in the mission control. The screen tracking ASLV's projected trajectory along with the actual one went blank. Telemetry data from ASLV stopped after 164 seconds. The ASLV-D1 met a watery grave in the Bay of Bengal.

The ISRO chairman U.R. Rao was supposed to address the customary press conference after the launch. We were wondering whether that would happen at all now that the mission had failed. A few minutes later, Rajiv Gandhi walked into the conference room with a sullen-looking Rao wearing a checked bush shirt and Andhra Pradesh chief minister N.T. Rama Rao in his typical saffron-coloured dhoti and kurta. The prime minister spoke first. In a measured tone, he said setbacks were bound to happen when one worked in cutting-edge areas of technology. However, he said, 'The setback will only be in time. The morale of our scientists is high. ISRO will analyse what went wrong, correct it and move on to the next generation rocket – Polar Satellite Launch Vehicle [PSLV] as planned.'[8] Addressing the visibly crestfallen ISRO chairman, Gandhi said, 'Don't lose heart. It is only when you stumble that you can get up and walk better.' Priyanka and Rahul, who had accompanied Rajiv to witness the launch, sat in the last row of the conference room as their father addressed the press. The teenage siblings wore a grim look as they walked out along with the prime minister's entourage.

Over the next few weeks, the Failure Analysis Committee pored over data relating to about 366 parameters gathered during the short flight and examined thirty-seven possible reasons for the mission failure. The first stage did not ignite, probably because of the failure of a component in the ignition command chain. Armed with findings, engineers went back to workshops to build a new rocket. They were back with the second developmental flight of ASLV on 13 July 1988. My editor K.S. Jayaraman deputed me once again to cover the launch. By this time, I had been transferred from Bangalore to Hyderabad. ISRO was lukewarm to the press. No arrangement was made to take us to the spaceport from Chennai. We hired taxis and reached Sriharikota but were not allowed to enter SHAR. There were no VIPs to witness the launch like the last time. We were all waiting outside the gates, while the same drill of countdown was being followed inside.

The ASLV-D2 took off at 14:48 hours. The two strap-on motors ignited and got separated at the designated time. Before the separation, the command of the first stage was issued, and it ignited. However, soon thereafter, the first stage started tumbling, eventually leading to a splashdown into the Bay of Bengal from an altitude of 25 km. The press was eventually called in. A nervous-looking Rao briefed us. He said, 'We are disheartened. We know that similar failures have marked the development of rocket technology in other countries. But that can't be a point of consolation for us.' The opening line of my despatch was similar to what I wrote a year ago with a minor tweak: 'Disaster struck the Indian space programme for the second successive time today when the second developmental flight of ASLV failed in its mission soon after take-off.'[9] In some circles, the joke about SLV failures was extended to ASLV; it was dubbed 'Always Sea Loving Vehicle'.

The third flight of ASLV took place on 20 May 1992. It was a success with the rocket injecting a Rohini satellite into the LEO. However, the satellite malfunctioned after being in orbit for two months, and it was lost. The next ASLV was launched on 4 May 1992 with yet another Rohini series satellite. Meanwhile, work on the next-generation rocket PSLV was progressing well. This made the space agency discontinue ASLV launches and terminate the Rohini satellite project. Though two out of the four ASLVs launched failed, the programme provided invaluable insights into technologies useful for the next set of launch vehicles. Both SLV-3 and ASLV provided a technological base for the second generation of launch vehicles.

The immediate target was to move to the operational phase of the space programme with the capability to launch 1000-kg class applications satellites into the Sun-synchronous polar orbit (SSPO) from Indian soil. Satellites in SSPO orbit Earth over its poles – from north to south – and are 'synchronous' with the Sun. It means they remain in a 'fixed' position relative to the Sun, allowing them to travel past the same place on Earth every day at the same time. Therefore, remote sensing satellites are usually placed in an SSPO. The PSLV was designed for this task. The ASLV was only good enough for experimental satellites. For launching operational satellites, a larger launch vehicle was needed, and PSLV was going to be that.

A Workhorse Is Born

The efficiency of a rocket depends on how effectively it uses propellant to produce thrust for the rocket to lift off and propel into space. An efficient rocket should be able to produce more thrust with less propellant. Solid propellants generally have lower specific impulse compared to liquid ones. The SLV-3 was fully based on solid propellants while ASLV deployed liquid propulsion only for the limited purpose of controlling the second and third solid stages. To be able to launch heavier satellites, new rockets based on liquid propulsion were needed. Liquid propellants produce higher thrust per unit of propellant used. Making a rocket engine based on liquid propellants is far more complex, involving high-precision fabrication. A liquid propellant is held in tanks made of special steel, from where it flows into the combustion chamber to produce the necessary thrust. The flow of propellants, combustion rate and the like have to be well controlled.

Indian scientists experimented with liquid propulsion at Thumba in the late 1960s, but there was no defined development programme. While the focus in the 1970s was on first mastering the solid propulsion technology needed for SLV-3, ISRO engineers were working on the possible configuration of a launch vehicle that should follow SLV-3. They suggested that it should include liquid propulsion engines. However, simultaneously working on a liquid propulsion system needed expertise as well as funding. Around the same time, the French space agency, CNES, with whom ISRO was working closely since the sounding rocket years, was also planning to develop liquid engines for a new launch vehicle, Ariane. This was after a series of failures of Europa, a launch vehicle developed collaboratively by France, Germany and Britain.

In 1973, CNES and ISRO formed a joint commission to deepen further cooperation in the space sector. One of the immediate outcomes was the French assistance in establishing a critical testing facility – the Static Test and Evaluation Complex at SHAR. It was executed by the Societe Europeenne de Propulsion (SEP), which then was also working on a liquid propulsion engine for the Ariane launch vehicle. During the meetings of the joint commission in 1974, the French side made an interesting offer, a kind of barter deal. The SEP was willing to transfer the technology of the liquid propulsion engine, Viking, in return for ISRO manufacturing pressure transducers for SEP and deputing its engineers to work on the Ariane launch vehicle development. ISRO agreed to provide 100 man-years of its engineers and scientists to SEP as it faced a shortage of skilled technical workers and had to deliver Ariane in a short period of six years.[10]

As per the agreement, forty ISRO engineers were working at any given time at SEP, embedded in its Ariane development teams. This allowed them to absorb the technology of the Viking liquid propulsion engine through participation in the development process, including all associated activities such as procurement of components and sub-systems from the industry. The division of 100 man-years of ISRO engineers was like this: 25 man-years were provided by ISRO engineers to the French group directly engaged in developing sub-systems of the Viking engine, while the rest of the man-years were for teams working on the stage and ground systems for Ariane's Stage 2. A few ISRO personnel were deployed with the French group working on the cryogenic engine and Stage 3 of the Ariane vehicle. 'The deployment helped ISRO to acquire substantial information on the second stage of Ariane and gave the engineers good exposure to its cryogenic third stage,' recounted Muthunayagam, who was the project director, in his memoirs.[11] A formal technology acquisition methodology was adopted with a backup team of the Liquid Propulsion Project (LPP) at VSSC that worked closely with Indian engineers in France. In Bangalore, a pressure transducers unit was established on the campus of the National Aerospace Laboratories to manufacture transducers based on the technology SEP supplied. The unit manufactured some 7000 units of transducers of different types.

Upon their return to India at the end of the five-year contract, the engineers trained at SEP were inducted into LPP to develop an Indian version of the Viking engine. T.N. Seshan signed the agreement with SEP on behalf of the Indian side in his capacity as the additional secretary of DoS. He coined an Indian name for Viking: Vikas, an acronym for Vikram A. Sarabhai. The prototype of the Vikas liquid propulsion engine was ready in 1985, and it was ground tested at SEP in France as a testing facility was yet to be established in India.

The development of the Vikas engine was a crucial step, but several other technologies were needed to develop a full-fledged four-stage PSLV. The solid rocket motor of SLV-3/ASLV with strap-on boosters of the type used in SLV-3 formed the first solid stage of PSLV. The second stage of the rocket was based on the Vikas liquid propulsion engine, followed by a solid third stage and another liquid upper stage that was developed indigenously. The configuration of PSLV was somewhat similar to the Ariane launcher that had the second stage powered by the Viking liquid engine.

Besides the fourth-stage liquid engine, Indian scientists developed several new technologies like the gimbal control system for liquid propellant engines, a flex-nozzle control system for solid propellant motors, digital autopilot, closed-loop guidance system and digital avionics. A special guidance software was developed for the unique configuration of alternate solid and liquid stages. Some critical materials such as maraging steel (for making the solid motor case) had to be developed as they could not be bought off the shelf.

The first PSLV was ready for its maiden flight on 16 September 1993 from SHAR. During the countdown, a snag was detected in a pyro arming connector. The launch was called off, and the snag was addressed along with all associated circuits. It finally took place on 19 September at 10:45 hours. The rocket lifted off perfectly. The strap-on motors separated as planned, and so did the first stage of the rocket. The second stage of the rocket powered by Vikas also performed well. But soon after the third stage ignited, the vehicle started tumbling. The mission ended in a failure and huge disappointment for thousands of scientists and engineers in ISRO as well as dozens of institutions and industries who had worked on PSLV for over a decade. As the failure analysis later revealed, it was a software problem, a computation error by the digital autopilot of the guidance and control processor.

In a year, the second developmental flight of PSLV was ready for launch. On 15 October 1994, PSLV lifted off from Sriharikota, all its stages performed as planned and the satellite, IRS-P2, was injected precisely into its predetermined sun-synchronous orbit. It was the culmination of twelve years of hard work by dozens of teams that worked on PSLV's design, fabrication, testing, integration and, finally, the launch.

It was the first time India successfully delivered a large, multidisciplinary and multi-sector engineering and technology project. It demonstrated the capability to launch operational satellites into a precise orbit from Indian soil. India could design and build satellites, launch them using home-built rockets, and had ground facilities to manage the satellite and harness the benefits of space technology. 'On that day, through PSLV-D2, we gave notice to the world that we are potential competitors in the world's space market,' N. Narayanamoorthy, a member of the PSLV team, later commented.[12]

The PSLV is a giant rocket – 44 m high – the height of a twelve-storeyed building and having a diameter of 2.8 m. At lift-off, its mass is 320 tonnes. The thrust it produces is six times that of all four engines of a Boeing 747. It can take up to 1750 kg of payload to sun-synchronous polar orbits of 600 km altitude.

Since 1994, PSLV has not looked back. Till January 2024, it has had sixty launches, with dozens of consecutive successful missions, putting over 360 satellites in the weight range of 1000 kg to 1750 kg each into their orbits. The launch vehicle has four variants – the core-alone version with no strap-on motors and versions with two, four and six strap-on motors. It has been deployed for multiple types of missions from launching large, single satellites to orbiting a record-making 104 micro-satellites in a single flight. The satellites launched by PSLV came from nearly 300 customers from thirty-six countries. They include earth observation, geostationary and navigation satellites. The crowning glory of PSLV came in 2008 when it launched Chandrayaan-1, India's first deep space mission to the lunar orbit, followed by the Mars Orbiter Mission (MOM) in 2013. Its remarkable journey since 1994 has made PSLV a reliable workhorse of ISRO.

Taming the Naughty Boy

After a gap of two decades, I returned to Sriharikota to cover important space missions. In 2008, I witnessed the landmark launch of PSLV that propelled India's first moon mission, Chandrayaan-1, into space. (More on this is in the chapter on interplanetary missions.) Two years later,

ISRO scheduled another mega launch, the first flight of the Geo-Synchronous Launch Vehicle-D3 (GSLV) with the indigenously developed cryogenic engine. As I drove to Sriharikota on 15 April 2010, it was typical coastal weather for the time of the year, hot and sultry. My mind went back to the 1980s when I came here for the first time to report on the first two ASLV missions, both of which failed. The 17-km road from Sullurpeta to the barrier island of Sriharikota was much smoother and had a lot more habitation than before; yet, the Pulicat Lake retained its serene beauty.

The journalists were ushered into a large, well-furnished hall named after Brahma Prakash, an ISRO veteran. There was a large screen showing the launch pad on one side and the control room on the other. The GSLV stood majestically, as tall as a seventeen-storeyed skyscraper, dwarfing the palm trees in the background. The ISRO chief K. Radhakrishnan sat in the control room, flanked by senior team leaders on both sides. A trained Kathakali dancer and vocalist, the bearded Radhakrishnan retained a calm and composed posture despite the palpable tension as the countdown continued smoothly. Much was at stake for the space agency: the rocket was powered by Indian cryogenic technology that had taken years to develop, and it was to launch a large satellite, GSAT-4, which was critical for the communication systems of India. In the visitor gallery were sitting two former chiefs of the space agency, U.R. Rao and K. Kasturirangan, and veteran space scientist Yashpal.

The rocket, weighing 416 tonnes, lifted off majestically at 16:27 hours, generating a massive triangular trail of fire and smoke in a clear evening sky. Some of us took the flight of stairs to the rooftop to see the rocket rising at a distance. 'Beautiful! Beautiful!' people murmured and cheered. Inside the control room, there was joy all around as the strap-on motors functioned well, the first stage separated and the second stage ignited. Everyone was waiting with bated breath for the next stage, the cryogenic engine, to ignite. The steering engine ignited first and then the main engine and the gas generator, as planned. Still, the engine could not operate.

The first signs of trouble were noticed at 16:32 hours. The voice of the commentator from the control room sounded ominous: 'There is a deviation in the flight path … there is a reduction in the altitude. This was not expected. Let's see how the flight will be recovered.'[13] A few seconds later, the commentator went silent. At this time, the GSLV had been in flight for 304 seconds of its total planned journey of 1022 seconds. Soon it became clear that the rocket, along with the 125-crore-rupee satellite in its uppermost tip, descended and splashed into the Bay of Bengal. The mild cheers that were heard a few seconds ago turned into gloom. The former ISRO chiefs were seen consoling Radhakrishnan, who remained stoic. A few minutes later, he emerged in the Brahma Prakash Hall to address the customary post-launch press conference. 'We have a long way to go,' he said in an expressionless tone.[14] 'All ISRO scientists and employees have worked hard for eighteen years to bring the cryogenic engine stage to a level of flying. This in itself is a major accomplishment.'

Cryogenic technology has indeed been a long tale in India's space journey. It is both strategic and complex. It is strategic because any nation or space agency mastering it can claim entry into the club of countries with commercial space launch capability. The commercial space launch market is worth US$20 billion and is growing. Cryogenic technology also makes a country self-dependent in the field of space, allowing it to pursue ambitious missions such as human space flights and the building of space stations.

Cryogenic propulsion is a highly complex and challenging technology to master, much more complex than the liquid propulsion India has mastered. Cryogenic is a type of liquid propulsion but is called cryogenic because the oxidiser and the fuel (typically liquid hydrogen and liquid nitrogen) have to be maintained at an extremely low temperature (minus 250 degrees Celsius or so). The fuels remain in a liquid stage till the combustion starts to generate a high-energy reaction. They need to be encased in special chambers in the engine. A rocket with a cryogenic upper stage, like GSLV, is referred to as an 'icy hot' vehicle because when the solid and liquid stages are burning and generating temperatures of 3000 degrees at one end of the rocket, the cryogenic stage is insulated and remains super cool till its turn comes for ignition. Cryogenic propulsion produces a higher capacity to convert fuel into thrust than solid and liquid systems. This allows rockets with cryogenic engines to attain higher speeds and transport heavier payloads.

The early leaders of the space programme were fully aware of the importance of cryogenic propulsion as their vision was to attain the capability to launch large communication and earth observation satellites, which needed powerful launch vehicles. Yet resource constraints and the need to prioritise available funds resulted in a step-by-step approach to launch vehicle development. Several technical and expert committees in the 1970s and the early 1980s suggested a structured cryogenic development project, but it did not happen. The SEP, which transferred the liquid propulsion technology to ISRO in the mid-1970s, was engaged in developing cryogenic technology. It was willing to sign a similar deal for cryogenic engines as well, but ISRO decided against it. 'Since ISRO had just started a new initiative on liquid boosters with SEP, we did not pursue the idea then. Resource limitation was a major factor behind the decision,' recalled Muthunayagam, who headed the Liquid Propulsion Systems Centre (LPSC) then.[15]

Therefore, importing cryogenic engines for GSLV emerged as an option if India wanted to quickly acquire the capability to launch larger application satellites from SHAR. The space agency approached SEP for a technology transfer deal for the cryogenic engine, but it demanded a very high fee. An offer came from Western aerospace companies General Dynamics and Arianespace, but the price quoted was too steep – US$800 million for two cryogenic engines and no transfer of technology. Moreover, depending on an American or European company was too risky as the MTCR had kicked in. It was a grouping of industrialised countries that sought to control the flow of technology to limit the proliferation of missiles. In 1990, America amended its domestic laws to allow it to apply sanctions against entities it thought violated MTCR. India was already facing problems with America over the import of a supercomputer from Cray Inc.

Meanwhile, the Soviet space agency Glavkosmos was exploring foreign markets for its space technologies. It was ready to supply India with a 12-tonne cryogenic engine to power the upper stage of GSLV at a fraction of the cost and with the transfer of technology. The Soviet engine KVD-1 was built for the Proton rocket, which was to carry cosmonauts to the moon but that mission never took place. As per the contract that was signed in January 1991, Glavkosmos was to deliver the first engine in 1994, and ISRO was to develop all associated control electronics and integrate it with the rest of GSLV.

The deal evoked a sharp reaction from America, which feared India might deploy the technology in intercontinental ballistic missiles, and it was projected as a violation under MTCR. India hit back, saying America was trying to block the deal due to commercial reasons – as India had refused to buy the engine from General Dynamics – rather than non-proliferation reasons. Over the next two years, it blew into a full-fledged diplomatic row involving Washington, New Delhi and Moscow. The United States enlisted the support of Canada, France and Japan to pressurise Moscow, which was already in domestic turmoil. Boris Yeltsin, who succeeded Gorbachev, wanted to improve relations with America and buckled under its pressure. In 1992, America imposed sanctions on both ISRO and Glavkosmos. In October 1993, Glavkosmos amended the contract with ISRO; it removed the technology transfer clause and agreed only to sell seven cryogenic engines. Around the same time, ISRO initiated a development programme for GSLV with an indigenous cryogenic engine called GSLV Mark II to differentiate it from the GSLV that was to use the Russian cryogenic engine.

The development of the indigenous cryogenic stage suffered a jolt in October 1994 when two senior scientists at LPSC, S. Nambinarayanan, project director of the Cryogenic System Project, and D. Sasikumar, deputy project director of engine fabrication in CSP, were arrested on charges of alleged espionage and were suspended from service. The Kerala Police, which conducted the initial investigations, botched the investigation, and the case was handed over to the Central Bureau of Investigation. After several levels of enquiry and legal battles, the Supreme Court acquitted both scientists in 1998.

The case also exposed the rift between ISRO chairman Kasturirangan and the LPSC director. Muthunayagam alleged that the ISRO management bypassed him while initiating action against LPSC scientists, and Kasturirangan allowed central agencies to act without ISRO conducting an internal enquiry. 'He appeared to lack confidence in me because I was once his senior and a former unwelcome competitor to his new position. This is probably why he did not discuss the case with me,' Muthunayagam has said in his autobiography *From Space to Sea: My ISRO Journey and Beyond*.[16] He quit ISRO in April 1995 to take up a new assignment in the Department of Ocean Development.

The first flight of GSLV from SHAR on 18 April 2001 was a success after it was aborted just 4 seconds before take-off a month earlier. The GSLV injected the GSAT-1 satellite into an elliptical orbit but not in the desired orbit because the cryogenic engine did not perform optimally and the thrust generated was only sufficient to place the satellite in a lower orbit. In this sense, the mission was not a full success. The satellite lasted just for a year. Between 2001 and 2010, six missions of GSLV with Russian cryogenic upper stage took place. Of them, two failed, and one was partially successful.

In parallel to the GSLV programme with the Russian cryogenic engine, ISRO got ready its cryogenic engine, the first of which was flown in the GSLV launched in April 2010, but it failed. The second and third launches with indigenous cryogenic engines in January 2014 and August 2015 were successful. With this, India could rightfully declare it had mastered cryogenic technology. The GSLV Mark II enabled the launch of the GSAT series and Insat-3D series satellites, ending altogether the dependence on foreign launchers for any size of satellites.

The next was a larger, more powerful version, GSLV Mark III or Launch Vehicle Mark3, which launched Chandrayaan-2 and Chandrayaan-3 missions in 2019 and 2023 respectively. This vehicle can transport satellites weighing up to 4000 kg and inject them into the geosynchronous transfer orbit. A human-rated version of this vehicle is to be used for India's maiden human space flight. The overall height of the vehicle is 43.5 m and a 5-m diameter payload fairing. It has a gross lift-off weight of 640 tonnes. Given its wayward ways and patchy success record, GSLV was nicknamed a 'naughty boy'. After the seventh consecutive successful flight of GSLV Mark III in February 2024, the project director declared, 'GSLV is now a disciplined boy.'

3

A Revolution from the Sky

IN OCTOBER 1945, Arthur C. Clarke, a twenty-eight-year-old British science fiction writer and budding futurologist, wrote a landmark paper in *Wireless World*. In the paper, which was titled 'Extraterrestrial Relays', he unveiled a new concept of orbiting satellites broadcasting directly to home receivers. Clarke proposed that by combining advances in rocketry and microwave engineering, it was possible to place artificial satellites in an orbit from where the satellite would remain stationary in relation to the Earth and use such a satellite for broadcasting signals over a large geographic area. When Clarke thought of this, the Moon was the only satellite known to humans, and radio and television broadcasting was still terrestrial – signals were beamed from a transmitting tower and received by sets within a geographic region. No technologies existed to realise extraterrestrial broadcasting from a geosynchronous orbit predicted by Clarke.

In less than a decade, however, artificial satellites became a reality, and Clarke's ideas seemed feasible. In 1964, two engineers, Richard B. Marsten and Samuel Gubin, working with a private company, the Radio Corporation of America, prepared a blueprint to design, build and launch a broadcasting satellite that could beam television signals directly to American homes using 'a lightweight, erectable antenna with steerable feed'.[1] The series of technical papers by the two evoked great interest in NASA, and it commissioned further studies by the National Academy of Sciences. All this resulted in the plan to develop broadcasting satellites and earth stations to receive signals. Marsten joined NASA in 1969 to become the director of Communications Programmes. The plan was to launch three applications technology satellites (ATS) to test not only direct-to-home (DTH) broadcasting but also other applications like telehealth and navigation.

A series of technical and geopolitical developments at the height of the Cold War in the 1960s pitch-forked India to the centre of DTH technology development. NASA was founded in 1958 after the Soviet Union launched its first satellite, but American scientists were already engaged in space-related research like atmospheric and weather studies. Indian scientists often interacted with scientists from other countries and conducted joint experiments with them during the IGY as discussed in Chapter 1. Such scientific cooperation was also an extension of American diplomacy. The Department of State used NASA's division for international cooperation for such diplomatic goals. One of the major objectives of ATS was to evaluate the efficacy of direct broadcasting in a geographically vast country with no terrestrial television.

NASA developed a programme, Satellite Instructional Television Experiment (SITE), to test the feasibility of direct broadcasting using ATS satellite. 'The whole point of SITE was that it could broadcast directly into home receivers, [obviating the need for an extensive] ground network of ... stations to receive television from a satellite and rebroadcast it through a diffusion [system]. You could skip that whole step, and go right to home receivers. So [the] infrastructure was unnecessary,' NASA scientists proposed.[2] The technology could be field-tested only in a country that was geographically large and yet had no terrestrial television. India looked like a good place to go, recounted Arnold W. Frutkin, who headed NASA's international programmes.[3]

Frutkin was acquainted with Sarabhai from the COSPAR days. He called him up and explained the idea of conducting SITE using ATS in India. Sarabhai instantly said yes. Frutkin asked Sarabhai to write a letter expressing willingness to participate in SITE to enable approval of the Department of State. This resulted in NASA signing a memorandum of understanding with DAE in 1965. The project, according to historian Asif Siddiqi, may have been a part of the American strategy to engage Indian scientists and divert them from nuclear proliferation in the light of a possible Indian response to the Chinese atomic bomb testing in 1964.[4]

The memorandum of understanding required the Indian side to design, develop, produce, deploy and operate 5000 receive-only earth stations, while the Americans provided the communication transponder in ATS-6 to beam local programmes over the Indian subcontinent 3 to 4 hours a day, 5 to 6 days a week, for one year (1 August 1975 to 31 July 1976). The programmes were uplinked from a large earth station in Ahmedabad and watched directly on community television sets installed in 2500 remote villages in six states. Some of them were not yet electrified; so, they were provided with battery-operated sets. Each television set was connected to a large chicken-mesh antenna (a large parabolic dish of 3 m diameter) that received the signals. About 24 lakh people had access to community television sets. Some 24,000 teachers were trained with training capsules designed for them.

The hardware (antenna, television sets, adapters and so on) was developed and manufactured in India. Software – programmes on birth control, basic literacy, hygiene and modern agriculture techniques as well as entertainment capsules – was developed by multidisciplinary teams consisting of sociologists, scientists, health experts and film-makers led by anthropologist Binod Agrawal. In addition to direct broadcasts to community television sets, satellite signals were also retransmitted through terrestrial networks in some cities.

SITE was not just a technology demonstrator but a sociological experiment bringing together scientists, sociologists, communication experts, meteorologists, agriculture scientists, and film and television producers to work collaboratively. The Space Applications Centre, headed by Yashpal, became the cradle for innovative programming. Developing science programmes for children in villages that did not even have proper schools was a challenge. Where schools existed, they did not have any science equipment and sometimes even a blackboard. 'I wrote down a credo which was that the objective of the science programmes would be to help children realise that science is everywhere. Science is in the kitchen, science is in the village pond, science is in the bicycle, science is in the flora and fauna, science is everywhere,' Yashpal recalled.[5]

SITE successfully demonstrated to the world the feasibility of DTH as well as satellite television using terrestrial networks. It helped Indian scientists and industry to develop capabilities to design, manufacture and maintain a large network of earth stations.

Aryabhata Shows the Way

Almost in parallel to SITE, Sarabhai began work on developing indigenous satellites. Sometime in 1968, he suggested to Udupi Ramachandra Rao (more famous as U.R. Rao), who was in PRL and a visiting professor at the South West Centre for Space in Dallas, Texas, to prepare a note justifying the need for India to build a satellite programme. Based on a preliminary note he submitted, Sarabhai wanted Rao to form a satellite group and lead it, given his interest in astronomy research and emerging satellite technology. These ideas crystallised further sometime in 1971, and ISRO formed a satellite development group. The SSTC had the Satellite Electronics Unit, while PRL scientists helped them out sometimes. Some members of the electronics team were trained in NASA. Rao assembled a group of about twenty-five scientists and engineers from PRL and SSTC's electronics unit and formed a new group named Satellite Systems Division. He also inducted specialists in thermal control, power control, orbital mechanics and so on.

The 1960s saw a series of satellites launched by America, the Soviets and some European countries. These satellites carried scientific, communication and earth observation payloads. If India wished to be a space-faring nation, it needed to develop the capability to design and fabricate satellites and payloads and rockets large enough to launch them. India could not wait for all the technological building blocks to be developed indigenously as it would take a lot of time and resources. The satellite group proposed to design and fabricate a modest-sized 100-kg satellite with a few scientific payloads and launch it from America using NASA's Scout rocket, which propels small satellites to a LEO. 'Scout was the cheapest launch vehicle we could think of at that time,' recalled Rao later.[6]

While the satellite design work was underway in Trivandrum, Sarabhai received a letter forwarded by the prime minister's Secretariat. It was from D.P. Dhar, the Indian ambassador in Moscow, and gave details of an offer from the USSR Academy of Sciences to strengthen Indo-Soviet ties in a range of areas – medicine, oceanography, space, etc. It specifically mentioned the possibility of the Soviets helping Indian scientists launch their first satellite. The USSR academy had provided equipment and a reconnaissance helicopter for TERLS, and the Soviets had perhaps come to know about the Indian plan to use an American launcher for the proposed scientific satellite.

Sarabhai was called for a meeting with the Soviet ambassador in Delhi in May 1971. At this meeting, Soviet ambassador Nikolai Pegov asked U.R. Rao the weight of the first scientific satellite launched by the Chinese. 'On hearing that it weighed around 190 kg, ambassador Pegov told us that the first Indian satellite must be heavier than the first Chinese one and the Soviet Union was ready to launch it for us whatever be the weight,' recounted Rao in his book.[7]

This placed ISRO in an advantageous position at the beginning of the 1970s and helped it quickly build the necessary building blocks of a full-scale space programme. On one hand, it was working with NASA on SITE, and with the Soviet Union on its maiden satellite project on the other. As it transpires, both the cooperation deals were somewhat driven by the geopolitics of the two superpowers.

The satellite project was named the Indo-Soviet Satellite Project, subsequently changed to Indian Scientific Satellite Project (ISSP), with a total budget of ₹3 crore including ₹1 crore foreign exchange component. The launch cost was to be borne by the Soviets. All that ISSP had in 1972 was a set of industrial sheds, a group of young engineers and scientists in their late twenties and a target of building a satellite from scratch in three years. None of the group members had even seen a satellite before, let alone built one. Even the Soviets refused to show them one during visits to Moscow. All meetings were held at the office of the space agency Interkosmos. The only exception was Rao, who had developed an X-ray astronomy payload and placed it in the Pioneer rocket as part of his postdoctoral work in Texas some years ago.

Rao was acutely aware of the absence of any capability of the Indian industry to supply the space-grade components, electronic systems and sub-systems needed to build a satellite. Importing such things through the normal government process of tendering would have delayed the project inordinately. He proposed a novel way out, and Dhawan agreed. A three-member committee with Rao as chair was constituted. T.N. Seshan, a young Indian Administrative Service officer who joined DoS as the joint secretary in charge of administration, and Y.S. Rajan, who was the scientific secretary to the ISRO chairman, were the other two members.

The committee toured France, the United Kingdom and America with a shopping list. It was empowered to select components and parts, negotiate the price and place the order on the spot. This way everything needed could be procured within months and at a good price, while following all government purchase rules. Rao also utilised his contacts in NASA, MIT and other places to access non-space-qualified parts to build an engineering mock-up of the satellite. In its final version, the satellite employed 12,000 electronic components, 20,000 solar cells and other structural parts, and 25,000 interconnections, and the total length of connecting wires was over 6 km.[8] The satellite weighed 360 kg, way more than the first Chinese satellite.

When ISSP was in the advanced stage, it was suggested that it should have a popular name and not a technical nomenclature or a numerical code. In the last meeting of the Project Management Board before the satellite was to be shipped to the USSR, Dhawan proposed three names for the satellite: Aryabhata (ancient Indian astronomer and mathematician), Mitra (friend in Hindi, to commemorate Indo-Soviet friendship) and Jawahar (to celebrate the spirit of Independence and the memory of India's first prime minister, Jawaharlal Nehru). The shortlisted names were sent to the prime minister, Indira Gandhi. She chose Aryabhata.

Aryabhata was launched from Kapustin Yar, near Volgograd in the Soviet Union, atop the giant Interkosmos rocket on 19 April 1975. This was the first India-built satellite in space, orbiting Earth. It marked India's entry into the space club. Aryabhata became an instant hit in the media and the popular imagination. Its typical shape and design, quasi-spherical with twenty-six flat faces having solar panels, was intriguing to people. The Department of Posts issued a special commemorative stamp on Aryabhata, while the Reserve Bank of India printed its image on two-rupee banknotes.

The satellite established contact with the ground station in Moscow as well as the station at SHAR, as planned. However, a drop in signals was noticed after the satellite orbited the Earth seventeen times. Command operations showed power supply to the three scientific payloads could not be established. It was then decided to switch off the supply to the payloads to keep the satellite technologically functional and prevent it from tumbling. The satellite remained in orbit for seventeen years and was considered a success from the point of view of design, fabrication, launch and orbital performance of a space-worthy satellite.

Aryabhata was followed with two experimental earth observation satellites, Bhaskara-I and Bhaskara-II, named after another ancient astronomer and mathematician. Both were designed and fabricated in India and launched from the USSR, Bhaskara-I on 7 June 1979 and Bhaskara-II on 20 November 1981. The first satellite had two types of sensors – a television camera and a microwave radiometer for land use, forestry and geology-related studies.

Another key building block in the satellite building story of ISRO is the Ariane Passenger Payload Experiment (APPLE). It was named so because it was to be launched as a co-passenger with the European satellite Meteosat on the Ariane launch vehicle. The European Space Agency (ESA), which was to launch APPLE, had a very tight deadline and specifications. The Ariane launch took place from Kourou in French Guiana, and APPLE was declared operational on 13 August 1981. It was designed to have a mix of payloads: communication, broadcasting and meteorological. It was to test Indian capabilities to build a multipurpose communication satellite, a long-term goal of ISRO to have operational satellites. It was a technological milestone for the space agency as it allowed the testing of several new technologies like 3-axis stabilisation, static earth sensor, solar array drive and solid apogee boost motor.

An iconic picture connected with APPLE shows the full-scale flight model of the spacecraft being transported on a bullock cart with rubber tyres. This was not due to lack of any transport facility but to subject the satellite to an important test that needed to be conducted in a non-magnetic environment. Conducting this test in a test facility abroad would have cost a lot of money and time, so the team decided to create the required environment on a bullock cart. 'The solution was found in about five hours and at a cost of one hundred and fifty rupees for hiring a cart,' remembers R.S. Vasagam, who was the project director of APPLE.[9]

Communication Revolution

SITE was not only a technological landmark for NASA and ISRO, but it also presented to Indian policymakers and the political leadership a glimpse of the potential of satellite technology to address some of the basic challenges India was facing in the 1970s, such as lack of literacy and numeracy, basic education and health. Although SITE was planned long ago, the timing of its execution (August 1975 to July 1976) coincided with the internal emergency declared by Prime Minister Indira Gandhi. Her Independence Day speech delivered from the Red Fort was broadcast for the first time via SITE. The SITE broadcasts also included publicity capsules on the prime minister's twenty-point economic programme.

The success of SITE made the space agency actively pursue plans to develop Indian communication and broadcasting satellites. A tentative plan for an Indian communication-cum-broadcasting satellite – Indian National Satellite (Insat) – was prepared in 1968 at Sarabhai's instance. Though Insat was formally approved in July 1977, its concept was in the minds of Indian scientists and their American counterparts involved in SITE from 1967 to 1969. The Insat system was going to be the first major national effort in harnessing space technology for practical applications in national development. It was an operational domestic satellite system for telecommunications, meteorology and direct television broadcasting. It was a unique concept because till then no satellite combined these three elements. Some media reports criticised the decision, saying a multipurpose satellite like Insat had no future as both the USA and USSR till then had launched only single-purpose satellites.

India was the first country to go for an operational domestic multipurpose satellite. This was possible because of the very detailed and systematic studies preceding the choice by experts from all the ministries and departments of the Government of India. 'Obviously, in this sense, pioneering in space need not be an exclusive preserve of the developed nations. Of the feasibility of the INSAT-1 mission and the large economy from integration of services, there can be no doubt,' ISRO chairman Satish

Dhawan explained in a letter to Krishnaswamy Rao Sahib, secretary to Prime Minister Morarji Desai in 1979.[10] The Insat spacecraft, Dhawan said, was 'indeed relatively more complex than what a set of single-mission satellites might have been but then such trade-offs can be expected for every new mission'.

Developing such satellites indigenously and launching them with Indian rockets would have taken a long time. So, it was decided to use the commercial options available. In October 1977, ISRO floated a global tender for Insat-1 spacecraft and allied equipment and services. The configuration and the transponder capacity of the satellite were decided through consultation with all potential users like Doordarshan, IMD and the Department of Telecommunications. ATS pioneer Richard Marsten was appointed as a consultant to Dhawan for Insat procurement.

Two American firms responded to the call, and after a detailed evaluation of their bids and initial negotiations, Aeronutronic Overseas Services Inc., a subsidiary of Ford Aerospace Communications Corporation, was shortlisted and eventually awarded the contract to build and launch a set of four Insat satellites in July 1978. The US Department of State gave the go-ahead after American government agencies cleared the sale. In January of the same year, another agreement was signed with America to establish a satellite earth station at Hyderabad to receive remote sensing data from the American Landsat satellite. Despite the thaw after the peaceful nuclear explosion at Pokhran in 1974, Indo-US relations in the space sector were on an upswing. Ford sent Wernher von Braun, the famed missile scientist of the Second World War era who was now working with Ford Philco as emeritus scientist, to lobby its case for the contract.

ISRO teams were deputed to work with Ford Aerospace during different stages of the fabrication, integration and the launch of these satellites, which gave them first-hand experience of working on large commercial satellites. APPLE, fabricated in India, weighed about 600 kg while Insat series satellites were 2500–3000 kg and far more complex to handle.

Insat-1A was launched on the Delta 3910 rocket from Cape Canaveral on 10 April 1982, but its C-band antenna did not open once it was in orbit. Manoeuvres from the ground station at Hassan did not help. The onboard fuel depleted, which led to the satellite drifting from its slot in the geostationary orbit and, eventually, to the failure of the mission in September 1982.

The American press blamed ISRO for the mission failure. 'ISRO was reported "caught off guard" by the amount of fuel it had used to correct early malfunctions,' a news report in the *Washington Post* said.[11] ISRO was dubbed overambitious in launching a multipurpose satellite. The report went on: 'Because INSAT was built to ISRO specifications, the blame would probably fall on Satish Dhawan, head of India's space programme, who had argued for a multifunction satellite to bring radio and television to thousands of remote villages and give India international communication links. He considered mass communications the best hope for progress in a country with a 36% literacy rate.'

The mission faced troubles even before the launch, which was put off twice because of mechanical failures. Domestically, the Insat project faced massive delays as finance minister Charan Singh in the Janata Party government stalled the release of funds, saying the project was a waste of money.[12] Facilities needed in user departments like IMD and Doordarshan to utilise the satellite were also delayed. The project was back on track only in 1981.

For launching Insat-1B a year later, the space agency chose the space shuttle *Challenger* because it cost less than a Delta launch and was more accurate. The satellite was ejected from the cargo bay of the shuttle in space by astronaut Guion Bluford Jr, the first African American to go to space. 'The mission required a night launch and a night landing because of the orbital requirements of Insat-1B. This was a weather and communication satellite with a Payload Assist Module (PAM) rocket that would boost the satellite into a geosynchronous transfer orbit [GTO],' Bluford recalled.[13] 'Forty-five minutes after deploying the satellite, we ignited the PAM which rocketed the satellite into a GTO of 22,300 miles above the earth. Ground control took over command of the satellite and fired its onboard solid propellant kick motor to circularize the orbit.'

While the ejection took place as planned and the satellite cruised to its slot in its orbit, its solar array developed a snag and refused to deploy. The problem was overcome through ground manoeuvres, and the satellite started functioning fully soon after. It remained operational beyond its designed life of seven years, providing broadcasting, telecom and met services.

The third satellite in the series, Insat-1C, was launched by an Ariane rocket on 22 July 1988. The snags with Insat continued. This time, the satellite suffered a power bus malfunction after a few days in orbit. Like 1A, Insat-1C was also declared a total failure. The last satellite of the series, Insat-1D, launched on 12 June 1990, was a success.

Though only two of the four planned Insat-1 series satellites became operational, these satellites had tremendous societal impact. In 1980, India had just seven television centres and four relay centres. The television network covered a mere 6.1 per cent of the geographic area and 15.2 per cent of the population. Insat changed this dramatically. SITE created an appetite for television in India. ISRO wanted the government to push satellite-based television broadcasting from the mid-1970s, but the broadcasting lobby (All India Radio, which also controlled Doordarshan) constantly opposed it. The situation, however, changed in the 1980s when Insat satellites became operational.

The Doordarshan network expanded rapidly, covering 90 per cent of the population and 80 per cent of the Indian land mass by the end of the 1980s. The number of television transmitters increased from forty-two in 1984 to 220 in 1988. Doordarshan centres received TV signals from the satellite and retransmitted them terrestrially for local distribution. This way, the national programmes could be watched all over the country simultaneously. Given the low penetration of television sets and the technical and practical difficulties of installing large chicken-mesh antennas, India did not opt for the DTH model demonstrated during SITE. Instead, a hybrid model was adopted: satellite signals were received by Doordarshan centres and retransmitted terrestrially. The Insat-led spread of the Doordarshan network also inaugurated the era of television soaps in India with serials like *Hum Log*, *Ramayana* and *Mahabharata* garnering massive pan-Indian viewership in the 1980s. *Hum Log*, which addressed social issues like small family size, women's status, dowry and alcoholism, garnered 65 to 90 per cent audiences in North India and 20 to 45 per cent in South India during its seventeen-month run in 1984–85.[14]

IMD used weather information from the satellite for weather summaries and forecasts. The satellite imagery of the Indian land mass with cloud cover and other information shown in prime-time news bulletins of Doordarshan made Insat a household name.

Keeping in line with the strategy of parallel development, Dhawan created the Insat-2 Study Group in 1981, and based on its report, the government gave the go-ahead for the second series in April 1985. Such advance preparation for operational satellites is necessary to ensure continuity of services once national services like broadcasting and telecommunications are delivered through a satellite platform. This not only requires new satellites at the end of the designed life of old ones but also a backup if the launch or satellite fails.

Insat-2 was planned as a second-generation series, with extended C-band telecom transponders, a higher resolution meteorological payload and a transponder for search and rescue operations, in addition to the set of transponders used in the Insat-1 series. At this point, broadcast transponders were becoming a much sought-after commodity in the emerging global market. Insat-2A and Insat-2B, built by Indian scientists and engineers, were launched on 10 July 1992 and 23 July 1993 respectively on Ariane launchers. Both the satellites were categorised as 'test satellites' to validate new technologies, but they functioned so well that they were declared operational. They were followed up with 2C, 2D and 2E and, subsequently, by the next-generation Insat-3 series. This makes Insat the crown jewel of ISRO.

An Eye in the Sky

In addition to using space technology to improve communication, broadcasting and weather services, another fundamental objective of the Indian space programme was monitoring natural resources using space technology. Remote sensing, the technique of acquiring information about Earth's surface as well as the atmosphere using airborne sensors, was identified as one of the peaceful uses of outer space by the UN. Till this point, high-altitude balloons and aircraft fitted with special cameras were used for imaging areas of interest on the Earth. Remote sensing satellites were still in the planning stage.

While wheat and rice production in India was improving as a result of high-yielding varieties introduced under what came to be known as the Green Revolution, Dr M.S. Swaminathan, who was leading this effort, was concerned about other commercial crops as well. Potential losses due to root-wilt disease affecting coconut trees in Kerala was a matter of concern. During a meeting with Sarabhai, he asked if remote sensing techniques could be used to get some advance information about its movement and spread. Sarabhai seized the opportunity, though the newly formed ISRO in 1969 did not have any project in remote sensing but only a few young scientists who had just returned after attending a conference on remote sensing in America. He asked them to prepare an experiment and made a short presentation on the potential of remote sensing in India to Prime Minister Indira Gandhi.[15] For the experiment, her approval was needed as it involved the use of a special camera from NASA.

TERLS had a Soviet helicopter. The imaging instrument and films were lent by NASA. The small team, which included ISRO and agriculture scientists, flew over coconut plantations taking images in different spectral bands. For navigation, small fires were lit on the ground. An examination of the photographic data showed identifiable changes in the crowns of disease-affected trees and also the severity of the disease. The leaves of the affected trees were examined in the lab, and the virus could be seen. This meant the disease could be detected before it spread or became severe. P.R. Pisharoty, who led the experiment, later came to be known as the father of remote sensing in India.

The Kerala experiment was followed by a larger project, the Agriculture Resource Inventory and Survey Experiment (Arise) in Anantapur in Andhra Pradesh to assess the area under rice cultivation. Meanwhile, a separate agency, the NRSA, was established in Hyderabad for remote sensing data analysis. It had a fleet of aircraft to collect remote sensing data. An Indian remote sensing satellite was still a few years away.

America launched the world's first dedicated remote sensing satellite, Landsat, in 1972, inaugurating the era of satellite-based remote sensing. Remote sensing satellites acquire information about Earth's surface (land and oceans) and the atmosphere using different types of sensors, cameras and radars. Different land cover features – water, soil, mountains, snow, vegetation – reflect visible and infrared light in different ways. By collecting, analysing and interpreting this information, scientists develop images that yield information on different parameters. Based on the analysis of Landsat data, NRSA in 1985 suggested that India's forest cover had declined from 16.9 per cent to 14.1 per cent between 1972 and 1982. This led to a major controversy as the finding was at variance with that of the Forestry Survey of India. In the end, it was decided to use remote sensing data along with 'ground truthing' to arrive at the extent of forest cover. The episode made policymakers appreciate the usefulness of satellite-based remote sensing in important decision-making areas.

Two Indian satellites, Bhaskara-I and Bhaskara-II, launched from the Soviet Union were the first Indian remote sensing or earth observation satellites. Though the resolution of images obtained was coarse, about one kilometre, it allowed Indian scientists and engineers to gain valuable experience in space imaging and associated technologies.

This experience helped ISRO plan operational remote sensing satellites. At the same time as Insat-2 development, the agency started work on another operational series: IRS (Indian Remote Sensing Satellite). The first two satellites of the series (IRS-1A and IRS-1B) were launched in 1988 and 1991 respectively on the Soviet Vostok rockets. Several ground and aerial instruments were developed indigenously. IRS-1A could provide high-quality images at a low cost due to an Indian innovation – the use of solid-state detectors (charged couple devices), which did not have any flight pedigree then.[16] Dr George Joseph led this effort, which facilitated simplified design and novel optical systems leading to low spacecraft weight and better reliability.

The migration from a two-band 1 km resolution camera to a four-band camera with a resolution of 26 m was a big leap in technology. The IRS series was followed by specialised, thematic remote sensing satellites with powerful sensors, Resourcesat, Oceansat and Cartosat series, establishing India as a global leader in remote sensing. The launch of RISAT-1 in 2012 with a synthetic aperture radar (SAR), which enabled the imaging of the earth's surface features during both day and night under all weather conditions, was another landmark. A team led by Tapan Mishra developed SAR technology at the Space Applications Centre, Ahmedabad.

During the 1962 war with China, the armed forces urgently needed some critical electronic parts, which had to be urgently fabricated at TIFR in Bombay. After the war, this experience led to the formation of the Electronics Committee chaired by Homi Jehangir Bhabha with Vikram Sarabhai among its members. The panel reviewed the requirement of electronics for communication, broadcasting, medical and other instruments used in both military and civilian sectors and proposed a blueprint for indigenous technology development.

A similar moment came during the Kargil War in 1999. It was felt that infiltration from across the border had gone unnoticed despite India having advanced in remote sensing technology. During the war, America reportedly denied India access to location data from its GPS satellites. This experience triggered two major projects at ISRO – building India's spy satellite and a constellation of Indian navigation satellites. The Technology Experiment Satellite, launched in October 2001, had a resolution of 1 m, allowing it 'to pick up images even of a truck moving along the border area of Pakistan', as a BBC report put it.[17] RISAT-2, developed by an Israeli company and launched in 2009, is also considered a spy satellite.[18]

By the turn of the century, India emerged as a space-faring nation with capabilities to design, fabricate and launch a range of satellites, track them, process satellite data and deploy space technology to a wide range of applications from education and health to navigation. The biggest impact of space technology has been felt in weather forecasting and cyclone warnings. In November 1977, when a severe cyclone in the Bay of Bengal hit the Andhra coast at Diviseema, it killed 15,000 people, and the resulting storm surge affected nearly 2 million people. The forecasters could see the eye of the storm on radar screens, but they had no means to predict its path or time and location of its landfall. A series of weather and ocean monitoring satellites have helped scientists to monitor the progress of any storm almost in real time. Combining satellite data with that from other instruments, IMD is able to predict the precise time and place of landfall of cyclones days in advance. This gives the local administration enough time to evacuate people to safer places. As a result, no human lives are lost even when cyclones of an intensity similar to or greater than Diviseema hit the Indian coast.

Satellite data from ocean monitoring satellites is helping Indian fishers in many ways. Sophisticated instruments like scatterometers provide data about sea surface temperatures and the movement of oceanographic features. This data, in turn, helps in understanding the transport of phytoplankton, zooplankton, fish eggs and juvenile fish. Along with information on waves, currents and mixed layer depths, scientists prepare 60-hour forecasts and potential fishing zone advisories during the fishing season.[19] This has helped reduce search time, saved fuel and increased the productivity of Indian fishers.

Space Start-ups Emerge

The vision document titled 'Atomic Energy and Space Research – A Profile for the Decade 1970–1980', prepared by Sarabhai, stated the prime objective of the space programme was 'to develop indigenous competence for designing and building sophisticated hardware' for rockets and satellites for scientific research and practical applications. It was an ambitious plan, seeking to develop everything – satellites, launch vehicles, ground facilities and applications. ISRO could not have achieved all this through in-house technology development and production. It needed industry and academic support from within India and outside.

The technology denial regime under the Treaty on the Non-Proliferation of Nuclear Weapons and MTCR was meant for defence-related technologies, but it affected the procurement of critical materials, components, devices and equipment for the civilian space programme as well. This forced the space agency to look for industry sources domestically or to produce the technologies in-house. Industries in diverse sectors such as electronics, computers, telecom, chemicals, scientific instruments, materials and fabrication were identified and nurtured so that they could produce and supply space-grade components and sub-systems. In the SLV-3 project, for instance, fifty-four industries participated due to the proactive engagement undertaken by the project director, A.P.J. Abdul Kalam. The ISAC, engaged in developing satellite technology, sourced 70 per cent of its electronic fabrication needs from industry.

Large sub-systems and rocket engines are produced in private- and public-sector units. The liquid-propelled Vikas engine of PSLV was productionised at Godrej & Boyce in Mumbai and MTAR Technologies in Hyderabad. Liquid engines and stages, tankages and cryogenic materials for the space programme are produced in Thiruvananthapuram at BrahMos Aerospace Thiruvananthapuram Limited. The space agency also consolidated the electronics and avionics requirements of different groups so that bulk orders could be placed. Bharat Electronics Limited formed a dedicated division for this. An aerospace division was created in Hindustan Aeronautics Limited (HAL), partly funded by ISRO, as rocket fabrication needs went up with PSLV becoming operational.

Building upon the industrial base developed in the aerospace industry, ISRO in September 2020 took the next step: opening the sector for the private sector to take up space projects independently. It formed a new wing, IN-SPACe or Indian National Space Promotion and Authorisation Centre, in 2020 as a mechanism to allow private companies to participate in core space activities. Besides allowing non-government entities to build, operate and control satellites and all associated infrastructure, the space agency allowed private companies to access its technical facilities.

The policy changes boosted the space start-up ecosystem and encouraged large industrial houses to expand their space business. Agnikul Cosmos, incubated in the Indian Institute of Technology Madras, and Hyderabad-based Skyroot Aerospace are developing independent rockets. Bengaluru-based firms Pixxel and Astrome plan to launch a constellation of LEO satellites. The Hyderabad-based

Ananth Technologies, founded by Subbarao Pavuluri who earlier worked with ISRO, is building satellites for customers in France and Sweden. In August 2024, Ananth announced that it had completed 'assembly, integration and testing' of two 400-kg-class satellites for ISRO. This was the first time the space agency tasked a private company to do this. Tata Advanced Systems supplied a military satellite to an American company, Satellogic.

Several other start-ups are working on a range of activities – satellite constellations, small satellite launch vehicles, ground stations, geospatial services, propulsion systems and application products.

The Hyderabad-based Dhruva Space designs and makes space-qualified solar arrays and has constructed satellite deployment systems compatible with PSLV. Bellatrix Aerospace in Bengaluru is focused on developing advanced in-space propulsion systems and rocket propulsion technologies. It works on propulsion systems or thrusters for heavy, micro, and nanosatellites. InspeCity, incubated in IIT Bombay, specialises in satellite life-enhancing and deorbiting services. The Ahmedabad-based PierSight is developing an SAR and Automatic Identification System integrated satellite technology for ocean monitoring. Satellize, founded by Hyderabad entrepreneurs Mahesh Murthy and Ashhar Farhan, specialises in customised nanosatellites. Private space companies, however, face challenges like lack of adequate funding and a hazy regulatory and legal environment.

4

To the Moon, Mars and Venus

IT WAS ABOUT 5 AM on 22 October 2008. The Sriharikota spaceport presented a serene yet bustling scene. After the overnight rains, the tarred roads, avenue trees and manicured lawns around scientific and administrative blocks were all wet. Puddles formed on the ground, reflecting the faint light of dawn breaking in the eastern sky. Plants and trees were glistening with droplets of water, while birds chirped in the surrounding trees. The mild sea breeze wafting from the Bay of Bengal was moist. I was in SHAR to cover a space mission after almost two decades. A lot had changed since the last time I was here in 1988.

The Brahma Prakash Hall, in which the press teams were seated, was large, well lit and air-conditioned and had a huge screen on which we could see the live feed from the mission control room. Given the size of the press contingent and the importance of the mission, an adjoining hall was converted into a press room where journalists could write their stories and transmit visual feeds. We were eager to witness the launch of Chandrayaan-1, India's maiden mission to the Moon. Soon, daylight broke, and clouds started clearing, as if to signal the beginning of a new chapter in India's space exploration journey.

At 5:40 AM, ISRO chairman G. Madhavan Nair walked into the control room, taking his place along with members of the Launch Authorisation Board and mission directors. Though PSLV had thirteen consecutive successful flights by then, this flight was crucial because it was going to place Chandrayaan-1 on a trajectory that would take it to an orbit around the Moon. It was a prestigious mission as the international lunar community was keenly watching it because it was among the first attempts by any country to return to the Moon after decades. The spacecraft carried payloads from NASA, ESA and the Bulgarian Academy of Sciences, along with those developed by Indian scientists. Scientists from these agencies sat in the VIP gallery in the mission control centre.

The Launch Authorisation Board, which met at 1:30 AM to review the mission preparations, considered all options, including a possible postponement if the weather did not clear. It was going to be a very close call, as the launch window available in the morning was just 15 minutes long. The continuing rains on the island due to the north-eastern monsoon the previous day caused much anxiety. To provide location-specific weather forecasts, a team of weather scientists stationed in the spaceport was working on multiple computer models, observational inputs from met satellite Kalpana-1, data from Doppler radars, automatic weather stations and GPS atmospheric sounding equipment. The previous night, the team gave a 6-hour prediction for the island, which appeared to be precise as the countdown progressed. During the 52-hour countdown, as many as 814 specific activities took place and hundreds of parameters were checked.

The four-stage launch vehicle, PSLV-C11, an upgraded version of the standard PSLV configuration used in earlier launches, lifted off majestically at 06:22 hours. It used larger strap-on motors to be able to achieve a higher payload capability. At lift-off, the 44-m-tall rocket weighed 316 tonnes. Even after a smooth lift-off, Nair continued sitting motionless with tension writ large on his face. It took nearly 18 minutes for all the stages of the rocket to ignite and separate, finally injecting the Chandrayaan-1 spacecraft into its initial orbit. Only then Nair clapped, smiled and hugged his colleagues. Later he went around the hall, shaking hands with fellow scientists.

A few minutes later, Nair walked into the Brahma Prakash Hall to address the press conference. 'This mission had a lot of dramatic moments after the vehicle was moved to the launch station. We were working against all odds,' Nair said in his opening remarks. 'What we have faced in the last five days has really been an ordeal.' While the launch was successful, Chandrayaan-1 had a long way to go before it reached its intended lunar orbit. 'There are many technological challenges ahead, as the spacecraft goes through different gravitational forces and extreme thermal environments. Our scientists have not taken any chance, they have simulated the environment. Still, there are many unknowns,' Nair spoke cautiously to the press.

PSLV injected Chandrayaan-1 into an elliptical orbit around Earth, about 22,860 km at its farthest point (apogee). Over the next two weeks, Chandrayaan's onboard propulsion system called Liquid Apogee Motors (LAM) was fired five times when the spacecraft came close to Earth. Each firing increased the speed of the spacecraft, and it went farther. The orbit-raising operations were executed from the Mission Operations Centre in Bangalore, and the spacecraft was being tracked from a new facility, the Indian Deep Space Network, established at Byalalu near Bangalore.

By gradually increasing its apogee, the spacecraft was brought into the lunar transfer trajectory with an apogee of 380,000 km on 4 November. The spacecraft eventually came under the gravitational pull of the moon and started orbiting it on 8 November 2008. The Indian Moon mission finally reached its destination – a circular orbit just 100 km from the Moon. It was the first Indian mission to deep space.

Once the spacecraft settled in the lunar orbit, Indian scientists had a novel experiment in the offing: the ejection of the Moon Impact Probe (MIP) from Chandrayaan-1 and its crash landing on the lunar surface.

On 14 November 2008, the scene inside the mission operations centre of the ISRO Telemetry Tracking and Command Centre in Bangalore was similar to the one during the launch from Sriharikota three weeks earlier. MIP, weighing about 34 kg, consisted of a C-band radar altimeter for measurement of altitude of the probe, a video imaging system for acquiring images of the lunar surface and a mass spectrometer for measuring the constituents of the lunar atmosphere. The shiny cubical object had the Indian flag printed on all its sides. Before it was detached from the spacecraft, its camera was switched on so that it could record its 25-minute journey to the lunar surface.

The free fall of MIP was planned such that it would land at a designated place near the Shackleton crater in the South Pole region of the Moon. As the probe descended towards the Moon, it photographed the lunar surface below and collected data about the lunar atmosphere. The spot where the MIP crash-landed was later named Jawahar Sthal as the day of its landing happened to be the birthday of India's first prime minister, Jawaharlal Nehru.

The idea of an Indian object touching the lunar surface came from A.P.J. Abdul Kalam during his visit to VSSC as the President of India in 2003. He was keen that an Indian payload should land on the lunar surface. 'It was a tough call because the probe was thought of much after the configuration of Chandrayaan was frozen. This placed constraints on the weight of the probe. Another crucial technology that was developed was a special motor with a safe propellant that could be used for MIP without affecting other payloads of the satellite. A commercial camera was used after it was space-qualified,' recalled

Madan Lal, who led the MIP development project, in an interview with the author.[1] By the time the mission became a reality, both Kalam and Lal had retired, but they were present in the control centre to witness MIP hitting the lunar surface.

Like all ISRO missions, Chandrayaan, too, has a long story. The possibility of Indian interplanetary missions was first mentioned to the public in a lecture ISRO chairperson K. Kasturirangan delivered in New Delhi at a function in May 1999 to mark the first anniversary of the nuclear device testing at Pokhran. The government decided to celebrate 11 May every year as National Technology Day. Towards the end of his presentation on the Indian space programme, Kasturirangan showed a couple of slides on how the capabilities of PSLV and GSLV could be exploited to reach the Moon, Mars and Venus. The slides were based on the conceptual work done by Dr Adimurthy and Dr R.V. Ramanan at VSSC. The mention of interplanetary missions using the existing technological capabilities caught the attention of scientists, policymakers and journalists present in the audience. The news was splashed in the next day's newspapers with headlines like 'India now aiming for the Moon'.

The mention of interplanetary missions in Kasturirangan's speech was a departure from the guiding philosophy of using space technology for national development that ISRO followed from the beginning. Sarabhai had famously said, 'There are some who question the relevance of space activities in a developing nation. To us, there is no ambiguity of purpose. We do not have the fantasy of competing with the economically advanced nations in the exploration of the Moon or the planets or manned space flights.'[2]

Three decades after Sarabhai made the statement, ISRO was embarking upon the same path that its founder had warned against.

Given the wide interest the idea generated over the next few months, the space agency thought it prudent to discuss it with the larger scientific community. A presentation was made to the Indian Academy of Sciences in October 1999, followed by a discussion at a meeting of the Astronautical Society of India in February 2000. A detailed feasibility assessment study was completed in 2001, and the idea of a lunar mission was presented before the Parliamentary Standing Committee in April 2002. A political consensus on the mission was thought necessary because it signified a deviation from the well-proven path of launching operational satellites. The Lunar Mission Study Task, chaired by Dr George Joseph, concluded in its report submitted in July 2002 that 'it is feasible to have a mission to the Moon with the present capabilities of ISRO and the sensor development competence available in the country'.[3] The report referred to the proposed mission as Somayana-1 (meaning the moon craft in Sanskrit).

After necessary approvals from the Space Commission, the file was sent to Prime Minister Vajpayee. By now, the parliamentary panel had submitted its report, putting its seal of approval on the interplanetary plans of the space agency. Vajpayee told Kasturirangan: 'Now there is political interest in this, there is general societal interest also. I will make the announcement [about it] on the Independence Day.'[4] As promised, the prime minister announced India's plan to launch a lunar mission in his speech from the Red Fort on 15 August 2003. But ISRO was in for a little surprise. Vajpayee did not use the suggested name, Somayana, for the Moon mission but called it Chandrayaan. When Kasturirangan met the prime minister the next day, Vajpayee told him that he consulted some Sanskrit scholars who felt that Chandrayaan was more apt. From then on, it took another four years to get the mission ready for launch. Mylswamy Annadurai was named the Project Director.

While India had the technological feasibility to launch a lunar orbiter with the proven capability of PSLV and had a conceptual work on the lunar trajectory ready, what new scientific goal was India's lunar mission going to achieve? It was a pertinent question. The first race to the Moon in the 1960s and 1970s saw humans land on the lunar surface. The Apollo and Luna missions of the 1960s collected lunar rock and dust samples, analysis of which gave important clues about the origin of the Moon and its evolutionary process. Such missions, however, were limited to equatorial regions or the near side of the Moon. The scientific data they collected was not sufficient for modelling the chemical and physical evolution of the Moon.

Unlike the landing missions, which could explore only limited parts of the Moon, orbital missions like Chandrayaan were considered more valuable as they could gather data continuously, covering large swathes of the lunar surface. The turn of the century witnessed a renewed interest in the Moon and the beginning of a so-called second race to the Moon. ESA launched a lunar mission in 2006, followed by the orbital missions by Japan and China in 2007 and Chandrayaan in 2008. The next year, NASA launched its Lunar Reconnaissance Orbiter.

The second Moon race was an attempt to fill the gaps in the understanding of the Moon. A key objective of Chandrayaan-1 was to undertake chemical, mineral and topographic mapping using an array of cameras at different wavelengths. Since the spacecraft was designed to circle the Moon for two years, it was expected to yield valuable information. A big hope was to detect the possible presence of water and helium-3.

However, the orbiter faced many challenges, and it remained in orbit only for ten months. The first inkling of trouble came within a month of the launch when the spacecraft began getting heated due to lunar summer. It experienced abnormally high temperatures within a month of being in orbit. This necessitated the gradual switching on of different onboard cameras. Just one camera was switched on at a time, but ISRO downplayed this, saying, 'There is nothing unusual about it.' The heating was due to the failure of the tiny DC/DC converters. The second trouble was the failure of star sensors, which, as scientists later revealed, made 'the spacecraft operation to be carried out without star sensors which are normally required for attitude referencing of a satellite'.[5] By this time, the spacecraft had circled the Moon 3400 times, and ISRO claimed that 95 per cent of the mission objectives were achieved.

It became apparent in May 2009 that the mission was in serious trouble when ISRO raised the orbit of Chandrayaan-1, which was at a height of 100 km from the lunar surface since November 2008, to 200 km.[6] The reason given was that higher altitude will enable studies on orbit perturbations and gravitational field variation, and enable imaging of a wider swathe of the lunar surface. This seemed odd because all along the space agency had touted lunar orbit at an altitude of 100 km as the unique selling point of Chandrayaan-1, and all imaging instruments were geared for taking pictures from this altitude. The communication with Chandrayaan-1 was lost on 29 August 2009, and the mission was terminated.

The taint of premature termination of a prestigious scientific mission, however, was short-lived as scientists made a dramatic announcement on 29 September 2009 – a breakthrough discovery of water on the Moon – in the top scientific journal *Science*. Among the eleven payloads on Chandrayaan-1 was the Moon Mineralogy Mapper (M3) jointly developed by Brown University and the Jet Propulsion Laboratory of NASA. It was designed to study lunar geology by measuring characteristics of sunlight reflected from the lunar surface. As different materials on the lunar surface absorb and reflect sunlight in different ways, it could give an idea of different molecules, including water.

'When the first hint for the presence of these two [water and hydroxyl] molecular species in the sunlit polar region of the Moon was seen in the [M3] data, it was both a surprise and a suppressed delight,' recalled Jitendra Nath Goswami, principal scientist of the Chandrayaan-1 mission.[7] It was a surprise because it was believed till then that if there is water on the Moon, it will be in the permanently shadowed areas like the base of deep craters. Over the next few weeks, M3 collected data from different polar areas and made repeat observations of some areas. In all this, signals of absorption due to water and hydroxyl were clear. The landmark discovery was announced to the world jointly by Indian and American researchers. What a landing mission could not find half a century ago, an orbiting mission could. India's journey to the Moon did not go in vain.

MIP carried an instrument, Chandrayaan Altitude Compositional Equipment, that collected data on the composition of the lunar atmosphere as MIP descended on the Moon. Analysis of data collected by this instrument during its 20-minute journey revealed signals of water and carbon dioxide molecules as well as traces of other molecules in the lunar environment. This was also a surprise discovery.

Other important discoveries followed – sub-surface ice and permanently shadowed craters, mini-magnetosphere and refractory rocks not identified earlier. Chandrayaan-1 data also resulted in the preparation of a three-dimensional, high-resolution map of the lunar surface. The Terrain Mapping Camera captured some 70,000 images of the

Moon, including six points where Apollo had landed in the 1960s and the 1970s. The findings, including the presence of water molecules, were reconfirmed by subsequent lunar missions like the Lunar Reconnaissance Orbiter and Lunar Crater Observation and Sensing Satellite of NASA.

The second lunar mission, Chandrayaan-2, was an advance over the first one. While Chandrayaan-1 was an orbiting mission, its successor included a landing capsule with a rover inside it. Unlike MIP, which achieved hard landing, Chandrayaan-2 was supposed to soft-land a lander named Vikram with a robotic rover (Pragyan) through controlled descent. The satellite onboard GSLV Mark III was launched on 22 July 2019 from Sriharikota and was elevated to the lunar orbit on 20 August 2019 following a series of orbit-raising manoeuvres. Chandrayaan-2 was placed in a 100-km lunar polar orbit, very much like its predecessor. On 2 September 2019, a crucial operation was planned: the separation of Vikram and its controlled descent on the lunar surface.

Given the experience with Chandrayaan-1, which discovered water on the Moon, and the success of the MOM (discussed in the next section) in 2014, the planned soft-landing of Chandrayaan-2 evoked great public interest. Television channels arranged live commentaries on the landing mission and were showing ISRO's live feed from the control room. This time, I was sharing the excitement from a television studio in Noida and participating in the accompanying discussion. The show went on and on as the soft landing was planned between 1 AM and 2 AM. Everybody was reminded of the statement of ISRO chairman K. Sivan about the powered descent of Vikram after its detachment from the spacecraft at an altitude of 35 km above the lunar surface. Sivan had described the descent sequence as 'fifteen minutes of terror', given the uncertainties involved in the operation. Soft-landing is a tricky proposition, and not many space agencies succeeded in achieving it in their first attempt. Till then, only 50 per cent of thirty-eight soft-landing lunar missions were successful.

Vikram got detached as planned and began its descent to the lunar surface around 1:40 AM. There was no cheer in the control room. Everyone was glued to their screens. Prime Minister Narendra Modi sat in the VIP area, along with retired space scientists and officials. The screen showed an animated model of Vikram as it descended, along with altitude and other parameters. Suddenly, the 1477-kg lander started deviating from its intended trajectory, and at 1:52 AM, when it was just about 2 km away from the lunar surface, Vikram stopped communicating. It had a hard landing. The landing mission failed though the Chandrayaan-2 orbiter continued in its orbit and remained there for the rest of its designed life.

The soft landing was finally achieved with Chandrayaan-3 launched on 14 July 2023. Vikram made a soft landing on the Moon at 18:03 hours on 23 August 2023, making India the fourth nation to have achieved the feat.

The Indian lunar missions have rekindled global interest in the Moon and are helping redefine lunar science. The new scientific findings from these missions have busted several notions about the Moon, such as it being bone-dry, geologically dead and lacking a gravitational field. Indian scientists have not only found the signature of water on the lunar surface but have shown that the lunar surface is dynamic and volcanically active and has mini magnetospheres, according to P. Veeramuthuvel, project director of Chandrayaan-3.[8]

A Slingshot to Mars

Man's interest in Mars began as soon as space exploration started sixty years ago. In the very beginning, scientists from America and the Soviet Union tried to send missions to the Red Planet. In the first pictures of the planet taken by these missions, Mars appeared like a fuzzy red ball. Over the decades, we have reached a stage where we know so much about this planet that we are even thinking of sending humans there. The discovery of the likely presence of water on Mars is the most important landmark in this fascinating journey of Mars exploration.

After the success of Chandrayaan-1, it was natural for India to think of exploring deep space beyond the Moon. Mars was an obvious choice for several reasons. In many ways, it is the most Earth-like planet that holds the secrets of our past and possibilities of the future. Mars was formed around the same time as Earth but is only half the diameter of Earth. The surface temperature on Mars is like extreme temperatures in some regions on the Earth. Mars has days and nights almost corresponding to the day-night cycle on Earth as well as gravity, though much weaker than Earth. The Martian environment also depends on the interactions of atmosphere, hydrosphere, cryosphere and lithosphere. It has an abundance of iron oxide, giving it a red hue. In science fiction and popular imagination, Mars is seen as a habitable planet or a place where aliens come from.

For such reasons, Mars has captured the imagination of space explorers since the beginning of the space age. The very first Soviet and American interplanetary missions were aimed at reaching Mars. Reaching Mars, however, is a tough call. It is some 55 million km away when it is closest to the Earth (the Moon is about 400,000 km away). At other times, it is 400 million km, and it could take up to nine months for any spacecraft to reach Mars, braving the harsh space conditions for such a long period.

No wonder only half of some sixty missions to Mars (fly-by, orbiting and landing types) since 1960 have been successful. The first successful fly-by mission occurred in

1965 when NASA's Mariner 4 flew past Mars and sent the first-ever images of the planet. Mars missions of the Soviet Union in 1971 and ESA in 2003 succeeded but none of them in their first attempt. India launched its MOM on 5 November 2013, and the spacecraft was inserted into the Mars orbit on 24 September 2014. India made history by becoming the first country to successfully get to the Red Planet in the very first attempt.

The idea of an Indian mission to Mars germinated in the recommendations of the Advisory Committee for Space Science chaired by U.R. Rao. The space vision document prepared by the panel identified missions to Mars as an important component of ISRO's interplanetary foray. K. Radhakrishnan, who took over as ISRO chairman in November 2009, formed the Mars Mission Study Team in August 2010. He chose Vipparthi Adimurthy to head this panel that had members from all key units and centres of the space agency. For many years, Adimurthy, a doctorate from IIT Kanpur, led space dynamics studies at VSSC and played a key role in designing the Chandrayaan-1 mission.

After studying different possibilities and technological options available to ISRO, the task force recommended an orbiting probe to be launched using the PSLV-XL quickly. The urgency was because of the favourable Earth–Mars geometry, which provided a window between November 2013 and January 2016. If ISRO wanted to launch a mission to Mars with the available rocket technology and by optimally using onboard fuel, it had to do it at the earliest. The next such window would have been in mid-2018. The agency opted for the earliest opportunity even though it meant readying the spacecraft and scientific payloads in less than twenty-four months. The project was approved by the central government on the very same day it was submitted in June 2011.

Designing a spacecraft for the mission posed challenges in power management, communication and onboard propulsion systems. Spacecrafts usually draw power from solar panels fitted on them. MOM was to do the same, but given the lower solar irradiance during its long journey, it had to have larger solar panels. A communication signal from a Martian orbiter takes about 20 minutes to travel the 400-million-km distance to the ground stations as against the 1.5 seconds it takes from the Moon. This meant no real-time interventions were possible if something was to go wrong. So, the probe had to have onboard autonomy for critical operations. Another challenge was restarting the onboard propulsion system after a long period of hibernation during the trans-Mars journey. Alongside the work on designing and fabrication of the orbiter, the mission teams designed the complicated pathway for sending the probe to Mars, divided into three phases – the Earth orbital phase, the trans-Mars phase, and the Mars orbit capture phase.

The journey of MOM began on 5 November 2013 when PSLV-XL took off from SHAR at 02:38 hours. The mission sequence was different from the one for launching routine satellites. The first three stages of the rocket separated in 9 minutes. Then, for 24 minutes, the rocket continued without the fourth stage burning in what was called the 'coasting phase'. After this, the fourth stage of the rocket ignited and separated, releasing MOM into the parking orbit around Earth. In this highly elliptical orbit, MOM was 248 km from the Earth at its closest point and 25,553 km at the farthest point. A series of six orbit manoeuvres were conducted between 7 and 13 November by firing the onboard propulsion systems, LAM. These operations raised the farthest point to about 193,000 km. On 1 December, the LAM was fired once again. When it gained enough velocity, it was manoeuvred to escape the gravitational pull of Earth and move tangentially towards Mars. The Mars Transfer Trajectory was the second and longest phase of MOM's journey. Over the next 300 days, it travelled a total distance of 653 million km.

While the distances involved in the mission are astronomical, every operation right from the launch had to be executed precisely. Even a micro-second delay or deviation could have jeopardised the mission. As the spacecraft left Earth, the accuracy needed for the overall attitude (orientation) had to be the order of 0.01 arc second. This accuracy level is like shooting a 1 cm diameter coin placed at a distance of 200 km, according to Adimurthy.[9] An error of a mere 1 m per second in the velocity given to the spacecraft by the propulsion system could lead to up to 200,000 km error in the position when the spacecraft approached Mars. Closer to Mars, a delay of a few seconds in initiating the retarding burn of LAM could have resulted in a deviation of lakhs of kilometres.

In the early hours of 24 September 2014, the LAM was fired once more, this time to retard the velocity of MOM so that it could enter the 'Sphere of Influence' of Mars. Another firing of the onboard propulsion system at 7:17 AM further slowed down MOM, and it was inserted into the Martian orbit. While the satellite had travelled 653 million km, the distance between it and Earth was 224 million km. At this distance, it took 12 minutes for a command sent from mission control to reach the spacecraft.

Ritu Karidhal, project manager and deputy operations director of the Mars mission, recalled: 'Our preparations for Mars Orbit Insertion began two months in advance. We had extensive reviews about the configuration and the commands to be given. On D-day, the sequence of operations went off as planned, including the blackout when the spacecraft went behind Mars. It was as if time had stopped for those 26 minutes. At 8 AM IST history was made when MOM entered the Martian orbit.'[10]

With this, MOM finally reached the orbit around Mars, and India became the first country to do so in the very first attempt.

Over the next few days and weeks, scientists carried out finer corrections in the orbit and switched on MOM payloads like the methane detector. The sensors and cameras threw new light on the Martian atmosphere and its topography.

The Mars mission has meant a great deal for ISRO. It propelled India into a select club of nations with the capability of not just launching satellites but also highly complex deep space missions and managing them. From approval to launch, MOM took an incredibly short time of fifteen months. This demonstrates that a government agency like ISRO has the capability to execute complex technology projects within a very tight deadline and with available resources. Executing such a project in a tight time frame, with no room for failure, needs a very high level of project management, teamwork, review mechanism and quality control. India's ability to successfully realise the complex mission to Mars in its first attempt, in a cost-effective (₹450 Cr) manner, captured the world's attention and propelled India's image as a credible space-faring nation to greater heights. This capability could pave the way for greater opportunities for space commerce, including launch services and marketing of satellite imageries, according to ISRO.[11]

For a country steeped in ancient beliefs around Mars and other planets, a mission to deep space was more than just a scientific endeavour. In the marriage market of 21st-century India, being born on a day when Mars is in a so-called unfavourable constellation (being a *manglik*) is still considered a curse. All this when we know that the planet being blamed for the misfortune of mangliks is located several hundred million kilometres away and there is no way its sphere of influence could extend to the marriage prospects of individual earthlings. Though ISRO has had a very good track record with a gamut of operational satellites, it was challenging missions like the Chandrayaan and MOM that provided the opportunity to boost public understanding of science.

The Secret of Cost-effective Missions

India's success with MOM attracted global attention, particularly in the West, because NASA's Mars probe, MAVEN (Mars Atmosphere and Volatile Evolution Mission), reached its orbit around the Red Planet in the same week. The two missions were compared for their cost. MOM's cost was about US$74 million while MAVEN's was US$671 million. Media reports also compared MOM's cost with that of the 2013 space fiction movie *Gravity*, which had a budget of US$100 million. 'Just Rs 450 crore. That is Rs 12 per km. Equivalent to auto fare. Truly Indian,' read an intrepid comment on ISRO's Facebook page on the Mars mission, summarising a layperson's understanding of the discussion on the cost of space missions.[12] The tabloid *Mail Today* dubbed the mission as 'ISRO's Martian Garib Rath'.[13]

The cost of an interplanetary mission depends on several obvious factors like the size of the spacecraft, the launch vehicle and payloads, the cost of man-hours spent in the project and so on, but an equally important contributor is the design of a mission's trajectory. Both MOM and Chandrayaan-1 were appreciated in the global space community for the creatively frugal and cost-effective ways in which the two missions reached their respective destinations.

Designing an interplanetary mission requires deep knowledge of space dynamics or astrodynamics. Planets and celestial bodies like the Moon are in motion all the time, and they are hung together through the forces of gravity. Everything – the selection of launch vehicle, the design of spacecraft, sub-systems and payloads, launch window and time of launch, flight duration, the velocity to be attained during flight – is determined by the trajectory design. All of this influences the mission cost. Scientists who work in astrodynamics are the back-room people of space missions and the unsung heroes of India's cost-effective space programme. R.V. Ramanan is one such pioneer who has designed several key mission trajectories at ISRO. Ramanan, born in a middle-class family in a village near Madurai, was inspired to become a space scientist by a book on rockets that he got as the prize for winning a science quiz in school. Ramanan recalls: 'When I joined VSSC, we had a lot of spare time because launch missions used to take place once in two to three years. We were told to utilise the time to work in any area of our choice. I chose interplanetary missions because this subject fascinated me from my college days and we had a paper on space dynamics. I was cautioned that there was nobody [in VSSC] to guide me and there was no internet but the VSSC library was well stocked. I started exploring books and research journals to figure out how to design an inter-planetary mission.'[14]

Ramanan joined VSSC in 1984 after completing an MSc in mathematics from Madura College, Madurai. He wrote his first technical report on an Earth–Mercury mission in 1987. The calculations he made matched those given in the NASA data book. Ramanan's boss was impressed and encouraged him to continue his work. He then worked out Earth–Venus and Earth–Mars trajectories.

In 1994, ISRO formed a technical committee on interplanetary missions in which Ramanan started working with his senior Dr Adimurthy who was an expert in launch vehicle trajectory design. Ramanan said, 'We prepared a report on interplanetary missions, and at the end of it, we added a small chapter on the Moon as it was the closest celestial body though not a planet. The dynamics governing a lunar trajectory is different because planets are governed by the Sun while the Moon is governed by the Earth.'[15] He wrote a research paper on the lunar trajectory and sent it to a research journal. One of the reviewers wrote, 'Anyone needing a lunar transfer trajectory might well consider this one,' while another was sarcastic, saying, 'I am impressed that India has a space centre and they are interested in going to the Moon.'

Fellow scientists in ISRO, too, were dismissive of Ramanan's work, saying, 'NASA has gone to the Moon so many years ago, what new you are going to do.' Ramanan would tell them, 'We can find new ways of reaching the Moon. Which day to start, which time, at what velocity, relative geometry of the Earth-Moon position – these are all unknowns which we have to work out.'[16] The Apollo-11 mission in 1969 took 3 days, 3 hours and 39 minutes to land on the Moon. It used a very powerful rocket so the trajectory was short. On the other hand, Chandrayaan-1 took twenty-one days to reach the lunar orbit because it used a modest-capacity rocket but a novel trajectory.

For Chandrayaan-1, Ramanan said that the mandate was to use the available rocket, PSLV: 'So, we had to optimally use the propulsion system of the spacecraft. Therefore, we decided to use PSLV propulsion to get into a high-energy elliptical orbit and then push the spacecraft towards the Moon. Till then, others were all using a circular orbit around Earth because it allowed every day an opportunity to manoeuvre the spacecraft towards the moon. In an elliptical orbit, we get only two opportunities in a month and the time available is also restricted. Despite these challenges, we opted for an elliptical transfer orbit as it saved fuel and we could use the available rocket.'[17]

The innovation was born out of necessity. The strategy required no change in the configuration of PSLV, the spacecraft had good payload capability and the time taken for mission development was short. MOM trajectory was also designed similarly to enable the use of PSLV.

Chasing Space Weather

On 2 September 2023, another ambitious mission, Aditya-L1, to study the Sun was launched. Scientists have been observing the Sun for long using ground-based telescopes to study what the Sun is made of and its influence on the solar system.

After the space age began, scientists became interested in getting a clearer view of celestial bodies from space by launching space telescopes. A space telescope is nothing but a satellite with sophisticated instruments to watch celestial objects like stars, black holes, galaxies and so on. Space-based astronomical observations are important because all celestial objects cannot be seen and tracked from ground-based observatories. Celestial objects are detected by signals of various gases they emit. These signals either become faint or cannot be detected due to the Earth's atmosphere. Therefore, initially, scientists used balloons or observatories located at high altitudes for their studies. Then NASA launched the Hubble Space Telescope in 1990, followed by Chandra X-ray Observatory (named after India-born astrophysicist and Nobel laureate S. Chandrasekhar) in 1999.

Around the same time, Indian scientists started planning a space telescope, Astrosat. It was launched in 2015 with

India-made instruments. Most of the payloads were designed and developed by Indian astronomers from leading centres such as TIFR and the Inter-University Centre for Astronomy and Astrophysics, Pune. One of the unique features of the observatory was its capability to gather astronomical data in different wavelengths (optical, ultraviolet, low- and high-energy X-ray) simultaneously. This was a big deal for space observatories because most such missions till then were meant to capture data in one or two wavelengths. Astrosat made several significant discoveries: detection and characterisation of star formation in and around Jellyfish galaxies, detection of young main-sequence stars in the bulge of Andromeda galaxy outside the nucleus, and discovery of X-ray polarisation from the off-pulse region of Crab pulsar.

Encouraged by the success of Astrosat and the capability of the Indian astrophysical community, it was decided to launch a space-based solar observatory. It was first proposed to have a modest mission with one payload, Visible Emission Line Coronagraph, to observe the solar corona from an 800-km LEO. The mission was named Aditya (the Sun in Sanskrit). Subsequently, the scientific community felt it would be better to place an observatory in the halo orbit around the first Lagrangian point (L1) of the Sun–Earth system since it could provide continuous viewing of the Sun. The Lagrangian points are gravitationally stable spots in the direction of the Sun, providing the advantage of continuously viewing the Sun without any occultation/eclipses.

The mission was thus reconfigured as Aditya-L1, and it was decided to place it at L1, which is 1.5 million km from Earth towards the Sun. The Sun is about 150 million km from Earth. Instead of just one payload as originally planned, Aditya-L1 had a total of seven instruments. Besides the instruments to study the solar corona (the outer layers of the Sun with a temperature of over 1 million degrees Kelvin), Aditya-L1 had instruments to observe the Sun's photosphere and chromosphere as well. The suite of Aditya-L1 payloads is expected to provide the most crucial information to understand the problems of coronal heating, coronal mass ejection, pre-flare and flare activities and their characteristics, study of the propagation of particles, fields in the interplanetary medium and so on.

Placing the solar observatory in the L1 point was a major challenge. After its launch from SHAR on 2 September 2023, Aditya-L1 embarked on an extraordinary journey to the L1 point. In a series of manoeuvres executed from the ground, the onboard propulsion system was fired at an appropriate time to increase the size of the satellite orbit progressively and move it towards the L1 point. Five liquid engine burns were executed during the Earth orbit phase; the fifth burn set Aditya-L1 in the trans-L1 injection trajectory. The velocity was managed in a way to minimise the spacecraft's exposure to the high-radiation Van Allen radiation belts. The spacecraft underwent a cruise phase lasting for about 110 days before it was injected into the halo orbit on 6 January 2024. The project director of the Aditya mission was Nigar Shaji, who has been a part of several satellite projects at the U.R. Rao Satellite Centre. She was born as Nigar Sultana in a farming family in Sengottai town in Tamil Nadu and did her engineering degree from Madurai Kamraj University, Tamil Nadu. An important objective of Aditya-L1 is to study the space weather, which refers to the changing environmental conditions in space in the vicinity of Earth and other planets. Space weather is determined by the radiation, heat and flow of particles and magnetic fields from the Sun. The flow of high-energy protons from the Sun is known as solar wind, which fills nearly all the space in the solar system, along with the solar magnetic field.

The explosive eruptions during the coronal mass ejection (CME) events also affect the solar weather. The interaction of Earth's magnetic field with the field carried by CME can trigger a magnetic disturbance near Earth. Such disturbances can affect the functioning of space assets like communication satellites. 'Activity of planet-sized sunspots – dark areas of strong magnetic field on the Sun's surface – affect solar wind influencing space weather. These magnetic fields fan out in loop-like structures, permeating different layers of the Sun's atmosphere, from the chromosphere to the super-hot outer corona,' explained Dibyendu Nandi, head of the Center of Excellence in Space Sciences India, Indian Institute of Science Education and Research, Kolkata.[18] Keeping an eye on the solar weather, therefore, is vital for commercial space assets. Aditya-L1 has been able to detect the impact of CME using an advanced detector, PAPA or Plasma Analyser Package for Aditya.

The next planetary stop of ISRO would be Venus. In September 2023, ISRO chairman S. Somanath announced that the Venus orbiter mission (unofficially referred to as Shukrayaan) had been configured, and a set of scientific instruments to study the Venus system science were in the making.[19] These instruments would study the planet's atmosphere and ionosphere.

II

Indians in Space

5

Rakesh Sharma: India's First Cosmonaut

MOST OF THE IDEAS about space travel, space stations, missions to other planets and space tourism first emanated in science fiction and later sci-fi movies. A Russian mathematics teacher, Konstantin Tsiolkovsky (1857–1935), was the first to envisage the idea of a space colony in his novel *Beyond the Planet Earth.* The novel was serialised in Russian magazines around 1900 and published as a book in 1920. He called such colonies 'mansion-conservatories' – structures floating around in a geosynchronous orbit and powered by solar energy harnessed through giant parabolic mirrors. Tsiolkovsky explained that artificial gravity could be generated in such a space colony by making it rotate.[1]

Austrian scientist Hermann Potocnik Noordung in 1928 proposed the idea of a possible human space station, which was a wheel-shaped structure with a living quarter, a power-generating station and an area for astronomical observations.[2] To produce artificial gravity, Noordung proposed that the space station be placed in an orbit synchronous with the Earth. Wernher von Braun, Hitler's rocket scientist who migrated to America after the Second World War, took Noordung's idea forward and talked about a spinning toroidal station to produce micro-gravity in 1946. A model of the space station made by von Braun was later used by film-maker Stanley Kubrick in his 1968 landmark sci-fi movie *2001: A Space Odyssey.*

To translate the ideas and concepts of space stations featured in science fiction into reality, scientists needed to design powerful rockets that could take capsules with humans into space and bring them back safely. The rocket and missile technologies developed and deployed during the Second World War became the starting point for early space exploration. The first satellite flown by the USSR in 1957 was proof of many concepts, though still far from human flights and space habitats imagined by Tsiolkovsky, Noordung and other pioneers. Inspired by Tsiolkovsky's ideas, an aerospace enthusiast, Sergei Korolev (1907–1966), took to rocketry in his teens.[3] As a Russian soldier deployed in Germany in 1945, he was asked to access and analyse the records of von Braun's work on guided missiles and liquid fuel rockets, according to some accounts. A few years later, he emerged as the chief designer of the Soviet space programme, then known as the OKB-1 design bureau working mainly on the Intercontinental Ballistic Missile (ICBM) project.

The design bureau's first success was the launch of the Sputnik 1 satellite using the R-7 rocket on 4 October 1957 after several failed missions. 'The road to the stars is now open' was Korolev's famous line after the success of Sputnik 1.[4] Sputnik 1 was followed by Sputnik 2 and 3 and eventually a crewed Sputnik mission. In Sputnik 3, the dog Laika travelled to space but died after being in orbit for some time. After Laika, a total of forty-eight dogs were sent to space in different missions. Of them, only twenty survived. Two of them, Belka and Strelka, flew into space in 1960 in the Vostok capsule and were brought back safely.[5] The same capsule was used for the first human space flight with cosmonaut Yuri (Iurii) Gagarin (1934–1968) on 12 April 1961. Gagarin became the first human being to travel to space.

America sent Alan Shepard (1923–1998) into space in Mercury-Redstone on 5 May, less than a month after Gagarin's flight in Vostok 7.

On 16 June 1963, Valentina Tereshkova (1937–) became the first woman in the world to fly into outer space. Both Gagarin's and Tereshkova's flights developed major life-threatening problems, which were revealed many years later.[6] Gagarin's Earthbound capsule, attached to a parachute, landed 500 km away from where it was supposed to land. Tereshkova detected an error in the automatic navigation system and found that the spacecraft was moving away from Earth instead of going back towards it. She somehow managed the system manually and completed the mission. Though Sergei Korolev was behind all these Soviet 'firsts', his name was a classified secret. He was merely known as the chief designer. Even the Nobel committee was denied the information about Korolev. His identity was revealed to the world only after his death in 1966.

Tereshkova remained the first woman in space for almost two decades, until 1982, when another Soviet cosmonaut Svetlana Savitskaya (1948–) travelled to space. The third one was Sally Ride (1951–2012), who, in 1983, became the first American woman and the youngest American astronaut to travel in space. After her death, Ride was also celebrated as the first known LGBT astronaut. Gender and race discrimination was prevalent in NASA in the 1960s and 1970s, famously depicted in the 2016 Hollywood movie *Hidden Figures*. As an act of redemption, NASA in 2020 named its headquarters building in Washington after Mary W. Jackson (1921–2005), the first African American female engineer at NASA and one of the key characters depicted in the film.

Gagarin zoomed into space as just another Soviet pilot, but his short journey turned him into a Soviet national hero and an international icon. Gagarin and Tereshkova became cultural ambassadors of the Soviet Union after their respective space feats. They went on tour of friendly countries, meeting presidents and prime ministers and attending public receptions. Gagarin came to India in 1961 and visited Delhi, Lucknow, Bombay, Calcutta and Hyderabad. In Delhi, he was a house guest at the Teen Murti House, Prime Minister Nehru's official residence, and was received by senior leaders and officials in other cities.

Nehru presented a sculpture, *Space Unknown*, made by Amarnath Sehgal, to Gagarin. He asked the Municipal Corporation of Delhi to arrange a civic reception for the cosmonaut. Nehru suggested that the reception should be held at the National Stadium, and not the Town Hall as was the practice for such occasions, and young students and children be invited to meet Gagarin.

At the reception on 29 November 1961, Gagarin was taken around the stadium in a flower-bedecked open jeep with Nehru in tow. Delhi mayor Sham Nath read out a message that said, 'In a world, which in spite of tremendous advances, is still full of conflict and fear of war, new vistas have opened out which may well give us new perspectives and pull us out of our narrowness of mind and lead us to a new era of tolerance and cooperation. We welcome you as a messenger of peace and goodwill and one who has given us glimpses of the future to come.'[7]

The draft of Nath's speech was prepared by Nehru. In his speech and the interaction with the press, Gagarin declared, 'A time will arrive when a space flight by a joint Soviet–Indian crew will be made.' Gagarin's words proved to be prophetic, coming true twenty-three years later.

At the time of Gagarin's visit, the Indian National Committee for Space Research was in its formative days, and the first sounding rocket from Thumba was yet to be fired. When the plan got going in 1963, both the United States and the USSR contributed generously to the making of TERLS.

Such cooperation fitted very well with the dictum of the two superpowers to use an emerging area of science and technology to increase their sphere of influence.

America opened its launch facilities to its allies and helped them develop their own. This contributed to the development of national space programmes in the United Kingdom, Canada, Italy, France, Australia and West Germany in the 1960s. America promoted Intelsat in 1964 and the communications satellite Early Bird for use by friendly countries. On the other hand, the USSR did the same with countries in the Eastern bloc through Intersputnik, a consortium of members of the Council for Mutual Economic Assistance. Vikram Sarabhai developed close ties with both NASA and the USSR Academy of Sciences. He visited the Soviet Union in 1967 to sort out problems with the Minsk computer and M-17 helicopter the Soviets had given for TERLS and work out further meteorological studies with the help of Moscow. With NASA, he developed the SITE programme.

Like Gagarin's visit to India and several other countries, American astronauts who walked on the Moon were sent on a world tour. The Apollo 11 astronauts returned and brought back some Moon rocks and presented them as a gift to President Nixon. He decided that such rock samples should be gifted to every head of state as a sign of American goodwill. The samples were sent to American ambassadors through diplomatic courier, and they were told to present the same to the head of state. One such sample was gifted to the then Indian president V.V. Giri on 28 December 1969 by Ambassador Kenneth B. Keating. It is on display in the Rashtrapati Bhavan Museum.

Between 1969 and 1972, six Apollo missions brought back 382 kg of lunar rocks, core samples, pebbles, sand and dust from six different exploration sites on the Moon. NASA decided to loan lunar soil samples to research organisations the world over for analysis. In India, a 100-g sample was given to TIFR in 1970. The analysis found that the lunar surface is restless; materials move up and down as a result of meteoric objects. The average time a rock of dust grain spends on the surface of the Moon is 10.5 million years. The intensity of heavy nuclei present in the cosmic radiation during the past tens of millions of years has essentially been the same as seen today near the Earth, according to a reply the minister for education Bhakt Darshan gave in the Parliament.[8] These studies were led by Devendra Lal, a professor of nuclear physics at TIFR who was also a visiting professor at the Scripps Institution at the University of California San Diego. Later, the samples were handed over to PRL for further studies and safekeeping.

Lal did his PhD at TIFR under the nuclear physicist Bernard Peters, who had been a student of Robert Oppenheimer, the father of the atomic bomb. Lal's work related to cosmic ray physics and nuclear interaction of high-energy cosmic rays. After taking over as director of PRL following Sarabhai's death in 1971, Lal shifted his attention to the application of stable and radioactive isotopes for the advancement of earth and planetary science research. 'Several of the now well-established sampling, synthesis, extraction and isotopic measurement techniques were developed for the first time by isotope geoscientists at PRL which later became the routine practice elsewhere,' explained Anil Bhardwaj, PRL director, in 2024.[9] This expertise in isotope geoscience, developed over the decades, helped PRL develop instruments for ISRO's lunar missions and analyse the data they gathered, leading to scientific discoveries, including the signature of water on the lunar surface.

Two astronauts who walked on the Moon – Neil Armstrong and Charles Conrad – visited India in November 1970. Among various public engagements was a visit to the Parliament where the duo was seated in the President's Box. The Lok Sabha Speaker made special reference to the two astronauts: 'Through them we have the first touch of the

Moon in this parliament. They belong to all humanity. We all differ, discuss and sometimes quarrel over earthly matters in this parliament, which I propose we shall not do today. Parliament itself at the moment is feeling like the Moon.'[10]

The House then gave a standing ovation to the visiting astronauts.

Soyuz, Salyut and Skylab

Gagarin's space flight triggered the space race between the two superpowers, with Kennedy announcing plans to land an American on the Moon by the end of the decade. While America's Apollo aimed at crewed lunar landings and scientific exploration of the Moon, the Soyuz programme of the USSR focused on crew transport to space stations and long-duration missions in the Earth orbit. The Apollo spacecraft had a command and service module for crew transport and the lunar module for lunar landings. The Apollo missions were launched using the Saturn V rocket, a powerful heavy-lift launch vehicle. The Apollo spacecraft also developed the capability to dock with the lunar module in lunar orbit and with the command module in the Earth orbit.

On the other hand, the Soyuz programme used the Soyuz spacecraft, a versatile and long-serving spacecraft for crew transport and space station missions, and the R-7 rocket to launch it. The Soyuz spacecraft was used to ferry crew to space stations like Salyut and could also dock with space stations for crew transfer and resupply missions. After a series of failures, mishaps and loss of human life, the Americans succeeded by landing on the Moon first. The Soviet failure to land astronauts on the Moon was due to several factors. The Soviet N1 rocket, which was intended to carry cosmonauts to the Moon, faced technical difficulties and reliability issues. The space programme itself suffered due to the demise of Sergei Korolev and the rivalry between design bureaus and entities involved. Unlike NASA, the Soviets lacked a cohesive space agency.

The Apollo programme ended in 1972 after six successful human landings on the Moon. Though the Soviets failed to land cosmonauts on the Moon, their space programme made significant advances. The Soyuz spacecraft demonstrated advanced docking capabilities, including automated and manual docking procedures, and extravehicular activities or spacewalks. Cosmonaut Alexei Leonov conducted the first-ever spacewalk by a human during the Voskhod 2 mission in 1965. In September 1970, the Soviet Luna 16 mission succeeded in a 'sample return' mission to the Moon, and the uncrewed mission brought back samples of the Moon to Earth. The next mission, Luna 17, carried the first lunar rover, which explored the lunar surface for almost a year.

The next frontier was building a space station where space crew could spend long durations in space and conduct experiments, like the space stations imagined a few decades back. It was again a race between the superpowers but was not bitter like the race to the Moon. For the first time, the United States and the USSR cooperated in space, resulting in the landmark Apollo-Soyuz docking in 1975.

On 19 April 1971, the Soviet Union placed into orbit Salyut, the world's first space station. The idea was to keep the station crewed, with crews replaced every few days and supplies sent through a regular Soyuz module that could dock with the station, allowing new passengers to enter the life modules of Salyut. The Salyut-1 station was designed for six months. On 23 April, Soyuz 10 lifted off with three crew members for a month-long stay aboard Salyut. However, the spacecraft could not achieve docking with

Salyut-1 and had to return to Earth the next day. The second mission, Soyuz 11, followed on 6 June. It had three crew members – Georgi T. Dobrovolski, Vladislav N. Volkov and Viktor I. Patsayev – and it docked successfully with Salyut-1. The three spent twenty-four days in space, conducting biomedical, astrophysics and Earth observation experiments and showed the feasibility of long stays in space. However, the mission ended in tragedy when the crew died due to the sudden depressurisation of the Soyuz 11 spacecraft on its return journey, shortly before re-entry into the Earth's atmosphere. The Salyut-1 was commanded to be destroyed after 175 days in space.

The death of the three cosmonauts sent shock waves across the world. Space travel was in the news all the time. The memories of humans walking on the surface of the Moon were still fresh in people's minds. There was euphoria all over about the triumph of science. The Soyuz tragedy was a grim reminder that humankind still had a long way to go. The Indian Parliament passed a resolution mourning the death of the cosmonauts. Prime Minister Indira Gandhi observed while moving the resolution on 1 July 1971: 'The exploration of outer space has re-awakened in all of us a sense of wonder. Whether the cosmonauts belonged to the Soviet Union or the United States of America, we have regarded them as representatives of all mankind. We have felt personally involved in their journey, following their every move, sharing the anxiety of their families, and of their country.'[11]

The Soviet space station programme resumed in 1974 with Salyut 4 after two more failed missions. Two sets of crews spent thirty and sixty-three days aboard the station in 1975, setting a new space endurance record. Then followed much improved next-generation space stations, Salyut-6 and 7, launched in 1977 and 1982, respectively. Meanwhile, NASA launched its space station Skylab 1 in

May 1973. The Skylab complex consisted of the orbital workshop, the airlock module, the multiple docking adapter and the Apollo telescope mount. The station was occupied by astronauts for periods ranging from twenty-eight to eighty-four days over the next year. The Skylab programme proved that humans could live and work in outer space for extended periods. The Salyut and Skylab programmes were a precursor to larger space stations in later decades – the Mir of the Soviet Union and the International Space Station (ISS) of NASA.

The Skylab became a part of folklore in India for a reason other than scientific. The space station's solar panels became damaged, which affected the power supply, and its thrusters also did not work properly. The Skylab's third and final crew left on 8 February 1974 after it emerged that the space station could not be fully repaired. In late 1978, NASA discovered the station was losing its orbit rapidly and had become a loose cannon. It became clear that the space station could crash in an uncontrolled manner. There was a widespread scare in India as NASA announced that it could crash somewhere in the Indian Ocean.

The D-day was 11 July 1979. The matter was raised in the Indian Parliament. Prime Minister Morarji Desai informed the Lok Sabha that ISRO was monitoring the situation from ground-based observatories and was in touch with NASA. 'Even if successful, these observations will be of limited utility in precisely predicting the re-entry point and if this occurs over India in alerting the public over a particular area,' Desai informed the House on 11 July.[12] The time window of Skylab's re-entry into Earth's atmosphere was between 17:20 hours IST on 11 July and 01:44 hours IST on 12 July.

Though the Indian land mass consisted of just 3 per cent of the region identified by NASA where the debris could fall, there was widespread fear in some districts in

Telangana. People abandoned their houses and sought shelter in safer places due to rumours in some cities. They sold their properties or hid their valuables in fields or wells in the event Skylab fell on their village. Those who could afford it went away to holy places like Tirupati. The streets wore a deserted look on the predicted day of the fall. Eventually, large chunks of Skylab fell into the Indian Ocean, with some parts of the space station littered over populated areas of Western Australia. A 2021 Telugu movie, *Skylab*, recaptured the space station scare in rural Telangana.

In the 1960s, the Academy of Sciences of the USSR, the highest Soviet scientific institution, initiated a programme for joint research in space physics, meteorology and related areas with scientific bodies of the socialist bloc and other friendly nations. That is how the USSR came to participate in a big way with TERLS. The president of the Soviet academy, the academician Boris N. Petrov, had personal links with leaders of the Indian scientific community. Satellites jointly developed by the Soviet Union and socialist bloc nations (Bulgaria, the German Democratic Republic, Cuba, Poland, Romania, Czechoslovakia) were launched using Soviet rockets, under the cooperation programme Interkosmos. When the USSR came to know about the Indian plan to develop a satellite and its possible launch from America, the USSR academy offered the launch from the Soviet Union for free. This resulted in the much-celebrated Aryabhata satellite, as discussed in Chapter 3.

After the Salyut space station started operating steadily, on 13 July 1976, Moscow signed an agreement with the governments of the countries involved in Interkosmos for the peaceful exploration of space. It authorised each of the nine socialist bloc countries to send one of its nationals on a Soyuz mission to dock with the Salyut. The only condition was that cosmonaut candidates should be military pilots because their prior flight training and experience would make them better prepared for space flight. The foreign travellers were to be designated as researcher-cosmonauts. The training of the guest cosmonaut would take about eighteen months, and two guest cosmonauts would be trained in each case. From these, a prime and an alternate candidate would be selected for each flight. Around the same time, America signed an agreement with ESA – a consortium of space agencies of West Germany, Italy, France and the United Kingdom – to allow European astronauts to participate in the Skylab programme.

On 2 March 1978, Vladimir Remek from Czechoslovakia became the first non-Soviet and non-American person to travel to space. Remek's flight to the space station was followed by a series of guest cosmonauts flying Soyuz missions to Salyut-6 between February 1978 and May 1981 – from Poland, East Germany, Bulgaria, Hungary, Vietnam, Cuba, Mongolia and Romania.[13] In 1982, a Frenchman, Jean-Loup Chretien, became the first guest cosmonaut from a non-socialist country to board a Soviet launcher. His flight docked with Salyut-7, which replaced Salyut-6 in the same year.

A year after the programme of guest cosmonauts began, Soviet president Leonid Brezhnev extended an offer to the Indian prime minister Morarji Desai to take an Indian onboard the Soviet rocket to the space station before Desai visited Moscow in June 1979. After the summit meeting at the Kremlin, Desai said, 'India will give deep consideration to the proposal.' It was subsequently discussed in the Union Cabinet where some ministers supported the idea since it would have brought prestige to India. Desai, however, was not in favour of accepting it. ISRO was also not keen to take it up because it felt that the goal of India's space programme was 'to use the space technology for the benefit of the nation' and 'not indulge in the grandiose plans of going to the Moon or establishing space colonies', as U.R. Rao recalled in his 2014 biography.[14] Just a month after his Moscow visit, Desai had to resign following a revolt in the ruling Janata Party. Charan Singh of the breakaway faction was sworn in as the caretaker prime minister. The general elections held in early 1980 saw Indira Gandhi return as the prime minister.

The proposal of a joint space flight was made public in May 1980 by Yuliy Vorontsov, the Soviet ambassador to India, along with other economic deals, such as the supply of heavy water for the nuclear power plants in Rajasthan, that were agreed to during Desai's visit. The Soviet engagement on economic and scientific matters came against the backdrop of the larger geopolitical fallout of the Soviet invasion of Afghanistan. The Soviets counted on India's support for their action and warned Pakistan not to meddle with Afghanistan and stop supporting anti-Soviet forces. Moscow saw New Delhi as a strategic partner in the region. Scientific cooperation, particularly the space flight, was seen as a sweetener in Indo-Soviet relations. In reply to a question in the Parliament on 1 June 1980, Prime Minister Indira Gandhi confirmed that the Soviet Union had offered to fly an Indian cosmonaut into space.[15]

Brezhnev, during his visit to India in December 1980, renewed the offer to Indira Gandhi. She readily accepted and directed ISRO, which was still lukewarm to the idea, to work with the Indian Air Force (IAF) to select two cosmonaut candidates and design scientific experiments for the mission. The joint Indo-Soviet human space flight was thus a political project and was not seen as part of the fledgling national space programme.

The Selection

As directed by the prime minister, the IAF began a programme code-named Project Pawan for the selection of two pilots to be trained as cosmonauts. The task of selection and initial training of future cosmonauts was assigned to the Institute of Aviation Medicine (IAM, renamed as Institute of Aerospace Medicine in 1987), a unit of IAF in Bangalore. Till this point, IAM's mandate was mainly to assist HAL in the aeromedical aspects of the design and development of aircraft and train medical officers of the armed forces in aspects of aviation medicine. It possessed simulators and equipment like the explosive decompression chamber, rapid recompression chamber and the human centrifuge to study aviation stressors on aircrew.

IAM conducted a medical evaluation of about 150 highly experienced and qualified test and fighter pilots who applied for selection as cosmonaut candidates. Forty pilots were shortlisted by a panel comprising members of both the Indian and the Soviet governments. The criteria for selection were aptitude and medical and psychological fitness based on the parameters provided by the Soviets. The final selection of the two candidates was made by the Air Force Selection Board. IAM was also tasked with the training of shortlisted candidates and the designing of the physiological experiments to be conducted by the Indian cosmonaut during the joint flight. The training was carried out in secrecy. The defence minister R. Venkataraman refused to divulge details, telling the Parliament on 5 November 1982 that 'the training programme for the selected Indian cosmonauts has been determined in consultation with the concerned organisations of the Government of the USSR. It is not in the public interest to disclose further details.'[16] After the training at IAM, the two candidates, Rakesh Sharma and Ravish Malhotra, proceeded for the eighteen-month-long cosmonaut training at Star City in the USSR.

At the time of his selection as a cosmonaut candidate in 1982, Rakesh Sharma was a squadron leader posted at IAF's Aircraft System Testing Establishment at Bangalore, while Ravish Malhotra was a wing commander in IAF.

Rakesh Sharma was born in a Punjabi family on 13 January 1949 in Patiala. His father, Devendranath Sharma, worked with Punjab National Bank, and his mother, Tripta, was a homemaker. As a young boy, he was raised in Hyderabad where his father was transferred in the 1950s. Rakesh passed his Senior Cambridge examination at St George's Grammar School, the oldest educational institution in Hyderabad, and enrolled for further studies at the Nizam College. He, however, discontinued the pre-university course (PUC) to join the National Defence Academy (NDA) at Khadakwasla. The NDA is the services academy where officer cadets are trained for the army, the air force and the navy.

Joining the air force and flying planes was Rakesh's childhood dream. He always wanted to be a pilot. He recalled that he was a young boy when he heard about IAF acquiring the de Havilland Vampire, the fighter jet with twin fuselage. These jets were stationed at the training establishment of the air force at Hakimpet, a World War vintage aerodrome on the outskirts of Hyderabad. The young Rakesh would cycle about 15 km just to have a look at the Vampires at the air base from behind the fence. 'I used to hear it fly overhead,' he reflected of that time.[17] One of his cousins was with the air force, and once he took Rakesh inside the airbase to see different aircraft parked there. The young boy got a chance to sit in the cockpit of his dream machine, Vampire. A few years later, when Rakesh got into the NDA, the air force was a natural choice for him. After his training, Rakesh was commissioned as an officer in the IAF in January 1970.

Rakesh was barely twenty-three when the 1971 war for the liberation of East Pakistan broke out, which would result in the making of Bangladesh. Among his first operational flights was the MiG-21. During the war, he flew twenty-one air defence and interception missions. He was then selected for test pilot training upon completion of which he was posted to the Aircraft Systems Testing Establishment (ASTE) in Bangalore. There, he operated a range of aircraft – the English Electric Canberra, Hawker Siddeley HS-748, Hawker Hunter, de Havilland Caribou, Polish Iskra jet trainer and HAL planes including HPT-32 Deepak, Kiran, Ajeet and Marut. By the time he was selected as a cosmonaut trainee, Rakesh had logged over 1600 hours of flying.

Ravish Malhotra also belonged to Punjab. He was born in Lahore in undivided Punjab on 25 December 1943. After the Partition in 1947, his family moved to Calcutta where Malhotra went to St Thomas High School. He enrolled in armed forces training at NDA in 1959, but the air force was not his first choice. 'Three of my cousins were in the Navy, and I had made up my mind to join them,' Malhotra revealed in a rare newspaper interview in 2019.[18] However, he was drafted for IAF instead of his first preference. 'It was destiny that I joined the Air Force, and not the Navy,' mused Malhotra.

Malhotra was commissioned into the IAF in October 1963, and he was posted as a test pilot at HAL Bangalore in 1975. He also attended the US Air Force Test Pilots Course at Edwards Air Force Base. Incidentally, two of his fellow trainees from the course later became NASA astronauts. At the time of his selection for the space flight, he was the wing commander and was the officer commanding at ASTE. The two cosmonaut candidates knew each other before their selection for the space flight training, as both had trained in NDA (in different years) and worked as test pilots for IAF in Bangalore. Malhotra served during the 1965 and 1971 wars with Pakistan, flying several operational squadrons. In the 1971 war, he flew eighteen operational missions in Su-7 ground-attack aircraft with No. 26 Squadron based at Adampur. At the time of his selection as the cosmonaut candidate, he was the chief test pilot at ASTE and had test-flown the Vampire, MiG-21, Ajeet, Canberra and Kiran aircraft, logging about 3400 hours of flying time.

The Training

The Soviets drew up an elaborate training plan and protocol for the two cosmonaut candidates selected by the IAF. Since the training duration was eighteen months, Sharma and Malhotra were permitted to bring their families along, and arrangements were made for them to stay in Moscow. The training took place at the Yuri Gagarin Cosmonaut Training Centre located in the Star City, a designated military area near Moscow. The two arrived in Moscow, along with their families, on 20 September 1982, and the training began on 23 September. Boris Volynov, a Soviet cosmonaut, was the commander of the training team.

The training group included six cosmonauts divided into two teams of three each. Each team consisted of a flight commander, a flight engineer and a research cosmonaut. As per the protocol, all foreign candidates were to be designated as research cosmonauts. After the training, one team was named the primary crew, and the second one became the backup or stand by crew. The first team included Yuri Vasilyevich Malyshev as the commander, Nikolai Nikolayevich Rukavishnikov as flight engineer (he was replaced by Gennady Mikhailovich Strekalov as he caught flu) and Rakesh Sharma as research cosmonaut. In the second team was Anatoli Nikolayevich Berezovoy as the commander, Georgy Mikhaylovich Grechko as the flight engineer and Ravish Malhotra as the research cosmonaut. All of them underwent identical training.

In the very first week of their arrival in the Star City, the cosmonaut trainees had a high-level ceremonial engagement – a visit from Prime Minister Indira Gandhi, accompanied by her son Rajiv. Indira Gandhi was on a week-long official visit, reciprocating Brezhnev's visit in 1980. In the Star City, she also posed for pictures with two women pilot-cosmonauts Valentina Tereshkova and Svetlana Savitskaya and signed the visitor's book. She wrote: 'The achievements of cosmonautics are a symbol of man's indomitable spirit and his inexhaustible courage to endeavour and to rise to great deeds.'[19]

The first part of the training was learning the Russian language as all consoles in the Soyuz and Salyut were in Russian. This was followed by courses on space science and technology, covering topics like space navigation, design of spacecraft and space stations, radiation protection, control systems and the like. Course modules included bio-medicine and biology, earth resources and materials sciences as well. All the lectures and notes were in Russian, and the two trainees had to write their exams in the same language. The second part of the training was space flight-related training using simulators and the Soyuz training module. The hydrological laboratory simulated the condition of free-floating. The two were also taken on flights of a converted Ilyushin (popularly called IL-76) transport aircraft to simulate the condition of weightlessness through a series of parabolic arcs. The fitness training included physical exercises and sports. In all, it was a gruelling schedule from 7 AM to 7:30 PM on most days.

Along with the general and space-related courses, the cosmonaut trainees underwent general physical and medical-biological training. This helped instructors to learn more about the individual psychological and physiological traits of each candidate. These inputs helped them while they formed the core and backup teams for the joint flight.

Elaborate training was conducted with large models of the spacecraft with instruments and controls as well as a mock-up of the Salyut space station. The cosmonaut trainees learned how to handle the onboard systems and intricate mechanisms of the spacecraft docking and undocking with the space station. While each cosmonaut on the flight had a specific role and the controls were auto-controlled, the trainees had to learn about the controls and systems so that they could handle them in case of an emergency at any point of the mission: entry into orbit, docking, undocking and descent. They were also trained to render first aid and handle still film cameras, in addition to specific scientific experiments they were to carry out during the flight.

An important part of the training in June 1983 was the splashdown training in Feodosiya on the coast of the Black Sea. As per the flight plan, the module with three astronauts would re-enter the Earth's atmosphere and then descend to Earth on land. However, in case of an emergency during the launch, there was a provision for a rescue module that could splash down in the sea. The sea training was to familiarise the trainees with the escape and survival procedures.

Just a month before this, Rakesh Sharma suffered a setback on the personal front. His six-year-old daughter, Mansi, passed away in a Moscow hospital where she was admitted for a surgical procedure. Her death was attributed to 'post-surgery complications', but the cause of the illness was not disclosed, according to an account published in *Interkosmos: The Eastern Bloc's Early Space Program* by Colin

Burgess and Bert Vis.[20] Despite such a tragic incident in the family, Sharma continued with the cosmonaut training, showing exemplary courage and dedication. His son, Kapil, who was eight then, was studying at the American School in Moscow. It was decided before the training that the children would continue their studies in Moscow since the training period was close to two years.

The training was occasionally covered in the official Soviet media. In one such report, Malyshev told Soviet news agency TASS: 'Our Indian colleagues are experienced test pilots. They are knowledgeable specialists and responsible people. All this has helped them to master space technology fairly quickly. During the time set aside for their training at Star City outside Moscow, they developed basic skills in performing operations needed in orbital flight.'[21]

About the training in Feodosiya and the exercise related to the docking of Soyuz with Salyut, he said, 'A thorough attitude to the forthcoming flight, enviable industry and inquisitiveness have helped my Indian friends to gain skills in coping with quite a few emergencies and now to pass a crucial test in space docking.'[22]

After one year of training, the two cosmonaut trainees took a short break in India. They shared their training experience with Indian journalists, saying, 'We will feel at home aboard the Soyuz.' Both spoke highly of the Soviet space technology. Sharma said that there was hardly any chance of error, while Malhotra was quoted as saying, 'The Soyuz spacecraft is a very reliable one and easy to control. It is easier to steer than a car.'[23] In Hyderabad, Sharma visited Nizam College, his alma mater for a while, shared his memories of the college and talked about the cosmonaut training.

However, a major accident involving the Soyuz spacecraft that happened while the Indo-Soviet crew was training was not revealed to the world. It became public many years later. This involved the Soyuz T-10 (the joint space flight that was scheduled with Soyuz T-11) mission on 26 September 1983, roughly six months before the joint flight. All the six cosmonaut trainees were taken to Baikonur to watch the rocket take off with Soyuz having two Soviet crew members – Gennady Strekalov and Vladimir Titov. A third crew member was to be Irina Pronina, but authorities pulled her out of the mission a few weeks earlier. If included, she would have been the third female Soviet cosmonaut. It was supposed to be an important mission during which Titov and Strekalov were to carry out a spacewalk to attach additional solar panels to Salyut-7, while Pronina was to create a record of the longest stay in space by a female cosmonaut.

None of this could happen as the rocket caught fire at the launch pad a few seconds before the lift-off, resulting in a massive explosion. A few seconds before the rocket exploded, the launch escape system of the Soyuz module at the upper end of the rocket was activated. The module separated with the two cosmonauts inside it. Just 3 to 4 seconds after the cosmonaut module departed, the entire rocket exploded on the launch pad, destroying the ground infrastructure as well, according to researchers Dwayne A. Day and Asif Siddiqi.[24] The Soyuz descent module came down about 3.7 km from the burning pad, and the cosmonauts were rescued safely. The Soviet authorities did not provide details of the accident but merely said that the launch faced some problems.

Both Sharma and Malhotra watched the deadly accident. Sharma later revealed to an interviewer that he did not share anything about the accident with his wife 'as had been my practice right through my flying and testing career'.[25] Gennady Strekalov, who survived the explosion, returned to the launch pad six months later to join the Soyuz T-11 crew to replace Rukavishnikov, who had taken ill.

The information about which of the two cosmonaut teams would be the main crew to fly on Soyuz T-11 was kept a closely guarded secret. On 15 March 1984, General Vladimir Shatalov, the head of the cosmonauts training programme, announced at a press conference in Moscow that the decision taken about the main and backup was in coordination with the Indian government. As per this decision, Rakesh Sharma was designated a member of the main team while Malhotra was in the backup team. Yuri Malyshev was the commander of the Soyuz T-11 spaceship that was to take Sharma to the orbital station Salyut-7 for a week-long stay. The third crew member in the main team was Gennady Strekalov. It was announced that the backup team would fly if any of the members of the primary crew fell sick or were disabled for any reason.

At the press conference, all the six cosmonauts spoke and fielded questions. Malyshev recalled his two visits to India on his way to Kathmandu and mentioned that he found Indian people friendly to the Soviets during his visits to Agra and Bombay. Throughout his mission, he said, he would remember his memories of India and the persistent desire of Indian people for peace and friendship with all nations. The team members paid their respects to the memory of Gagarin and visited the room he had stayed in at the Star City. Sharma and Malhotra wrote in the memorial book:

'Yuri Gagarin on his visit to India had expressed the hope that an Indian would one day fly on a joint Indo-Soviet space mission. This wish of his is now being realised as cosmonauts from India, it is our proud privilege to pay our respects to his memory on the eve of this historic Indo-Soviet joint crewed space flight.'[26]

The cosmonauts shared some lighter moments from their eighteen-month-long training with the media. Malhotra had the habit of lapsing into Punjabi during the initial period of his training as both he and Sharma spoke the language. However, team commander Berezovoy had to remind them to speak in Russian as agreed to since there would be no time for interpretation in outer space. Grechko had a dig at Malhotra: 'I tried to speak to him in Hindi but he does not know Hindi as he is from Punjab.'[27] In the media interaction, Malhotra and Sharma fielded questions in Russian, English and Hindi from Soviet and Indian reporters.

Asked for a message to family and friends in India, Sharma said: 'After many sessions in simulators and completing other courses of training, we are on time for the mission. We are sure we can fulfil the mission and carry out our responsibilities. All the people of the world will see the flight as a demonstration of Indo-Soviet friendship.'[28]

The Flight

The six-member Indo-Soviet crew left the Star City for the Baikonur Cosmodrome in Kazakhstan on 23 March. The members of the first team were Yuri Malyshev (commander), Gennady Strekalov (flight engineer) and Rakesh Sharma (researcher). The backup team had Anatoli Berezovoy (commander), Georgy Grechko (flight engineer) and Ravish Malhotra (researcher). In an interview with TASS before leaving for Baikonur, Sharma recollected Gagarin's visit to India and public rallies where thousands of people enthusiastically chanted 'Gagarin Zindabad'.

After a week, the Soviet space authorities announced that the joint Indo-Soviet flight would take off on 3 April evening IST. Analysts pointed out that never before had an exact schedule of a Soviet space mission been announced in advance. It was probably to facilitate a live television link between the Mission Control Centre at Kaliningrad near Moscow and New Delhi, given the interest the mission had generated in the two countries. Meanwhile, the crew members continued pre-launch preparations in Baikonur. They were housed in isolation in a contamination-free environment. If any member caught even a common cold, it could lead to a change in the composition of the team that would fly, officials told Indian media covering the event.

A day before the launch, on 2 April, it was announced that it would be the first team that would fly in Soyuz T-11 with Rakesh Sharma set to become the first Indian to go to space and the 139th human to do so. The Soviet State Space Committee approved the choice of Sharma originally made by the Government of India after receiving final reports on the condition of the cosmonauts and the test results of their preparedness. Soon after the announcement, Sharma briefly addressed the media from behind a glass screen. Sitting under a banner that said in Hindi 'Soviet-Bharat Maitri Ki Jay', he said: 'I am happy to have this honour.' Malhotra congratulated Sharma and said: 'I will be there to receive you when you come down to earth after your space journey.'

Sharma disclosed he was taking with him portraits of Mahatma Gandhi, Jawaharlal Nehru, President Zail Singh, Prime Minister Indira Gandhi and Defence Minister R. Venkataraman, besides a pinch of soil from Rajghat, Gandhiji's samadhi in New Delhi. In addition to the Indian national flag, the mementoes that he carried included the crests of the Indian organisations involved in designing experiments. He also carried video cassettes of Indian films for the Salyut-7 crew and a music cassette of classical music by Pandit Ravi Shankar and Alla Rakha Khan for himself. He said he was not carrying any books or films as he expected to have no time for such distractions.

On 3 April, two and a half hours before the launch, a special bus rolled into the launch pad and dropped the three-member crew at the foot of the giant 50-m rocket painted grey and capped by the gleaming white Soyuz T-11 spaceship. Sharma and Soviet cosmonauts wore snow-white space suits sporting the specially designed mission emblem – Lord Surya (the Sun god) in a chariot drawn by seven horses across the sky, flanked by national flags of the USSR and India. The three crew members boarded an elevator in the launch tower, ascended to the top and stepped into the 5.3-tonne spacecraft at the top of the 14-storey tall, 300-tonne rocket. At the count of zero, the first stage of the monstrous rocket roared into life. The time was 18:38 hours IST. In Baikonur, it was a freezing spring morning.

Just before the launch, Sharma's wife, Madhu, called on the wives of other cosmonauts in the Star City, a custom before each crewed mission. She then settled down in her flat to watch the launch on television. Mira, Malhotra's wife, watched the lift-off on television at her flat in the Star City. A small Indian delegation was in Baikonur to witness the launch: Nurul Hassan, the Indian ambassador in Moscow; V.S. Arunachalam, the scientific adviser to the defence minister; U.R. Rao, the director of ISRO Satellite Centre; and A.P.J. Abdul Kalam, the director of Defence Research and Development Laboratory.

The Indian officials were standing a few miles away, watching the rocket getting fuelled. When the fuelling was complete, a siren announced the imminent lift-off of the rocket. 'I saw a silent giant flame first; within a few seconds, a shock wave with a giant roar from the blast pushed us all to the ground. I nearly lost the cap the ambassador had loaned me for protection against the insistent wind and cold. The rocket had a perfect lift-off, and the programme director announced that Rakesh Sharma was now in space,' recalled Arunachalam in his autobiography.[29] Abdul Kalam was visibly excited at the launch, and he whispered in Arunachalam's ears, 'We should do this again but from India.'

The PTI correspondent in Moscow, S.P.K. Gupta, described the launch graphically:

> The rocket rose vertically for eight seconds belching fire and thundering and then bent 51 degrees to fly in a north-easterly direction. The spectacle changed every few seconds. It was soon a Sun brighter than the Sun to the left of the launching pad. Now it was a long white snake's sloughed skin right overhead. The snake's sloughed skin moved away as the bright Sun continued its date with space. The bright, round Sun soon changed into an elongated red bird with a red nose cone. And, it then just disappeared leaving behind some spreading smoke. The humans on the ground now waited in hushed silence as the count continued the seconds until, on the basis of radar tracking data, it was confirmed and announced that the spacecraft carrying India's son and India's space exploration aspirations went into orbit some 510-odd seconds after the launch.[30]

The rocket placed Soyuz T-11 into an initial orbit with an altitude of 202 km at perigee and 240 km at apogee (the point in the spaceship's orbit where it is farthest from Earth is called apogee, while its closest approach is known as perigee), an inclination of 51.6 degrees. In this orbit, Soyuz T-11 completed one revolution of Earth in 88.6 minutes. On the same day, an important operation, a dual-impulse corrective manoeuvre, was carried out during the fourth and fifth orbital revolutions, raising the orbit of Soyuz T-11 to altitudes of 222 x 295 km. At this time, the Salyut space station complex (Salyut-7 with Soyuz T-10 docked with it) was in an orbit with a perigee of 294 km and apogee of 305 km and inclination at 51.6 degrees. It was revolving around Earth every 90 minutes.

After several careful corrections in Soyuz T-11's orbit and 25 hours and 25 minutes after the lift-off, Soyuz T-11 docked with Salyut-7. After a few hours of docking, Sharma and the Soviet crew members crossed over to the space station's quarters. They were welcomed in Salyut-7 by Leonid Kizim, Vladimir Solovyov and Oleg Atkov, who had been in the space station since 28 February. It was the first time the space station was supporting a crew of six. The orbiting space station was to be the residence of Rakesh Sharma for the next seven days.

The docking was a critical operation of the mission and had some moments of anxiety before it was finally achieved. It was timed in a way that it happened over the USSR skies and could be televised. Sharma was the first to enter Salyut-7, followed by Malyshev and Strekalov. All three were hugged and kissed by Kizim, Solovyov and Atkov in turn. Within 20 minutes of arrival in Salyut-7, Sharma got an opportunity to see India from space as the space station made a 6-minute pass over the Indian subcontinent. On the ground, Indira Gandhi announced the successful launch and docking in the Parliament: 'It is a great achievement. Such adventures are fraught with risk. It is difficult and it is still rather new not only for us but even for those who have had previous experience.'[31] She had a special word of appreciation for Malhotra too.

The successful launch of Soyuz T-11 and its perfect docking with Salyut-7 led to a frenzy in Indian media. 'Squadron Leader Rakesh Sharma Conquered Space for India on 3 April,' said a headline. Another report described Sharma as a *Vayu Putra*, the sobriquet chosen by Valmiki for Hanuman in the epic Ramayana. A PTI report said:

> The perfect launch from the Soviet Cosmodrome at Baikonur in Soviet Kazakhstan was beyond description except by a Vyasa. The thunder and the lightning with

> which the launcher Soyuz rocket carried the tunicked space bird up into the azure Kazakh sky was indeed what the epic writer said of *Vishwaroopa* (appearance of God Almighty) on the battlefield of Kurukshetra in the time of *Mahabharata*. The analogy was inappropriate if only because the mission is devoted to the peaceful exploration of space for the benefit of all humankind.[32]

Madhu Sharma was quoted as saying 'If there is anything like being on top of the world, this is it. I am much more delighted than I was yesterday and am awaiting the next thrill – that of the landing.'

The event was front-page news in the Soviet press. While most newspapers had pictures of Malyshev, Strekalov and Sharma in that protocol order, *Pravda* placed Sharma's photograph in the middle of the three. Soviet newspapers described the mission as the Soviet–Indian carrier rather than an Indian in a Soviet space carrier, and commentaries talked about friendship between India and the Soviet Union rather than Soviet aid for the Indian space effort. Special postal stamps were issued with the Indian tricolour and the Soviet 'hammer and sickle' national flags along with images depicting the Soviet space programme. The Indian postal department released commemorative stamps and first-day covers to mark the event. TASS reported that a street in the Ukrainian village Znamanovka was named after Rakesh Sharma at the request of the local *Rassavat* (The Dawn) collective farm.

Academician Vladimir Kotelnikov, the chairman of the Soviet Interkosmos Council, told the media that the Indo-Soviet flight would be the last of the crewed space missions with cosmonauts of fraternal nations. Cosmonauts from nine socialist countries and one from France had previously made space flights with Soviet cosmonauts under the

Interkosmos programme. This ruled out any chance of Ravish Malhotra going to space in the future.

Yoga in Space

After settling down in the space station, the crew members got down to business. As a research cosmonaut, Rakesh carried out several scientific experiments specially designed for the flight. The Soviet crew members participated in many of them. The equipment needed for the work was sent to Salyut-7 in a cargo spaceship in advance. The experiments were of three kinds – space medicine or biomedical experiments, supercooling technological experiments and the Terra experiment – and data was collected for all of them. The experiments were designed by ISRO, IAF and DRDO laboratories. The material science experiment was designed by scientists from the Banaras Hindu University and the Defence Metallurgical Research Laboratory. It involved making a silver-germanium alloy using the undercooling process in micro-gravity conditions. Three experiments were done with alloys of different compositions.

For the Terra experiment, Sharma conducted photographic surveys of the Indian subcontinent during nine passes over the Indian territory, using handheld multi-spectral and cartographic cameras developed by ISRO. He also collected data about meteorological parameters, including cloud cover over India, and transmitted them to the ground stations. In all, some 2000 imageries of the Indian terrain were collected including those of Andaman and Nicobar, Lakshadweep islands, Ganga and Brahmaputra deltas, Indus River, Thar Desert and the Himalayas.[33] In addition to operating automatic cameras, Sharma clicked some 200 pictures of the ground below using a manual camera. In one of the mapping sessions, he spotted a massive forest fire in central Burma and informed the ground station.

The third and most important set of scientific experiments was a set of biomedical experiments. Human physiology behaves differently in micro-gravity conditions, and understanding these changes is necessary from the point of view of longer stays in space. Physiological changes occur due to cardiovascular deconditioning, vestibular disturbance, bone decalcification and redistribution of body fluid due to its headward shift. During the different phases of the joint mission, parameters like blood pressure, temperature and heartbeat were monitored. A method called Ballistocardiography was used to detect micro-changes in the body due to cardiac activity. Ballistocardiograms obtained during the flight showed that both the strength of cardiac contractions and coordination between the left and the right sections of the heart changed depending on the length of stay under weightless conditions and the amount of physical training. Another experiment was designed to study the bioelectrical activity of the heart.

A highlight of Sharma's space sojourn was the first-ever practice of yoga in space. He became the first cosmonaut to select yoga exercises in space to study possible use in preventing space sickness caused by weightlessness. Both Sharma and Malhotra trained for yoga in Bangalore as well as the Star City as part of their physical endurance exercises. In Salyut, Sharma performed a set of *asana*s (poses) and breathing exercises – *stithikaran pranayama*, *stithikaran vyayama*, *padahastha*, *parimita trikona* and *ustra asana*. Weightlessness is accompanied by changes in the body's motor apparatus (which affects biomechanics) and a disruption of coordination. There is deterioration of reflex muscle tone caused by loss of supportive weight and vestibular dysfunction. The yoga experiment was an attempt to see if it could prevent the harmful effects of weightlessness on the muscular-support apparatus.

Air Marshal Mulk Raj, the director of medical services of IAF, told the media that Sharma coped well with the micro-gravity conditions in the flight and this might have something to do with his conditioning by yogic exercises during the last forty-five days. He, however, cautioned journalists against drawing any hasty conclusions about the effectiveness of yoga in countering the effects of weightlessness in space. Any data from a single flight could at best be indicative and not conclusive. Dr Yeryomin, a Soviet space medicine expert, attached no significance to Sharma having the lowest pulse rate among the joint crew. He attributed it to psychological and other personal factors and pointed out that some Soviet cosmonauts, too, have had the same pulse rate.

In an interview with PTI in Moscow after the flight, Sharma credited yoga, particularly the ustra (camel) asana, with helping to overcome stiffness of the spinal column he suffered during the first two days of his space flight. Yet, he said, 'My observations are entirely subjective.'[34] Talking about the yoga experiment in his autobiographical account of the Indian space programme, U.R. Rao observed, 'While Mr Sharma did not suffer from any space sickness, a single example of this type of uncontrolled experiment cannot lead us to any meaningful conclusion regarding the effectiveness of Yoga exercises in space travel.'[35] By 'uncontrolled', Rao meant the absence of data from a 'control' group – astronauts who did not perform yoga – for comparison.

The metallurgical experiments suffered a setback as the Salyut crew ran into problems with the onboard furnace. It worked normally at low temperatures but did not attain the temperature necessary for the experiment. 'No such problems were encountered in previous Salyut flights,' an

Interkosmos spokesperson told Indian media in Star City. Samples of silver-germanium alloy made on Earth were to be melted in the furnace and 'undercooled' to produce some novel materials.

'Sare Jahan se Achcha'

In popular imagination, the high point of the Indo-Soviet joint flight was the conversation Indira Gandhi had with Rakesh Sharma on 5 April. It was broadcast live on national television in India and the Soviet Union. It was a unique event in the history of such joint flights conducted by the Soviet Union. While Soviet and American cosmonauts had previously spoken from space to their respective national leaders, no foreign cosmonaut onboard the previous fraternal Soviet flights had had such an opportunity.

The 15-minute television hook-up for the New Delhi–Salyut conversation was made possible through a telephonic channel using Soviet communication satellite Molniya and American satellite Intelsat. While Sharma could only hear the prime minister's voice, both the video and voice of Sharma and the Soviet crew were received in India. The images of Indira Gandhi speaking and the audio-visual of Sharma in a space station, as seen on a television set kept in front of Gandhi, were telecast on Doordarshan.

The space station chamber from where Sharma spoke to Indira Gandhi had colour portraits of Mahatma Gandhi, flanked by photographs of President Singh and Prime Minister Gandhi, on one side, and that of Soviet leader Chernenko on the other side. The national flags of India and the Soviet Union were spread on the table at which Sharma and Malyshev sat while the other four cosmonauts stood around. Sharma, Malyshev and Strekalov wore the Surya emblem on their left breast pocket and the

Interkosmos symbol over their heart. On the right breast pocket of Sharma was the IAF crest.

Indira Gandhi began by describing the space flight as a historic step towards generating awareness about outer space and its peaceful utilisation for humanity and hoped that Sharma's participation in it would inspire Indian youth to take up adventurous missions.[36] Congratulating Sharma and wishing him and all crew members well, she told Sharma in Hindi that she had many questions to ask but would restrict it to a few. She asked him if his experience in space was vastly different from what he had experienced during the rigorous training with simulators on Earth. Sharma said the training was tough, but he realised that it was very useful. Referring to the docking of Soyuz with the Salyut space station, the cosmonaut said that 'because of the training the docking manoeuvre went smoothly and we felt as if we were in a simulator on the ground when moving from the spaceship to the orbiting space station'.

The prime minister's second question was 'How does India look from space?', to which Sharma promptly replied, 'I can say without a doubt that *Sare Jahan Se Achcha*.' This became an iconic moment. Indira Gandhi gave a broad smile and moved on to her next question, enquiring about the health of Sharma and the crew members and their adaptation to the space environment. Sharma said he was feeling well and had had a good meal. Sharma, quoting the first line of the immortal poem penned by Mohammed Iqbal, was spontaneous and based on what he experienced in space. He was indeed awestruck at the sight of the planet Earth, particularly the Indian subcontinent, from space. Before Soyuz T-11 docked with the space station, Sharma sent a message to the cosmonauts in Salyut, saying, 'Crossing over from the blue of the Indian Ocean, I could see the green of the South [India] merging with the brown of the central region and then giving way to the beauty of the Himalayas. There is so much beauty.'[37]

In later interviews, Sharma recalled that he was nervous while speaking with the prime minister: 'In the Air Force, we are never trained for such occasions. When she asked the question, I confidently replied, "Sare Jahan se Achcha", since the Indian landmass indeed looked beautiful in its various hues from the hills to the sea. We used to sing Iqbal's poem in school like an anthem every day.'[38]

'It was certainly an achievement that Mrs Gandhi could politically benefit from. Some insinuated that she had "arranged" it with her "friends" in Moscow in the era of Indo-Soviet friendship. But the space mission was conceived way before and the training began in 1982,' commented journalist Mahendra Ved who was present in the IAF control room when the conversation between Indira Gandhi and Rakesh Sharma took place.[39] Ved felt that the prime minister praised Ravish Malhotra in her remarks specifically to counter the perception that former prime minister Charan Singh sought to create by saying that Malhotra lost out to a 'Brahmin Rakesh'.

Return Journey and the Aftermath

The Salyut station had room for the docking of two spacecraft modules. The Soyuz T-11 in which Sharma and the crew went to space was to remain docked, while they were to use Soyuz T-10, which had taken the host crew to the orbital station in February 1984. On 10 April, the eighth day of the space mission, Sharma and the two Soviet cosmonauts loaded the descent module. Sharma loaded the equipment to be returned to Earth along with exposed cine and photo films, samples of the space alloy and other materials used in the studies conducted during the week. The crew tested the functioning of the ship's onboard systems to ensure proper descent and the operation of its engine. The descent was scheduled for the next day, 11 April.

The three cosmonauts entered Soyuz T-10 around 10 AM IST after an emotional farewell by Kizim, Solovyov and Atkov, their hosts for a week in the space home. After 38 minutes, Soyuz T-10 separated from Salyut-7 and was in a separate orbit from that of Salyut-7 minutes later. The separation of Soyuz T-10 and Salyut-7 took place somewhere over the Siberian Far East near Usurisk. After jettisoning the living or transit module, the braking engines were fired at 15:33 hours, reducing the speed of the spacecraft. The module stopped orbiting and began the descent at 15:36 hours.

The descent module entered the atmosphere with its outer protective layer burning a fiery red with the temperature rising to 2500 degrees centigrade. The re-entry of the descent module into the atmosphere is a critical operation. 'The heat seal of the vehicle protects the crew and the temperature inside the capsule is regulated. However, the flames and blazes it causes are visible. The entire capsule is enveloped in flames and the ablative layers it is coated with keep slicing off,' Sharma said while describing the experience in an interview with *India Today*.[40]

While the capsule was descending, several planes, helicopters and vehicles were kept in readiness for the recovery and rescue of the capsule. The parachutes opened at 16:16 hours IST, and a helicopter received the beep of radio signals from the descent module and flew towards the landing site. 'Inches of snow had turned the bushy ground into slush by the exhaust of the descent engines which brought the capsule at almost zero speed at touchdown. The landing module was spotted in the air about 10 minutes before touchdown, appearing like a pendant attached to the orange-white parachute. Minutes earlier, the first recovery helicopter arrived at the landing site with Ravish Malhotra and two members of the backup team,' reported science journalist K.S. Jayaraman who was in the helicopter with Malhotra.[41]

Pushed by heavy winds, the module landed on its edge, slightly to the left, as rescue teams in six MI-8 helicopters converged on the spot. The first to emerge was Malyshev. Ten minutes later, the rescue team brought up Rakesh, looking tired but cheerful. The last to emerge was Strekalov. 'I am feeling three times heavier now,' said Sharma. The cosmonauts were lifted through the hatch and put on chairs just near the space capsule. Malhotra rushed forward to his friend for a warm embrace and kissed him on the cheek. Soon thereafter, the three crew members were taken in an ambulance to a nearby pressure chamber for examination and were then flown to Baikonur from the Arkalik airport.

The three cosmonauts underwent a re-adaptation process at Baikonur and were returned to the Star City on 17 April. The cosmonauts were brought to Star City in a motorcade, and their first stop was at the Gagarin statue in Moscow at which they placed floral tributes. The Indian and Soviet national anthems were played at both the opening and closing of the public reception held in the avenue before the House of Cosmonautics. After this, Sharma was reunited with his wife, Madhu, and son, Kapil. Over the next few days, Sharma and Soviet cosmonauts attended a series of public receptions, ceremonial meetings and press interviews in Moscow.

A grand investiture ceremony was held at the Kremlin on 20 April where President Chernenko presented the Order of Lenin and the Gold Star medal of the Soviet Union to Rakesh Sharma and the Order of Friendship of Peoples to Ravish Malhotra. Malyshev and Strekalov were awarded the Order of Lenin and second Gold Star medals of Heroes of the Soviet Union. Both Sharma and Malhotra received the honour in their IAF uniform. Chernenko said certain dates in the history of the Soviet Union and India would remain forever in memory. April was one such date as it was in April 1961 that Gagarin made the first human space flight in history, and it was in April 1984 that Rakesh Sharma made the first human space flight for India.

Malyshev, Strekalov and Sharma landed on 25 April on Indian soil for the first time after their space mission. While the Soviet Union honoured the first Indian cosmonaut with its highest civilian award, India chose its top gallantry award for the cosmonauts. The three cosmonauts were conferred the Ashoka Chakra, while Malhotra was decorated with the Kirti Chakra in a special ceremony at the Rashtrapati Bhavan on 12 May 1984. The two Soviet cosmonauts became the first foreign citizens to be awarded Indian military medals. The next day, a civic reception was organised for the space heroes by the Delhi Administration at the historic Red Fort.

The euphoria around Rakesh Sharma's space flight died soon, and both Sharma and Malhotra returned to their duties at IAF. ISRO did not have a human space flight programme, so there was no follow-up. 'It was not about science, it was more about politics, geopolitics,' Sharma said many years later.[42] Sharma's flight, according to ISRO chairperson U.R. Rao, remained 'an isolated artefact of curiosity' in the absence of an intensive programme for establishing human presence in space.[43] This, however, was not the end of the road for Indians in space.

6

Kalpana Chawla: A Citizen of the Milky Way

JUST AS RAKESH SHARMA captured the imagination of Indians in 1984, a girl from Karnal in Haryana – Kalpana Chawla – shot to fame thirteen years later. Sharma went to space as an Indian cosmonaut on a Soviet mission, while Chawla travelled to space as an American astronaut in 1997. She was the first woman of Indian origin and the first Indian American to become an astronaut. Her space career, unfortunately, came to a tragic end in 2003 when her second space journey ended in a space mishap. She remains a space hero, a symbol of grit and determination and a source of inspiration for generations of Indians, particularly girls interested in science and engineering. As A.P.J. Abdul Kalam put it, Chawla was 'a citizen of the Milky Way and a source of pride for all'.[1]

Her story is intertwined with that of the space shuttle programme of NASA. The space transportation system (STS), better known as the space shuttle, was the world's first reusable spacecraft that could carry large satellites both to and from orbit. The shuttle launched like a rocket, manoeuvred in space like a spacecraft and landed like an aeroplane. It was a winged spacecraft capable of launching crewed missions vertically into orbit and landing horizontally on a runway upon return to the Earth, unlike the Soviet Soyuz module that descended with the help of parachutes in open areas.

The STS comprised four major elements: the reusable orbiter vehicle to carry the crew and payloads; three main engines installed on the orbiter; a large expendable external tank with propellants for the main engines; and a pair of reusable boosters that provided initial ascent thrust for the vehicle. Unlike expendable rockets used to launch satellites, the orbiter and boosters of STS were reusable. The three main engines provided a combined thrust of over 1.2 million pounds, with the external tank feeding liquid hydrogen fuel and liquid oxygen oxidiser to engines. The two boosters with solid propellants provided a combined thrust of some 5.8 million pounds, mainly for the first 2 minutes of flight. The orbiter contained a pressurised crew compartment to comfortably accommodate up to seven crew members and a cargo bay.

NASA operated its shuttle programme from 1981 to 2011 during which it flew 135 missions with a fleet of shuttle orbiters – *Columbia*, *Challenger*, *Discovery*, *Endeavour* and *Atlantis*. During these missions, the shuttle transported astronauts into orbit several times; launched, recovered and repaired satellites; ferried materials to build the ISS and helped conduct important scientific experiments.

The work on developing a space shuttle was initiated in 1972, and the first shuttle, *Columbia*, was ready in 1981. Its first flight took place on 12 April 1981 with two astronauts onboard, and it was designated as a test flight. *Columbia* returned from its first mission lasting 54 hours safely, and it was followed by several crewed test flights between 1981 and 1982. The shuttle's first operational fight was in November 1982 when it deployed two commercial communications satellites. Meanwhile, three more orbiters joined the shuttle fleet: *Challenger* in July 1982, *Discovery* in November 1983 and *Atlantis* in April 1985. In its maiden flight in April 1983, *Challenger* successfully deployed a tracking and data relay satellite.

While the Shuttle programme progressed well, NASA planned to use it as a commercial space transportation system to deploy satellites and ferry co-passengers from other countries. The initiative was perhaps designed to counter the friendly space flights that the USSR was carrying out, but the Americans were not offering a free ride. The foreign astronauts were to travel as 'payload specialists' for a fee.

ISRO had signed a commercial agreement with America for the fabrication and launch of its Insat series of satellites. Under this, the first batch of Insat satellites were contracted to American company Ford Aerospace. Insat-1 A was launched in a conventional way using an expendable rocket, while Insat-2 B was deployed during the eighth flight of the Shuttle in October 1983. For the third one, Insat-1 C, the American space agency offered to take an Indian payload specialist onboard the shuttle to deploy the satellite. ISRO accepted the offer and began hunting for astronaut candidates in 1985.

Unlike Sharma and Malhotra who were test pilots working with IAF, ISRO looked for suitable candidates from among its scientists. The criterion was a science or engineering degree and 'health and fitness conforming to NASA Class III Medical Standards for Payload Specialists'. Some 400 applications were received. The applicants underwent a set of rigorous medical tests, including stress tolerance and psychological tests at IAM, and seven shortlisted candidates were interviewed by a selection panel chaired by U.R. Rao. The panel had the newly minted cosmonaut Rakesh Sharma and NASA astronaut Paul J. Weitz as members.

Two candidates were selected – P. Radhakrishnan from VSSC and N.C. Bhat from ISAC, Bangalore – for further training. Radhakrishnan, forty-two, was the head of the Test and Design Division at VSSC, while Bhat, thirty-seven, worked as a programmer in ISAC. The shuttle flight was to last for five days during which it was to orbit Earth every 90 minutes. The final selection of the Indian astronaut was scheduled to be announced two months before lift-off in September 1986.

Bhat was born in Sirsi and grew up in Gulbarga before joining IISc to study mechanical engineering. When asked about his family's reaction to his selection for astronaut training, he told a newspaper correspondent in 1986: 'The first thing my wife asked was whether I was going to get a pay hike.' His wife and kids were excited and showed no signs of worry as 'they knew travelling by a space shuttle is safer than by a night bus'.[2] It so happened that Radhakrishnan had interviewed Rakesh Sharma for All India Radio during Sharma's visit to Trivandrum a year ago. 'I didn't have the foggiest idea that I would ever come anywhere close to a space flight myself,' Radhakrishnan recalled.[3]

The initial training at ISRO was to familiarise the two candidates with the satellite to be deployed in orbit. In addition, the Indian astronaut was to carry out certain remote sensing experiments as well as repeat the yoga exercises that Rakesh Sharma conducted during his 1985 flight to see if it was effective in relieving space fatigue. The air experience of the two shortlisted candidates included flying in fighter jets that performed aerobatics like steep-turn, zero-dive and the like. In June 1985, the two were sent to the Johnson Space Centre (JSC) in Houston for the astronaut training programme, along with Group Captain Kuldip Rai who was designated as the flight surgeon as per NASA protocols.

'The medical tests at JSC were virtually a repeat of what was done at IAM except a test called Personal Rescue System. It is a contingency system to transfer the crew from a disabled Shuttle orbiter to a rescue vehicle,' recalled Radhakrishnan. He said: 'I was asked to get into a black flexible bag, just big enough for me to squat in. It was zipped up from outside and the lights went out. I could hear the thick door of the soundproof room shut. There was fresh air supply into the bag. Communication was forbidden though I could call for help through the microphone any time I felt uncomfortable. With the help of electrodes stuck to my chest, they could continuously monitor my heart rate for any untoward symptom including any tendency towards claustrophobia.'[4]

The two candidates then went to Ford Aerospace Corporation in California where the Insat-1 C was being fabricated.

It was a busy season at JSC when the two Indian astronaut candidates were training in America. 'I met Col. Loren Shriver who was to be the commander of our flight on the *Challenger* and Saudi Arabian Prince-Astronaut Sultan Abdul Aziz who had just then returned from a flight. At that time in JSC there was also a group of Japanese scientists undergoing tests like us,' recalled Radhakrishnan.[5]

As preparations for the next flight were on, the shuttle programme suffered a major setback when the tenth flight of the *Challenger* on 28 January 1986 ended in an explosion, killing all seven crew members 73 seconds after lift-off. After a long investigation, the cause was determined to be a failure in the right solid rocket booster aggravated by extreme cold weather in Florida before the launch. In the wake of the accident, NASA suspended the Shuttle programme, including the flight that was to take an Indian astronaut to space. The agency decided not to fly foreigners on the shuttle for the time being though the shuttle programme was resumed after two years with the launch of *Discovery*. Bhat and Radhakrishnan returned home as fully trained astronauts. Radhakrishnan, who now leads a retired life in Kerala, likes to call himself a 'stillborn astronaut'.

Challenger was replaced with a new orbiter, *Endeavour*, in May 1991, and the Shuttle programme was resumed.

The Girl from Karnal

While all this was happening, an Indian girl from Karnal was nursing her dream of flying high on advanced jets and perhaps a spaceship one day. Kalpana Chawla came to America in 1982, armed with a degree in aeronautical engineering from the Punjab Engineering College (PEC), Chandigarh, and an offer for admission to post-graduation courses in aerospace engineering. Flying was her childhood dream and first love, and she fancied the idea of becoming a 'flight engineer'.

She was dissuaded from pursuing a course in aeronautical engineering at every step. Her father wanted her to become a doctor or a teacher, while the counselling professors in PEC tried to convince her to opt for 'more suitable' streams for girls like civil or electronics. The college then had just seven girls, and she was the only girl in the aeronautical engineering class. After she graduated, she got an offer to join HAL, but she preferred to stay at PEC for a temporary teaching assignment till she got admission to a course of her choice in America. Her application was accepted by the Georgia Institute of Technology, Rensselaer Polytechnic Institute in New York and the University of Texas at Arlington. She finally enrolled at the Department of Aerospace Science and Engineering at Arlington.

Kalpana was born on 17 March 1962 (the date in school records is 1 July 1961 as she was underage for admission) to Banarasi Lal and Sanyogita in Karnal. The family hailed from Sheikhupura in the Multan District of pre-Partition Punjab. Banarasi Lal moved to the Indian side in the wake of the communal frenzy of the Partition and eventually settled down in Karnal. He began as a petty businessperson dealing with steel almirahs and then opened a cloth store. Subsequently, Chawla made it big in the tyre manufacturing business with his Super Tyre brand selling across India.

The family lived in the tony Model Town, and Kalpana went to Tagore Bal Niketan school. After she passed the tenth board examination in 1976, she enrolled at DAV College for Women for her pre-university course, like her elder sister, Sunita. However, DAV did not offer PUC for those wishing to pursue engineering. So, Kalpana shifted to the neighbouring co-educational Dayal Singh College and completed her pre-engineering course. This enabled her to seek admission into PEC. Like most Punjabi households, the Chawla kids had pet names: Sunita was called Pikki and Kalpana was Montu. Their brother, Sanjay, was Romi. The youngest sibling was Deepa.

All through her childhood, school and college years, Kalpana was obsessively passionate about stars, space and flying. During summer months when the Chawla family used to sleep on the terrace – as was a regular practice in those days – Kalpana would keep watching the night sky for hours, enamoured with twinkling stars and a rare shooting star. She had many questions about outer space but rarely got satisfactory answers. Once when her classmates drew a physical geography map of India on the floor of their classroom, Kalpana covered the ceiling with sparkling dots painted on black paper.

The town had a flying club, Karnal Aviation Club (now a part of Haryana Institute of Civil Aviation), where gliders and small planes like Pushpak were flown. The club was only a few kilometres from her house, and she would follow the planes flying overhead and wave at them. She got a chance to fly in one of them at the age of eleven. She pestered her father to take her on a joyride on Pushpak. From that day on, flying became her first love. Her biographer Dilip M. Salwi writes: 'She became as excited as a child whenever she saw planes or talked about them. And, one of the questions this inquisitive and sensitive girl asked after the joyride was, how can people be divided into classes, sects and religions, when they all look alike from the sky?'[6]

As a grown-up girl, she wanted to take flying lessons at the club, but her father did not approve of it.

Salwi recalls an incident at the DAV College where Kalpana's teachers encouraged her interest in science and mathematics. Her mathematics teacher, Swarn Arora, was once explaining the concept of 'null set' in modern algebra. As an example, she said an Indian woman astronaut was the classic case of a 'null set' since till then no Indian woman had become an astronaut. To everybody's surprise, Kalpana quipped, 'Who knows, Madam, one day this set may not exist?'[7] It was almost prophetic. Nobody knew that one day Kalpana herself would prove wrong the 'null set' example given by her teacher.

During her days at PEC, she was a voracious reader, interested in a range of authors from Ayn Rand to Salman Rushdie. Her favourite books were those by Kelly Johnson, the legendary aircraft designer. She was the joint secretary of PEC's Aero and Astro Club and arranged the screening of the iconic movie on aviation, *Those Magnificent Men in Their Flying Machines*. At the annual colloquium of the college, Kalpana presented a paper titled 'Time-lapse in Space' dealing with Albert Einstein's theory of relativity. She underwent a two-week exposure at the Aero Club of India in New Delhi.

After completing her MSc from the University of Texas in 1984, Kalpana joined the University of Colorado Boulder for a doctorate in aerospace engineering under Prof. Don Wilson. In Texas, she met Jean-Pierre Harrison, a French American who was a freelance flying instructor in the local flying club and lived on the same street as her.[8] The love for flying brought them closer, and Kalpana married JP, as Harrison was called, but chose not to change her surname. After moving to Boulder, JP started giving her flying lessons at the local flying club. They often flew together in gliders and aeroplanes, and soon, Kalpana secured licences to single and multiple-engine aeroplanes as well as single-engine seaplanes. She got the instructor licence as well. The couple subsequently bought a small turbo aeroplane and flew over the Rocky Mountains. She also did scuba diving over the weekends. In hindsight, all this appeared as if she was building endurance and stamina for a future career – as an astronaut.

In 1988, Kalpana started working at Ames Research Center, a NASA aeronautical centre in Silicon Valley focused more on aircraft and supercomputers than spacecraft, and was engaged in research on powered-lift computational fluid dynamics. She worked on the simulation of air flows encountered around aircraft like the Harrier. In 1993, she quit Ames to join Overset Methods Inc. as vice president and research scientist and led a team for the development and implementation of techniques to perform aerodynamic optimisation. Thus, she continued to work on the design aspects of high-tech aeroplanes.

Becoming an Astronaut

While working at Overset Methods, Kalpana came across a NASA advertisement for the selection of astronauts in aviation and space trade journals. It required applicants to hold a master's degree in science and engineering, three years' professional experience and US citizenship. Kalpana ticked all the boxes (she had become a naturalised American citizen in 1990), so she consulted JP about applying. He readily encouraged her to apply.

On the selection process, Kalpana said in a pre-flight interview later: 'They [NASA] seek [people in] particular fields, but I don't think that matters so much. You fill out the application and the committee goes through the applications and comes up with a smaller group. They then ask for recommendation letters – have you done your FAA [Federal Aviation Authority] medicals, and call you for interviews.'[9]

The security checks are done after the interview. Besides educational qualifications and experience, NASA looks for qualities like character, integrity, intelligence and team spirit among astronauts.

The first time Kalpana applied, she was asked to submit her FAA medicals but was not called for an interview. The second time around, she was called for an interview after the written test and selected in December 1994. In Kalpana's batch, twenty-three out of 2962 applicants were selected. Five were women among those selected. Kalpana was among seven non-Americans and the only civilian on the list.

It was a big decision for JP as well because he had to give up his flying instructor job in California and move with Kalpana to Houston where NASA trains its astronauts. The couple decided not to have a baby as it could affect Kalpana's career as an astronaut.[10] Kalpana joined the astronaut training centre at JSC, Houston, in March 1995 in NASA's fifteenth group of astronauts. JSC has been training astronauts since 1959, and its programme has evolved since then. Since the 1980s, candidates have been schooled in the Shuttle and space station systems along with several other disciplines – earth sciences, meteorology, space science and engineering.

The centre has highly realistic mock-ups and simulators to train astronauts. They are prepared for launch, landing, payload deployment, shuttle operations and docking. A motion-based training system simulates the vibrations and noise and views the astronauts experience during shuttle launch and landing, while a fixed-base simulator is used for docking and payload operations training. A space station simulator trains astronauts in the use of the on-orbit laboratory's systems. There is a full-scale mock-up of the shuttle's flight deck and mid-deck. Astronauts typically train for a total of 300 hours on simulators. The Neutral Buoyancy Laboratory, which is the world's largest indoor pool, is used to simulate the weightless environment of space. Astronauts train for spacewalks on full-sized replicas of space station modules under the water. They also train in land and water survival, aircraft operations and scuba diving.

At the end of the fourteen-month-long training, Kalpana became a member of the NASA Astronaut Corps. Unlike Rakesh Sharma who trained for a particular mission, Kalpana was a professional astronaut who could be drafted for any flying or ground duties at NASA. Her first assignment was to work as a crew representative dealing with technical issues for the Astronaut Office Extravehicular Activities/Robotics and Computer Branches. She was assigned to work on the development of 'Robotic Situational Awareness Displays' and testing space shuttle control software in the Shuttle Avionics Integration Laboratory.

Astronauts are assigned to flying missions based on mission objectives and the need for a specific role. The commander of a space mission, usually an aircraft pilot or experienced astronaut, is overall in charge of the mission. The flight pilot has the duty of manoeuvring the shuttle in space and terrestrial atmosphere. The mission specialist has a technical background and looks after all systems of the spacecraft and conducts experiments onboard. The payload specialist is a technical expert specially trained for a specific mission and handles scientific experiments concerning the payload. Radhakrishnan and Bhat of ISRO were trained to fly as payload specialists.

Kalpana did not have to wait long to fly on a space mission. On 7 December 1996, she got a telephone call

COURTESY GITA ARAVAMUDAN

The first group of engineers from TERLS during their training in NASA in 1963. R. Aravamudan and A.P.J. Abdul Kalam are first and second from the left

COURTESY GITA ARAVAMUDAN

An iconic picture of Aravamudan and Kalam assembling a sounding rocket in the Thumba church during the early days of TERLS

COURTESY GITA ARAVAMUDAN

A group of engineers pictured at TERLS sometime in the mid-1960s. In it are two future chiefs of ISRO (U.R. Rao and G. Madhavan Nair) and a future President of India (A.P.J. Abdul Kalam)

COURTESY P. RADHAKRISHNAN

ISRO's astronaut-candidate P. Radhakrishnan undergoing training on a gravity simulator at the Johnson Space Centre, Houston in June 1985. The mission to ISS for which Radhakrishnan was shortlisted was later called off

SOVIET PUBLICITY DEPARTMENT / PERSONAL COLLECTION OF S.P.K. GUPTA

Squadron Leader Rakesh Sharma in the customary pre-flight picture

SOVIET PUBLICITY DEPARTMENT / PERSONAL COLLECTION OF S.P.K. GUPTA

Prime Minister Indira Gandhi with cosmonauts Rakesh Sharma and Ravish Malhotra at the Star City in USSR

SOVIET PUBLICITY DEPARTMENT / PERSONAL COLLECTION OF S.P.K. GUPTA

Rakesh Sharma along with Soviet crew members soon after landing on the Earth

AUTHOR

The charred Soyuz T-10 descent module in which Rakesh Sharma and two Soviet cosmonauts returned to the Earth on 11 April 1984, on display at the Nehru Planetarium, New Delhi

NASA

Karnal-born NASA astronaut Kalpana Chawla poses for a picture with crew members of STS-107

NASA

NASA astronaut Kalpana Chawla with her husband, Jean-Pierre Harrison, during pre-launch activities of STS-87

NASA

NASA astronaut Sunita Williams talks on a microphone in the Destiny laboratory of ISS in October 2019

NASA

NASA astronaut Sunita Williams performing the 7-hour 55-minute spacewalk for the construction of ISS in January 2007

NASA

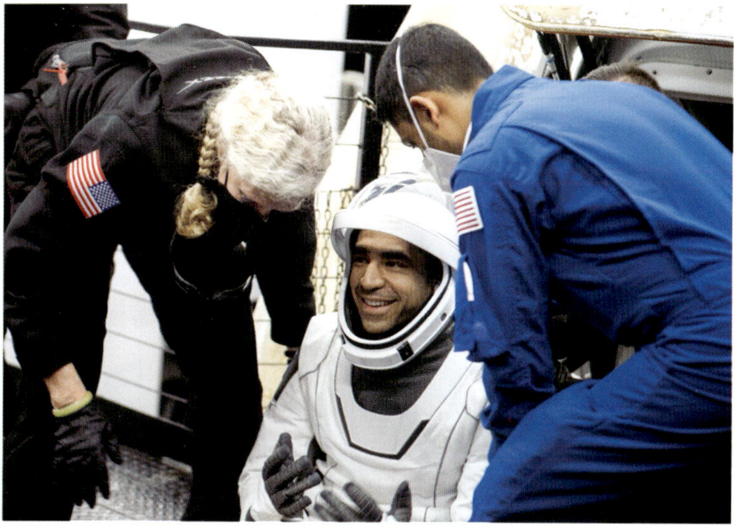

NASA astronaut Raja Chari is helped out of the SpaceX Crew Dragon Endurance spacecraft onboard the SpaceX Shannon recovery ship after he returned to the Earth on 6 May 2022 after spending 177 days in ISS

NASA

NASA astronaut candidate Anil Menon

ISRO

The Gaganyaan crew at the Star City in Russia: Wing Commander Shubhanshu Shukla, Group Captain Prasanth Balakrishnan Nair, Group Captain Ajit Krishnan and Group Captain Angad Pratap

NASA

Launch of Chandrayaan-1 from Sriharikota in October 2008

from the former mission specialist and astronaut David Leestma asking if she was interested in working for him. Thereafter, she was informed officially that she was selected for the STS-87 mission in the shuttle *Columbia*, scheduled for November 1997. She was designated the role of the mission specialist and prime robotic arm operator. Thereafter, she joined other members of the six-member crew to train specifically for her maiden journey to space.

Kalpana became the first Indian American to fly to space. Till then, not many women had become astronauts though the very first – Valentina Tereshkova – had gone to space way back in 1963. She went on a three-day space mission aboard the Vostok 6 spacecraft and returned safely. The second woman in space was also a Soviet, Svetlana Savitskaya, who flew aboard Soyuz T-7 in 1982, followed by Sally Ride of NASA the next year. Ride spent seven days on the shuttle *Challenger*.

The Cold War rivalry continued between the USSR and USA to secure many 'firsts' in the race of women in space too. Savitskaya was sent on her second mission to Salyut-7 in July 1984, this time becoming the first woman to participate in a spacewalk. NASA did the same within three months with Kathryn Sullivan who performed a spacewalk during the STS-41G mission of *Challenger* to become the first American woman to do so. The mission crew included two women, another first. NASA bettered the record with a mission with three women astronauts, STS-40, in June 1991.

In September 1992, Dr Mae C. Jemison became the first African American woman in space as a crew member of an eight-day flight of the shuttle *Endeavour*. She was selected as an astronaut in 1987. Then came Ellen Ochoa, the first Hispanic woman in space in April 1993 as a mission specialist on the shuttle *Discovery*. She was an accomplished flautist and played the flute during her spare time on the shuttle. Other 'firsts' by women astronauts in this period were a 169-day stay on Mir by Russian cosmonaut Elena V. Kondakova in 1994–1995 and a 188-day stay by NASA astronaut Shannon W. Lucid on the Mir in 1996 as part of the Shuttle-Mir Program.

Women of nationalities other than American and Russian who became early space travellers were British citizen Helen P. Sharman and Canadian Dr Roberta L. Bondar. Sharman was the first person from the United Kingdom in space and the first woman to visit the Russian space station Mir. Her eight-day Juno mission in May 1991 was privately funded. Bondar was a part of the shuttle *Discovery* flight in January 1992, becoming the first Canadian woman in space and the first neurologist in space. Dr Chiaki Mukai became the first Japanese woman in space in July 1994, spending fifteen days as a payload specialist on the shuttle *Columbia*. She was selected as an astronaut by the National Space Development Agency of Japan in 1985. In August 1996, Claudie André-Deshays became France's first woman astronaut. She stayed at the Mir station.

Kalpana's name was added to this select list in 1997. Many of the early women astronauts went on subsequent missions as well, creating new records. As of February 2024, seventy-five women have flown in space.[11]

Besides Kalpana, the crew for the STS-87 mission included mission commander Kevin R. Kregel; pilot Steve Lindsey; mission specialists Winston Scott, Takao Doi, Kalpana Chawla; and payload specialist Leonid Kadynuk. The composition of the crew was diverse and interesting. Four were NASA astronauts, two of whom were on their first mission. Doi was Japanese and the first Japanese astronaut to perform a spacewalk. Kadynuk was Ukrainian and had been a member of the USSR cosmonaut team; and Kalpana was of Indian origin. Kadynuk's inclusion in the mission had a geopolitical context. Ukraine had become an independent state after the break-up of the USSR, and America was in talks with Ukraine on the future of the nuclear weapons stockpile it had inherited from the USSR. It was believed that a seat on the shuttle flight was thrown in as a diplomatic sweetener in the ongoing negotiations.

The First Flight

NASA had an exceptionally busy year during which the Shuttle visited the Russian space station Mir thrice and carried out important upgrades to the Hubble Space Telescope. The STS-87 was the eighth and final Shuttle mission of 1997. All the preparations for the launch went off smoothly. *Columbia*, on its twenty-fourth flight, roared into the clear skies of the Kennedy Space Center in Florida at 2:46 PM EST.

The launch sequence of the mission was somewhat different from earlier Shuttle missions. Two minutes after the lift-off, *Columbia* shed its solid booster rockets and continued its onward journey under the impulse of its main engines. At 6 minutes into its ascent, a new manoeuvre was executed for the first time. For 20 seconds, the Shuttle's onboard computers steered the vehicle 180 degrees to the left. This meant the crew transitioned from a 'heads-down' to a 'heads-up' orientation. The manoeuvre was designed to allow the ground station to communicate with the Shuttle via the Tracking and Data Relay Satellite System a few minutes sooner than normal. This eliminated the usual 15-second loss of radio link with the mission control. The orientation manoeuvre allowed the crew to shoot some incredible pictures of the main tank in operation and the Earth below during the ascent.

On her first flight, Kalpana carried with her some educational and personal souvenirs, including a T-shirt with the logo of her school in Karnal and the college logo of PEC, besides a picture of herself with JP. A picture of aviation pioneer and industrialist J.R.D. Tata was also in her bag, JRD being one of her childhood heroes.

'I never thought, while pursuing my studies or doing anything else, about being a woman or a person from a small city or a different country. I pretty much had my dreams like anybody else, and I followed them. Fortunately, some people around me were always encouraging; they would say, "If that's what you want to do, carry on",' she said in the customary pre-flight interview released by NASA.[12] Watching the shuttle take off were members of her family – her mother, Sanyogita; her sister Sunita and her brother Sanjay. Being a vegetarian, Kalpana preferred vegetarian selections from the space food menu of NASA, including rice pulav, rice and beans, dried apricots and broccoli au gratin.

On the flight, Kalpana had a long set of duties as the mission specialist. Her main responsibility was operating the shuttle's 50-ft-long robot arm to deploy the Spartan (Shuttle Pointed Autonomous Research Tool for Astronomy) satellite and orchestrate spacewalks by two crew members.

Spartan was meant to observe the Sun in tandem with the Solar and Heliospheric Observatory or SOHO, which was already in orbit. SOHO had a problem shortly before the shuttle launched, so NASA decided to delay Spartan's release for 24 hours while SOHO's engineers fixed the problems. On the third day in the shuttle, Kalpana deployed Spartan, but the operation was not successful.[13] After its deployment, Spartan was supposed to execute a critical manoeuvre, but it did not due to a snag in its attitude control system. Kalpana then tried to re-grapple Spartan using the Shuttle's mechanical arm, but the satellite could not be captured. Instead, this imparted a rotational spin of about 2 degrees per second to the satellite.

The mission director, Kregel, then fired *Columbia*'s thrusters to match the satellite's rotation. From a routine satellite deployment, it became a serious situation. The crew assembled and drafted a plan to rescue the free-spinning satellite. It was decided that Spartan would be captured by hand by Scott and Doi during their scheduled spacewalk. Spartan was captured and brought back to the Shuttle during the 7-hour, 43-minute spacewalk on 24 November. According to later investigations by NASA, Kalpana accidentally skipped a step in the deployment procedure, resulting in Spartan's attitude control system not getting activated. Spartan was brought back to the ground and re-flown in 1998.

Two days before the Shuttle was to return to Earth, Indian prime minister Inder Kumar Gujral spoke to Kalpana on 3 December 1998.

Congratulating Kalpana, the prime minister said, 'When I think of you, I think of the long journey you have covered from Karnal to space. When I am talking to you, I feel I am talking to a person who represents India in space.' The poet Mohammed Iqbal figured in the conversation, reminiscent of the talk Indira Gandhi had with Rakesh Sharma in 1984. Gujral quoted a line of Iqbal – 'Sitaron Se Aage Jahan Aur Bhi Hain' (there are worlds beyond stars) – and asked Kalpana, 'You are in the midst of stars, and how do you feel?'

She replied, 'It's a very special feeling, you look at the night sky, what you are saying become very literal. A dome over the dark sky, stars everywhere and the earth covered by thunderstorms here and there, some sprays of lightning, every once in a while city lights twinkle. It is very much like a storybook.'

Recalling the poet Kalidas and his poem 'The Swim of the Swan', Gujral said, 'You are that swan swimming in the space.'

The prime minister had a question about the experience of weightlessness, to which Kalpana replied: 'It's not very difficult at all, you get very used to it very fast. When going from one place to another, you tend to tell yourself – take it easy, don't try to do it very fast – because otherwise you are just tumbling all over.' The crew, Kalpana, said, had people with different backgrounds who brought different cultures with them. She said she had been following the Indian space programme since her school days and had kept herself updated about it while in America. Gujral invited Chawla to India along with all the crew members and her family. 'You will be the guest of the Indian people and the Indian government. They all take so much pride and are excited about you. When you meet them, you will be extremely delighted.' She introduced the crew members to Gujral and showed the images of the Himalayas shot from the Shuttle. Gujral, a former diplomat, described Kalpana as 'a new, strong and formidable bridge between India and America'.[14]

After her space journey, lasting 15 days, 16 hours, 34 minutes and 4 seconds, the shuttle touched down with Kalpana and fellow crew members on 5 December 1997.

The successful space journey made her a celebrity in India. Special celebrations were organised, and sweets were distributed in Karnal. Students from her school wore T-shirts bearing the logo 'Tagoreans Are Proud of Kalpana' and marched from the school to the neighbouring Karna Stadium where the city's eminent citizens had gathered. The school had a special place in her heart. She was keen to visit India, along with her crew members, as per the invitation extended by Prime Minister Gujral. The visit did not materialise due to American government concerns over the prevailing security environment and the post-Pokhran thaw in Indo-US relations. Kalpana initiated a project to sponsor two students from Tagore Bal Niketan to visit Houston every year to see space training facilities and meet astronauts and experts.

Kalpana was invited to important Indo-American diplomatic events. During the visit of Prime Minister Atal Bihari Vajpayee to Washington in September 2000, Vice President Al Gore arranged for her to meet Vajpayee and invited her to the lunch he hosted for the visiting Indian leader.

The Final Odyssey on *Columbia*

After STS-87, Kalpana was given a technical assignment like other members of the NASA Astronaut Corps.[15] She was assigned to work with teams developing payloads for the Shuttle missions, giving an astronaut's perspective to the development teams. Astronauts are assigned to flying missions if their expertise and experience match with specific tasks or experiments to be carried out during a particular mission. Many NASA astronauts have flown more than once, and many have been on just one mission. Some opt out of further missions and retire to explore other opportunities. Kalpana continued with NASA and expressed her willingness to be part of any future mission.

That opportunity came soon. Sometime in 2000, Kalpana got a call from the Shuttle team leader asking if she was willing to join a future mission of the Shuttle. She was delighted and readily accepted the offer and was assigned STS-107, scheduled for January 2001. The mission was postponed several times due to technical issues and finally took place in 2003. This time she was to be the flight engineer – a role she had dreamt of as a child – while also being the mission specialist of the STS-107 mission onboard the workhorse, *Columbia*. Kalpana's second space journey began on 16 January 2003 with *Columbia* lifting off flawlessly at 10:39 AM EST. It was the first shuttle mission of the year.

The seven-member crew was a mix of experienced and new astronauts. Rick Husband, a former pilot with the US Air Force was the commander, while William 'Willie' McCool was the pilot. Other members were mission specialist 2 and flight engineer Kalpana Chawla; mission specialist 3 and payload commander Michael Anderson; mission specialist 1 David Brown; mission specialist 4 Laurel Clark and payload specialist Ilan Ramon from the Israeli Air Force. He was the first Israeli astronaut. Husband had served as the pilot of the STS-96 mission during which the Shuttle docked with ISS. For Kalpana and Anderson, it was their second space flight. Anderson first flew on STS-89 in January 1998, a year after Kalpana's STS-87 mission. McCool, Brown, Clark and Ramon made their debut as astronauts in this mission.

Unlike most previous missions, STS-107 was a dedicated science and research mission.[16] There were no operational tasks like the deployment of a satellite or spacewalks. As many as eighty experiments, designed by NASA as well as European, Canadian and German space agencies and universities, were conducted during the sixteen-day flight. The Shuttle carried a research module named SPACEHAB, a pressurised environment accessible to the crew while in orbit via a tunnel from the Shuttle's mid-deck. All the experiments were conducted in this module and the mid-deck. Given the large number of experiments, the crew worked in two shifts round the clock in two groups: the red shift had Husband, Kalpana, Clark and Ramon, while the blue shift had McCool, Brown and Anderson.

One of the studies, Water-Mist Fire Suppression Experiment (MiST) designed by the Colorado School of Mines, examined the physics of combustion, soot production and fire quenching processes in micro-gravity inside a large, rugged chamber. On Earth, gravity creates air currents that make it difficult to study the combustion process and fire-fighting techniques. In micro-gravity, these currents are reduced or eliminated. Kalpana and other crew members sought to determine the optimum water concentration and water droplet size needed to suppress fires. Angel Abbud-Madrid, who had worked in MiST for many years, was overjoyed when Kalpana showed from space the working of his instruments.

Another study was designed to gain insights into construction techniques in micro-gravity. Yet another experiment used pressurised liquid xenon to mimic the behaviours of complex fluids like blood flowing through capillaries. Different types of cell cultures were grown together in weightlessness to enhance their genetic characteristics to be able to improve crop yield.

For this mission, Kalpana had specially selected music CDs of Abida Parveen, Ravi Shankar and some American musicians – Thelonius Monk and Steve Vai suggested by JP – to be played as the morning wake-up call. For instance, on Day 15 of the flight, she played 'Yaar ko hamne ja ba ja dekha, kahin jaahir kahi chupa dekha' (I saw my beloved in all I saw; at times revealed, hidden at times), a Sufi ghazal sung by Abida Parveen. She carried with her specially designed insignia and mementoes from Tagore Bal Niketan, PEC, National Science Centre, Nehru Planetarium and the Aero Club of India. With her was also a white silk banner dedicated to her teachers, with a picture of a girl bowing before her teacher. Another example of her gratitude to teachers was her invitation to aerospace engineering professors from PEC, V.S. Malhotra and S.C. Sharma, for the launches of STS-87 and STS-107.

The mission control arranged a special video link for Kalpana with her family members. This was to compensate for the very few minutes she got to spend with them before the mission. It so happened that nine members of her family planned to travel to America to be in time for pre-flight meetings for families of the crew. Their flight from Delhi got delayed due to the winter fog, and they were further stranded on the way as they could not catch connecting flights to Houston. Her parents, brother and sisters reached America after a gruelling 36-hour journey and missed the time allotted for the meeting. At Kalpana's request, the mission authorities permitted a 5-minute meeting for each member of the family provided they were cleared by the medical team. This was necessary as the crew members were quarantined.

So, once Kalpana was in space, a video conference was arranged for the family. Kalpana was in a jovial mood, smiling and laughing. Her father, Banarasi Lal, spoke first. He joked to Kalpana, 'Your parents are old, they had to struggle so much to reach here. You could have arranged a special aircraft for them.'[17] Kalpana had a hearty laugh for a few seconds and then fished out a picture from her pocket and showed it. It was a photograph of Banarasi Lal and Sanyogita. It was a beautiful reply to her father's light-hearted banter. The entire crew had a short interactive session with President George Bush. The Israeli astronaut talked with the Israeli president and his family members, besides interacting with the Israeli media.

The STS-107 mission evoked great interest back in Karnal. The news was being closely followed with television channels providing live updates on the scheduled return of *Columbia* on 1 February. People were eagerly waiting for the final flash about Kalpana's safe landing even though it was late night in India. Kalpana's school arranged a special screening of television commentaries on the flight. People were in a celebratory mood and had arranged *dhol* (drum) players in anticipation of the conclusion of Kalpana's mission.

The crew onboard *Columbia* was in a good mood – laughing, taking pictures and exchanging banter – while preparing for the re-entry into Earth's atmosphere and finally landing.[18] The Shuttle commander, Husband, and the pilot, Willie, fired *Columbia*'s twin orbital manoeuvring system braking rockets at 8:15:30 AM EST to begin the Shuttle's glide back to Earth. They did not notice anything amiss on their consoles. At 8:41 AM, the mission control commentator said: 'This is mission control, Houston. *Columbia*'s altitude is now 90 miles above the Pacific Ocean to the north of the Hawaiian Islands, about 2 minutes away from entering the Earth's atmosphere. All activities continue to go smoothly en route toward a touchdown at the Kennedy Space Center.'[19]

Looking at the jet flames during re-entry through the window, Husband said, 'It looks like a blast furnace.'

Till about 8:51:19 AM, the re-entry was normal. Twenty-six seconds after the peak aerodynamic heating phase began, indications of an 'off-nominal external event' emerged. Landing gear sensors registered elevated temperatures while data from sensors at the back of the left wing stopped flowing. The control systems sensed unexpected aerodynamic drag on the left side of the spacecraft. The drag got worse as *Columbia* whizzed past south-western America. The mission control commentator announced at 8:52 AM that '*Columbia* is on target for runway three-three at the Kennedy Space Center Shuttle Landing Facility runway'.

Soon thereafter, the mission control reported a loss of communication with the Shuttle crew. Messages went unanswered. The tracking satellites and stations elsewhere, too, reported no communication with *Columbia*. Just before this happened, sensors reported an unusual rise in temperature, and ground observers saw some debris falling. *Columbia* just broke apart and exploded at about 207,000 ft above central Texas. It was travelling at about 12,500 miles per hour speed and was 1192 miles from its touchdown. At 9:20 AM, the mission control declared a contingency and loss of all communication. *Columbia* and all its seven crew members were lost forever. Kalpana Chawla became a distant star, a citizen of the Milky Way.

A seven-month investigation followed the disaster, including a four-month search across Texas to recover debris.[20] Some 85,000 pieces of orbiter debris were shipped to the Kennedy Space Center where the reconstruction teams identified pieces as to their location on the orbiter and determined damaged areas. About 38 per cent of the orbiter *Columbia* was eventually recovered. The investigation revealed that one large and two smaller pieces of insulating foam got detached from the external tank, and the large piece (27 inches long and 18 inches wide) revolving at a high speed impacted the underside of the left wing of *Columbia*. The impact cracked an external tile. During the re-entry, the superheated air and plasma made their way to the wing assembly through the crack, leading to its progressive failure.

The astronauts who perished in *Columbia* were declared America's national heroes. President Bush, speaking at the memorial service held at JSC on 4 February, said, 'None of our astronauts travelled a longer path to space than Kalpana Chawla. She left India as a student, but she would see the nation of her birth, all of it, from hundreds of miles above. When the sad news reached her home town, an administrator at her high school recalled, "She always said she wanted to reach the stars. She went there, and beyond." Kalpana's native country mourns her today, and so does her adopted land.'[21]

In 2004, Kalpana and the crew of STS-107 were awarded the Congressional Space Medal of Honor posthumously.

Karnal and India were devastated and shocked. The nation went into mourning. On 5 February, a memorial meeting was held at the Parliament House, attended by Prime Minister Vajpayee and leaders of all political parties. Vajpayee announced the renaming of an Indian meteorological satellite, Metast, as Kalpana-1. American scientists named seven asteroids after each crew member as a 'celestial memorial'. To mark the first anniversary of the disaster, NASA also named seven hills on Mars in memory of the lost crew. In 2020, a commercial firm, Northrop Grumman, named its cargo spacecraft launched to ISS as SS Kalpana Chawla.

Rakesh Sharma, while delivering the first 'Kalpana Chawla Memorial Lecture' in 2003, said, 'She was a small-town girl who dreamt big and then had the self-belief to chase that dream halfway across the world. She caught up with that dream and lived it. Kalpana personified the power of imagination. She imagined and therefore she was.'[22]

7

Sunita Williams: Marathoner in Space

IN JUNE 2024, a human space mission caught global attention and led to a media frenzy in India. The Boeing Starliner spacecraft was launched on 5 June for a ten-day rendezvous with the ISS. This was the first crewed flight of Starliner and was meant to validate its performance, safety and reliability as a space transport system. Its return journey, however, had to be postponed for several months as the spacecraft experienced a helium leak and problems with its thrusters during the docking with ISS, and astronauts needed time to fix them. Starliner returned to Earth in September 2024 but without its two passengers as NASA did not want to take any risks. Another spacecraft was arranged for the crew of Starliner.

On the Starliner flight were two experienced NASA astronauts, Butch Wilmore and Sunita Williams. Sunita's participation in the flight evoked great interest in India owing to her Indian connection – she is only the second woman astronaut of Indian descent to fly into space. Kalpana Chawla was the first. Sunita's space career started after Kalpana's, but she broke many records in space. During her two long-term stays on ISS, Sunita created many records – the longest continuous space flight by a woman (192 days), the highest number of spacewalks (seven) by a woman astronaut and the longest spacewalk time for a woman (50 hours, 40 minutes). She became the second woman ever to command the ISS. All these achievements made Sunita a household name in India though she was not born or educated in the country like Kalpana.

Tracing the Roots

During a visit to India, Sunita was asked about her role models. She said, 'The people who have inspired me the most are my parents – my father coming from India and my mother coming from not well-to-do family in midwestern America. Both went through a lot of struggles in their lives and have given everything they have had to my brother, my sister and myself, and have been amazing role models for us in morally, mentally, and physically what to do in life.'[1]

She considered herself lucky to have grown up in a multicultural environment, which she felt helped in shaping her space career during which she worked with the Russians on projects for building the ISS. We will further discuss ISS later.

Sunita's story represents the typical emigrant tale. She was born to Deepak Pandya, who immigrated to America in search of greener pastures, and Ursuline Bonnie Zalokar of Slovenian descent (Bonnie's grandmother came to America in the early 1900s). Deepak, a freshly minted doctor, arrived in America by the sea route, which took twenty-one days, met Bonnie, an X-ray technician, in his first job and got married to her. The two worked hard to raise three children and gave them a good education so that they could live the American dream. Bonnie was born and raised in Cleveland where the Zalokar family ran a delicatessen.

Deepak Pandya, born in a village called Jhulasan in the Mehsana District of Gujarat, got his medical degrees (MBBS and MD) from Gujarat University in 1957 and completed an internship at the Sheth Vadilal Sarabhai Hospital in Ahmedabad. He went to America when he got an offer for an internship and residency in internal medicine at the Case Western Reserve University in Cleveland, Ohio. After a postdoctoral fellowship in neuroanatomy, he was set on the path to becoming a leading expert in this field globally. He studied principles underlying brain organisation and published about 600 original research papers, monographs and books.

After he died in 2020 at the age of eighty-seven, the *Journal of Comparative Neurology* brought out a special issue in his honour, and Boston University, where he was emeritus professor of anatomy and neurobiology, organised a memorial symposium.[2] His colleagues affectionately called him Dee.

Sunita, Suni to her family and friends, was born in Euclid, Ohio, on 19 September 1965. When she was three, her family moved to Needham, Massachusetts, near Boston. Sunita was the youngest of three siblings. The eldest was Jay, followed by Dina. Sunita went to elementary, middle and high school in Needham, graduating in 1983. In her school days, she loved many sports – swimming, triathlon, biking, baseball, football, basketball and hockey.

The Pandya household was multicultural and multi-faith, values which Sunita, too, imbibed. Deepak was a gentle and spiritual person, a follower of Mahatma Gandhi and a believer in the philosophy of Sri Aurobindo. The family went to the local church on Sundays. Both Diwali and Christmas were celebrated with equal enthusiasm. Deepak would often narrate stories from the Ramayana and the Mahabharata to his children in their growing-up years. Given Bonnie's interest in baking and Deepak's love for Gujarati dishes, food was almost a family activity. Sunita likes pani puri and samosa (which were among the snacks she consumed in space).[3] Her husband can make samosas, while her mother makes jalebis.

This multicultural upbringing was reflected in the memorabilia that Sunita took with her on her first space journey in 2007 – a copy of the Bhagavad Gita, a statue of Ganesha and a St Christopher medallion (a Catholic symbol of protection and safe travel). 'Those were the things that were a part of our life when we were growing up. It was natural for me to take a part of my life with me to space. I took a little something from my father and some things from my mother,' she told an interviewer.[4]

The Pandyas shared a love for outdoor activities and sports, such as hiking, camping, windsurfing, swimming, skiing, soccer and tennis. The kids also got lessons in piano, ballet dancing and so on. Sunita was good at competitive swimming and ran the Boston Marathon when she was sixteen, without any preparation. All three siblings took lessons and practised swimming at the Harvard pool under the legendary coach Joe Bernal. The Pandya kids joined Bernal's swim club, Bernal's Gators. Sunita was also a swimming instructor for special-needs children.

Deepak Pandya and his family remained connected with relatives and friends in India. Sunita visited Gujarat in 1998 when her cousin Haren Pandya (Haren's mother is Deepak Pandya's sister) was elected member of the Legislative Assembly on a Bharatiya Janata Party (BJP) ticket. 'Sunita has been emotionally attached to Haren. In fact, in 1998 she had come from the US to campaign for Haren and had participated in his victory procession. She was so thrilled to see the large turnout,' Haren's father, Vitthalbhai, was quoted as saying in newspaper reports in September 2007 when Sunita visited Ahmedabad after her space flight.[5] Besides visiting Sabarmati Ashram and Dola Mata temple in Jhulasan, she visited the Haren Pandya memorial and garlanded his statue. In New Delhi, she met the prime minister, Manmohan Singh, and visited the American Embassy School.

A Career in the US Navy

As a child, Sunita was fascinated with fantasy stories and was not into science fiction, as one would expect of a future astronaut. In school, she was interested in science and related outdoor activities like exploring nature and the environment. She participated in experiments related to marine biology. At home, she was attached to her pet dogs and spent a lot of time with them. The Pandyas were popular among the neighbourhood kids for nurturing puppies and kittens of different types. Deepak was a medical scientist and a practising doctor, so discussions at home often included questions of science and philosophy. Sunita was aware of major events like the human landing on the Moon but never thought of pursuing any career in engineering or space. Deepak remembers Sunita watching the Moon landing on television and jumping with joy. As she grew up, Sunita wanted to be a veterinarian, given her love for dogs and other animals. After graduating from school, she applied for a course in veterinary science. Swimming, not flying, was her favourite outdoor activity.

It so happened that when she was trying to make a career choice, her brother Jay graduated from the US Naval Academy in Maryland. The family drove to the academy for the graduation ceremony. After the ceremony, Jay took the family around the academy, showing them all the facilities for athletics, swimming and the like. He was captain of the academy's swimming team and thought that the academy would be a good place for Sunita, too, to pursue her interest in athletics and swimming. Jay's suggestion was tempting to Sunita, and she agreed to apply for a course at the academy.

There were few girls on the campus as the entry of women into the US Navy had begun just a couple of years earlier. She applied for a course in physical science. At that time, applications had to be endorsed by a congressman or senator. Hers was endorsed by Massachusetts senator Edward Kennedy who was impressed by the credentials on her CV – from athletics to volunteering in a local hospital. Sunita entered the academy in 1983.

As Jay had predicted, Sunita excelled in a range of outdoor activities, from swimming to biking, at the academy. 'I really had fun and learned about leadership and followership going through the ranks there, and teamwork. I was on the swim team there, I was on the cross-country team, on the bike club, so a lot of sports, like my brother had suggested,' Sunita later confided to a biographer, Arvinda Anantharaman.[6] In academics, she was not a class topper but did reasonably well. Sunita graduated in 1987 and joined the US Navy where she was assigned the beginner's rank of ensign. After the induction training, ensigns could choose from navy air, marine or submarine services or special programmes like diving. Being an ace swimmer, her first choice was diving, but the application was rejected. She opted for the next special stream, navy air. While waiting for her air training to begin, she completed the diving programme and obtained a diving officer certificate though she was not commissioned as a diver.

At the Naval Air Training Command, she wanted to train on jets but was instead assigned helicopters. She became a naval aviator in July 1989 and was asked to join the Helicopter Combat Support Squadron 8 (HC-8) in Norfolk, Virginia. Here, a lot of exciting assignments awaited Sunita. She made overseas deployments to the Mediterranean, the Red Sea and the Persian Gulf for Operation Desert Shield and Operation Provide Comfort to provide humanitarian aid. She carried supplies and cargo to Saudi Arabia during the Gulf War in 1990. Two years later, she was named the officer-in-charge of an H-46 detachment for Hurricane Andrew relief operations aboard USS Sylvania.

In January 1993, she changed tacks once again and started training to become a test pilot at the US Naval Test Pilot School. She graduated in December 1993 and was assigned to the Rotary Wing Aircraft Test Directorate as a chase pilot. As a test pilot, she flew some thirty different types of planes and helicopters and logged over 3000 flying hours. She discovered that she was as good in the air as she was in the water.

Meanwhile, Sunita married Michael Williams, chief inspector in the Judicial Security Division of the federal government, in 1989, changing her name to Sunita Williams. He was her batchmate in the Naval Academy.

Becoming an Astronaut

Sunita's life journey is full of coincidences and second options. She never got to do what she wanted as the first choice, but second options opened new doors for her. She wanted to be a vet but ended up in the navy. There, her interest was in diving, but she became an aviator. In aviation, her first choice was to fly jet planes, but she was assigned helicopters. While doing all this, a career path in space was never on the cards. However, a visit to JSC changed it all.

It so happened that while training to become a test pilot, Sunita had to attend a training session at JSC. The exposure was a part of the test pilot course. The class was taken by a veteran astronaut of NASA, John Young. He was among the handful of astronauts who landed and walked on the Moon in 1972 and had flown six times on the

Shuttle. Before becoming an astronaut, Young was a naval officer and aviator and had been to the test pilot school. He mentioned that he had to learn to fly helicopters while training for the Moon landing. 'He landed on the moon in some type of vertical apparatus – that sounds like helicopters, and I was a helicopter pilot – so it seemed like it might fit. Then, I started looking at what I needed to do to become an astronaut,' Sunita recalled later of her meeting with Young at JSC.[7]

Soon, Sunita sent in an application to NASA for astronaut training. Though she ticked all the boxes like physical fitness, 1000-hour flying experience and team player, she did not qualify academically. A master's degree in science and engineering was mandatory. She noticed that several astronauts were from the US Navy, particularly from the test pilot school where she had been. So, she did not want to give up and enrolled for a master's course in engineering management at Florida Institute of Technology. After the two-year course, she returned to the test pilot school and logged in more flying hours before applying to NASA for the second time in 1997. She was called for the interview and was finally selected. After eleven years in the US Navy, she entered NASA in June 1998 as a part of the 18th Astronauts Group.

Sunita began her space career at a time when NASA was undergoing a churn in terms of the future direction because of dwindling budgetary support. The agency's focus was using the Shuttle to transport modules to assemble ISS in the orbit. ISS became a flagship programme of the agency, replacing the Space Station Freedom Plan which was originally designed to counter the Mir space station of the Soviets (by now it was Russian). Budgetary constraints and geopolitical necessities following the break-up of the USSR forced NASA to make the space station project 'international' and engage Russia as a partner.

The America-Russia cooperation in space saw NASA astronauts transported by Soyuz to Mir for long-term stay and returning by the Shuttle. This required NASA astronauts to actively train and work with the Russians. The training in Russia was in the Russian language, so the Americans had to learn the language before the flight or spacecraft training.

The massive structure of ISS, as it stood in 2010, was put together in space like a Lego set, piece by piece, with different elements and modules developed by participating space agencies from America, Russia, Japan, Canada and the ESA.[8] It was put together using the giant robotic arms of the Shuttle and then one of its own by astronauts and cosmonauts undertaking spacewalks. Once the habitable module was in place, humans started living in ISS for long durations.

The first module, Zarya, was launched by Russia in November 1998, followed by the America-built Unity module transported by the Shuttle a month later. Subsequently, other modules like Zvezda and SPACEHAB were attached, making ISS partially operational in 2001. Unlike Mir, which could accommodate only three crew members, ISS can support up to thirteen. It has multiple docking points for visiting spacecrafts to dock and transfer cargo or astronauts. Over the years, dozens of space missions have been executed for logistics, resupply and crew exchange at ISS by the Shuttle, Russia's Progress and Soyuz, Japanese H-II Transfer Vehicle, European Automated Transfer Vehicle and commercial spacecraft – Dragon, Cygnus and Starliner. ISS took its final shape in 2010.

After her training and evaluation at NASA, Sunita was assigned to work with the Russian space agency, Roscosmos, on the Russian contribution to ISS and the preparation for the first expedition crew that was sent to the station. She trained and worked in the Star City, where Rakesh Sharma and Ravish Malhotra were trained in the 1980s. Back in America, Sunita underwent additional training. NASA wanted to prepare future astronauts for long-term stays on the ISS. Unlike a typical Shuttle mission lasting a fortnight, the stay on ISS, could extend for several months. Besides living in isolation and under micro-gravity conditions for long durations, it meant living with people from different cultural backgrounds since the ISS was to host astronauts and visitors from different countries.

For this, NASA designed an underwater lab project in 2001, Neemo or the NASA Extreme Environment Mission Operations project.[9] Astronauts, engineers and scientists are sent to live in the undersea research station, Aquarius, for up to three weeks. The lab is located 5.6 km off Key Largo in the Florida Keys National Marine Sanctuary. The Aquarius habitat and its surroundings mimic conditions like space, a hostile and alien place for humans to live and survive. In the Neemo missions, astronaut trainees can simulate living on a spacecraft and test spacewalks in future missions. Sunita was a part of the Neemo-2 expedition in May 2002.

With induction training at NASA, operational work experience in Russia and underwater expedition, Sunita was ready for her maiden space flight. Then NASA suffered a jolt in 2003. *Columbia* was lost with its seven-member crew, including Kalpana Chawla. Sunita and Kalpana knew each other, though Kalpana was already an astronaut when Sunita joined NASA. The Shuttle programme was put on hold, and all ISS-related missions came to a halt. This was frustrating for Sunita because she had been informed in late 2002 that she had been selected for a mission. Her wait for a date with ISS only got longer.

Sunita's First Flight

The Shuttle flights were resumed in 2005, and Sunita was informed that she would fly on the STS-116 mission of the Shuttle *Discovery* in 2006. It was a complex mission – docking with the ISS, spacewalks to reconfigure and redistribute the solar power system of the ISS, attaching an integrated truss segment to the ISS and crew transfer from *Discovery* to ISS. The seven-member crew included Commander Mark Polansky, pilot William Oefelein and mission specialists Nicholas Patrick, Robert Curbeam, Joan Higginbotham, Christer Fuglesang from ESA and Sunita. Sunita was to replace Thomas Reiter (ESA) who was to return to Earth aboard *Discovery*, while she would stay till the next summer return on the STS-118 mission onboard the shuttle *Endeavour*. On ISS, Sunita's role was that of a flight engineer. On her first space trip, Sunita was going on a long haul.

The launch of STS-116 was originally scheduled for 7 December 2006 but was delayed because of bad weather conditions, and it occurred on 9 December. It was a night launch, planned in a way to ensure the shuttle's docking with the ISS with optimal propulsion. Sunita's family and several members of the Pandya and Zalokar clans were present to witness the launch. While in the mandatory quarantine one week before the launch, Sunita talked to her family members briefly from a distance and did namaste to all the elders. Deepak Pandya arranged for a priest to chant prayers for her safe trip. It was a perfect launch. 'We started to accelerate like nobody's business. Our stomachs and the rest of us are really getting squished now. We were still accelerating through the thinning of the atmosphere. Then everything got quiet,' Sunita described the experience on her blog.[10]

The shuttle docked with ISS on 11 December as planned, and the latches were opened to let *Discovery* crew enter ISS. On her first glance of the ISS from the Shuttle, Sunita exclaimed, 'Tally-ho on my new home. It is beautiful. The solar arrays are glowing.'[11] Soon, she was welcomed into ISS, her home for the next six months. She joined NASA astronaut Michael López-Alegría (he was of Spanish origin) and Russian cosmonaut Mikhail Vladislavovich Tyurin who were there on ISS.

The *Discovery* crew got down to the tasks of unberthing the truss from the Shuttle's payload bay, installing it on the main truss of ISS and rewiring the station's electrical system. Of the three spacewalks, two were performed by Curbeam and Christer, which lasted for a total of 11.5 hours. The third spacewalk was executed by Curbeam and Sunita during which they finished rewiring the power systems and installed a fixture to the robotic arm and debris shield on the Zvezda service module. The operation lasted for 7 hours and 31 minutes. It was Sunita's first flight and first spacewalk.

Sunita later recalled: 'My first mission was six and a half months. We weren't exactly sure how long it was going to be because I went up and back on the Space Shuttle which was dependent on weather for launch and landing. So, you might have to say goodbye a couple of times and you might get excited to come home and then have to wait. It was an emotional rollercoaster, particularly because it was my first space flight.'[12]

Shortly after docking with ISS, Sunita had a haircut. Instead of cutting her long, black hair before the flight (maintaining long tresses in micro-gravity becomes messy), she wanted to trim it in space. Her fellow astronaut Joan Higginbotham gave her the haircut and brought her hair back to Earth, where it was donated to a charity, Locks of Love, which works for children who lose their hair due to medical problems like cancer. There was a little Christmas celebration on ISS, and the crew took three days off from their duties on New Year's Eve.

People may wonder what Sunita and other crew members were doing on ISS for over six months. Astronauts and cosmonauts on the space station have a busy schedule in which every minute and hour is counted. The schedule includes exercise, maintenance work and scientific experiments. In addition, sometimes there are events like live interviews, ceremonial 'meetings' on national days, press conferences and phone calls with family. Over the weekends, there is cleaning and housekeeping work. ISS keeps getting cargo spacecraft and crewed missions. All the time, the ISS is connected to the mission control room.

In January 2007, Sunita and López-Alegría carried out two spacewalks to fix the Station-to-Shuttle-Power-Transfer System and the external thermal control system. On 4 and 8 February, the two astronauts were out in space again with specific tasks to work on ISS like attaching the Unpressurised Cargo Carrier Assembly Attachment System.

A spacewalk is a complicated affair though it may sound fun. Astronauts should prepare for them a day in advance, following the set protocol and safety procedures. The spacesuits are pressurised to keep the body inside comfortable with oxygen supply. Astronauts have to be well versed with all the procedures like getting the airlock depressed, tasks to be carried out with the robotic arm or by hand, emergencies like loss of communication and suit issues. After the walk, they should take care that no external contamination or radiation enters the ISS with them. During the spacewalk, astronauts remain tethered to the ISS.

Among the scientific experiments Sunita and López-Alegría conducted was one to see how cosmic radiation affects human brainwaves. Both wore soft caps with sensors to record brain functions and a hard cap with instruments to record cosmic rays passing through the space station. This was to generate data to help develop preventive measures for long-duration flights to the Moon and Mars in future. They also conducted a series of medical experiments to see how the human body adapts to space flights.

In the first week of April, it was time for another crew rotation at ISS. This time, López-Alegría and Tyurin were to return to Earth, with the crew from Russia replacing the two. Sunita made global headlines on 16 April 2007 when she ran the famed Boston Marathon from ISS. The marathon organisers had given her the race number 14000, which she pasted on the space station's treadmill. Within seconds of her starting the race on her treadmill, Houston told her that she had reached the finish line, running 42.2 km, because ISS travels at the speed of 7.7 km per second. She crossed the 'finish line' in about 4 hours and 24 minutes while circling the Earth at least twice. Sunita ran in tandem with fellow astronaut Karen Nyberg running in Boston.

During her long stay in ISS, Sunita partook in American, Russian and Indian food. While her love for samosas caught media attention in India, she also enjoyed palak paneer, chole chawal and halwa, packed specially for her by NASA. In interviews after the flight, she said she did not chant any mantras as such but kept a statue of Ganesha with her. 'I knew Ganesha was looking after me. When you are thinking about going away for a long duration mission, it has to be part of your mindset that you're leaving your family, but it's for the right reasons, for good reasons, and hopefully helping humanity,' was her response to questions about her experience.[13]

She missed her family and her husband, Mike, and her dog Gorby Williams (named after Gorbachev). She carried a stuffed version of Gorby to ISS, and Gorby became a darling in the mission control as well as outside. Her mother,

Bonnie, put together Gorby's stories and wrote a book for kids – *Little Tail, Big Tales: The Adventures of an Astronaut's Dog Gorby, and His Two and Four-Legged Friends*.

Sunita was scheduled to return in April, but for many reasons, the stay got longer. She ended her first space sojourn of 195 days on 22 June when she landed in the Shuttle *Atlantis* at the Edwards Air Force Base in California. The trip made her famous as the spacewalker as she conducted as many as four spacewalks, the highest by any female astronaut till then, and ran the Boston Marathon from ISS. She enjoyed her outings and described the experience thus: 'I looked up and saw the vastness of space with millions of stars crystal clear above me. I saw the Northern Lights shimmering and dancing green above the Earth's surface.'[14]

A Ride on Soyuz to ISS

Back from her mission, Sunita was appointed deputy director of the Astronaut Office. She got her second chance to fly to ISS in 2012. She was trained earlier at the Star City in Moscow and had learned the Russian language. These attributes were important because this time, Sunita was scheduled to fly on a Russian spacecraft from the Baikonur Cosmodrome in Kazakhstan. Her mission was called Expedition 32/33 and zoomed into space on 14 July 2012. The commander of this Soyuz flight was Yuri Malenchenko, while Akihiko Hoshide of the Japan Aerospace Exploration Agency was the flight engineer. The third passenger was Sunita.

Unlike the Shuttle, which was large and could accommodate up to seven astronauts and had room for payloads and experiments, the Soyuz is much smaller (having crew and descent modules) and is used only for transporting astronauts to the space station. It cannot carry any satellites or other instruments as payloads. This is how

Sunita described her ride on Soyuz in her blog post from space: 'The Soyuz ride was really fun and yes, the bulb thing in the "living" compartment. There is a "sofa" there – but you don't really need to sit and it was full of equipment we were bringing to the ISS. There is also water, food and a toilet. We try not to go number 2 in the Soyuz if possible.'[15]

She found that all the food was Russian – cans of meat and fish, cheese, cookies and juice in little juice boxes. The crew members had a lot of time between 'burns' for rendezvous, so they slept a lot, ate the food and used the toilet. 'Of course, we chatted and laughed. Luckily Dina brought me a Sudoku book, so I ripped out a couple of pages, put them in my flight books and did a couple of puzzles in my free time,' Sunita wrote on her blog.[16] The Soyuz docked with ISS on 17 July, and Sunita was welcomed by NASA's Joe Acaba and Russian cosmonauts Gennady Padalka and Sergei Revin.

On this visit to ISS, Sunita spent four months conducting research and maintenance tasks. Sunita found that although this was her second time living in space, it was different because 'not only is the station bigger and there are more people, the activities are different' and the core systems of the 'laboratory' were built and stable, allowing astronauts to live and work with more regularity. However, she wrote, 'some things remain the same – cleaning up, cleaning and working on the toilet, planning for trash, taking out the trash, restocking the "shelves", computer maintenance – but these are things that are common to any business or organization as well – I guess you call it overhead.'[17]

Along with Hoshide, she performed six spacewalks to replace a component that relays power from the space station's solar arrays to its systems and repaired an ammonia leak on a station radiator. The one on 30 August 2012 was challenging. The two astronauts were supposed to replace a failed power distributor installed in the truss that routed a fourth of the power coming to the station from the solar arrays. But a bolt that had been up there for ten years exposed to a harsh environment did not unscrew. Sunita and Hoshide tried for over 8 hours and returned to ISS without completing the task. A return spacewalk was required on 5 September to fix the problem.

With this walk, Sunita broke Peggy Whitson's record for the longest total time spent on a spacewalk by a woman. Peggy, who in 2012 was in the NASA Astronaut Office, congratulated Sunita from Mission Control: 'It's an honour to hand off the record to someone as talented as you! You go girl.'[18] In mid-September, there was a change of guard at ISS, and Sunita took over as commander of the ISS. She became the second female commander in ISS history after Peggy Whitson. It turned out to be a busy period on ISS: as many as nine spacecraft docked to the ISS within seventeen days.

During her second stay on ISS, she became the first person to do a triathlon in space, which coincided with the Nautica Malibu Triathlon held in Southern California in September 2012. She used the space station's treadmill and stationary bike, and for the swimming portion of the race, she used a device called Advanced Resistive Exercise Device to do weightlifting and resistance exercises that approximate swimming in micro-gravity. In the run lasting 1 hour and 48 minutes, Sunita ran 6.4 km, biked 29 km and swam 0.8 km. She ran the triathlon in tandem with CNN medical correspondent Dr Sanjay Gupta on Earth.

She landed in Kazakhstan on 18 November 2012 after spending 127 days in space. At the end of her second trip to ISS, Sunita had spent a cumulative total of 322 days in space.

In July 2015, Sunita Williams was selected to work closely with two private companies, Boeing and SpaceX, and help them develop their crew transportation systems so that they can be used to provide crew transportation services to and from the ISS. This was to end the full dependence on the Russian Soyuz after the end of the Shuttle programme. She was designated to be a member of NASA's Commercial Crew Astronaut Corps, who could be crew on test flights of Boeing CST-100 and Crew Dragon capsules. As part of the commercial crew programme, Sunita and Butch Wilmore lifted off on 5 June 2024 aboard Boeing's Starliner spacecraft riding on the Atlas V rocket. The crew docked to the ISS on 6 June. It was the first crewed flight of Starliner and was scheduled to return to Earth after a week. Sunita's stay on ISS, however, got extended to over eight months as some glitches were reported in the thrusters of Starliner. In October 2024, she sent greetings through a recorded message from ISS to guests attending the Diwali party hosted by President Joe Biden at the White House.

Raja Chari and Anil Menon: Set for the Moon and Beyond

In November 2021, Raja Chari (full name Raja Jon Vurputoor 'Grinder' Chari) became the third NASA astronaut with Indian roots. The son of an Indian engineer from Hyderabad, Chari was designated the commander of the SpaceX Crew-3 mission to ISS on his maiden space flight. Subsequently, he was assigned to the Artemis II mission, which is expected to orbit the Moon as a part of NASA's Artemis programme.

After a long career with the US armed forces, Chari was selected to join the 2017 Astronaut Candidate Class. At the time of his selection, he was serving in the US Air Force as commander of the 461st Flight Test Squadron and director of the F-35 Integrated Test Force. He has over 2500 hours of flight time in a range of fighter jets, F-35, F-15, F-16 and F-18, and has participated in combat missions in Operation Iraqi Freedom and deployments in support of the Korean peninsula. He graduated from the Air Force Academy in 1999 with a bachelor's degree in astronautical engineering and engineering science. He completed his master's in aeronautics and astronautics from MIT.

During his space mission, Chari served as a flight engineer on ISS and spent 177 days in orbit. He performed two spacewalks and helped capture and release three spacecraft and two cargo vehicles during his six-month stay. He also worked on dozens of scientific experiments in plant science.

America is a preferred destination for aspiring Indians, particularly from Telangana and Andhra Pradesh. Telugus constitute the largest group among Indians in America. Raja's father, Sreenivas Vurputoor Chari, immigrated to America after completing his engineering degree from Osmania University. His grandfather was a professor of mathematics at the same university. Sreenivas Chari married Peggy, a nurse and later teacher, and settled down in Cedar Falls, Iowa. Raja Chari told *Telangana Today* in 2021: 'He sacrificed a lot for his family. I have many relatives in the US, and most of them credit my father for helping them build a life in the States. As a child, I couldn't understand this, but now I believe that had my father not moved here, I wouldn't be what I am.'[19] About his interest in space, he said, 'Every child dreams of becoming an astronaut at some point. As a kid, the more sci-fi movies I watched, the more I wanted to be in the space.'

The year Raja Chari went to space, another Indian American, Dr Anil Menon, was selected to join NASA's Astronaut Candidate Class. He graduated to become an astronaut candidate in 2021 and is in line to fly on future missions of NASA to ISS and the Moon.[20]

He entered the portals of the space agency as a flight surgeon in 2014 and was associated with several ISS flights in that capacity. In 2018, he joined SpaceX as its first flight surgeon and medical director, providing necessary medical support for its first human missions. He returned to NASA after he was selected for the astronaut class. He has also lived in the Star City, working as the deputy crew surgeon for two Soyuz missions and the prime crew surgeon for a third.

Menon has an enviable list of medical and engineering degrees from Harvard and Stanford – bachelor in neurobiology, master in mechanical engineering, doctor of medicine, master in public health and a fellowship in wilderness medicine. He was deployed in Afghanistan for Operation Enduring Freedom and in the critical care air transport team. Menon taught general aviation as a certified flight instructor and has logged over 1000 hours as a pilot.

In 1999, Menon spent a year in India at the Jawaharlal Nehru University (JNU) as a rotary ambassadorial scholar to study and support the polio eradication drive. During his visit to Delhi in 2022, he recalled his days at JNU. 'I was lucky to attend Jawaharlal Nehru University for one year,' he posted on his X page while sharing a quote from Nehru that said, 'We live in a wonderful world that is full of beauty, charm and adventure. There is no end to the adventures we can have if only we seek them with our eyes open.' The quote, Menon wrote, 'always stuck with me and applies to space exploration as to every day'. He also shared a picture of him with his hundred-year-old grandmother, saying, 'I reflected on the tremendous change she has witnessed from discovery of penicillin to a moon landing. It's hard to fathom the transformation we will see in the next 100 years.'[21] His grandfather M. Gopal Menon was in the Indian Civil Service, and General Kunhiraman Palat Candeth was one of his uncles.[22]

'I am proud to be from Kerala. My father is from there and he lives in India now,' he told *Malayalam Manorama* in an interview in 2024.[23] 'I am looking forward to working with India's newest astronauts, one of whom is from Kerala very close to where my father is from,' he said, referring to the selection of IAF pilot Prasanth Balakrishnan Nair – who hails from Kerala – as one of the ISRO astronauts. Anil Menon's father, Sankaran Menon, hails from the Palakkad District. He moved to America in the 1970s and married Lisa Samoilenko, a Ukrainian immigrant, and settled down in Minneapolis where Anil was born. Anil's wife, Anna Menon, is the lead operations engineer at SpaceX and undertook her maiden space journey as part of the Polaris Dawn mission of SpaceX in September 2024. Commanded by billionaire Jared Isaacman, the five-day mission orbited around the Earth and, at one point, increased its apogee to 1400 km – the highest any human has reached since the last Apollo mission in 1972.

In July 2021, Sirisha Bandla became the fourth person of Indian origin to have travelled to space, after Rakesh Sharma, Kalpana Chawla and Sunita Williams, as part of the Unity 22 mission of the private space company Virgin Galactic, founded by Richard Branson. Her flight lasted for 90 minutes.

With a BSc in aeronautical and astronautical engineering from Purdue and an MBA from George Washington University, she works as the vice president of Government Affairs at Virgin Galactic. Her parents hail from Prakasam District in Andhra Pradesh, and they migrated to America in the 1990s when Sirisha was four. She became interested in a career in space science after she visited NASA on a school field trip.

India-born aviator and commercial pilot Gopichand Thotakura became India's first civilian space tourist in May 2024 as he travelled to space as part of the crew for the New Shepard-25 (NS-25) mission of Blue Origin, a space company founded by Amazon's Jeff Bezos. It was a short duration flight during which the spacecraft passed the Kármán line, the internationally recognised boundary of space. This allowed crew members to experience weightlessness for a few minutes.

The first Indian to enrol as a space tourist with Virgin Atlantic in 2007 was Santosh George Kulangara, an avid traveller and publisher from Kerala. He bought the ticket for US$200,000 and underwent preliminary training for space travel in 2008, but Virgin Atlantic's commercial space flight plan took a long time to materialise. Kulangara was still waiting to fly in 2024.

Shawna Pandya, an Indo-Canadian physician and scientist, is scheduled to fly to space under the Citizen Science Astronaut programme. She has undergone astronaut training as part of Project PoSSUM (Polar Suborbital Science in the Upper Mesosphere), which prepares civilian scientists for suborbital space flights. She will be a part of an all-women research mission on a Virgin Galactic flight scheduled for 2026. Pandya was born to Indian parents who immigrated to Canada from Bombay in the 1980s.

8

Gaganyaan: India's First Human Space Flight

When Prime Minister Modi presented astronaut wings to four Indian astronaut designates at VSSC in Thiruvananthapuram on 27 February 2024, it marked an important landmark in India's two-decade-long quest to place an Indian in space from Indian soil. 'An Indian is going into space after forty years. However, now, the time, the countdown as well as the rocket belong to us,' he declared after pinning the symbolic astronaut wings on the chests of four IAF fighter pilots – Group Captain Prasanth Balakrishnan Nair, Group Captain Ajit Krishnan, Group Captain Angad Pratap, and Wing Commander Shubhanshu Shukla.[1] Modi famously announced in his Independence Day speech in 2018 that India will place an Indian in space by 2022, in the seventy-fifth year of its independence. ISRO, however, could not meet the deadline set by the political leadership for reasons discussed later in this chapter.

The history of space exploration globally is intertwined with the Cold War, geopolitics, national pride and domestic political compulsions. Within weeks of the Soviet cosmonaut Yuri Gagarin becoming the first human to enter space in April 1961, America not only sent the first American astronaut Alan Shepard Jr into space, but President Kennedy declared that America's space objective would be to put a man on the Moon by the end of the decade. America did it.

It was against this backdrop that Vikram Sarabhai, founder of India's space programme, defined the guiding principles of space exploration for India. He said, 'We do not have the fantasy of competing with the economically advanced nations in the exploration of the moon or the planets or manned space flight.'[2] He wanted India to use space technology to solve 'real problems of man and society'. For this, international collaboration and help was necessary. The focus on deploying space technology to address pressing problems on Earth helped political leadership and policymakers justify the allocation of funds for the space programme. ISRO faithfully stuck to Sarabhai's vision and philosophy through the 1970s and the 1980s.

For the Indian space programme, international help came from the Soviet Union, America and France. The collaboration with the Soviets was strong in the 1970s with offers to launch Indian satellites from the USSR as a friendly gesture. As an extension of this, the Soviet leadership offered to take an Indian onboard a Soviet rocket to its space station. The offer was made by President Brezhnev to Prime Minister Desai in 1978 and renewed again during Desai's visit to Moscow in 1979.

It so happened that an Indian satellite, Bhaskara-I, was launched from Kapustin Yar in the same week as Desai's visit to the Soviet Union. ISRO chairperson Satish Dhawan and ISAC Director U.R. Rao were in Moscow for the launch and were asked to see the prime minister. In the meeting at his room in the Kremlin, Desai discussed the Soviet proposal for the human flight with the two scientists and said, 'How will it help if an Indian astronaut goes up into space and comes down?' The tone made it clear he was against human space flight. Desai then turned to Rao and asked, 'This is in line with what

Vikram believed, isn't it?' Rao has recalled this episode in his account of the space programme.[3]

A deviation from Sarabhai's philosophy occurred soon. A year later, Brezhnev renewed the offer to Indira Gandhi, and she accepted it. ISRO, however, did not budge from its focus on developing rocket technology and communication satellites. So, the task of selecting an astronaut was given to IAF, resulting in Rakesh Sharma's space flight in 1984. On human space flights, ISRO remained wedded to the path set by Sarabhai. Its plan to send an Indian scientist onboard the US Shuttle to deploy the Insat-1 C satellite also did not materialise.

Despite the public interest Rakesh Sharma's flight generated and the general political acceptance of the mission, the space agency thought it prudent to remain glued to its blueprint, which did not include any human space flight. The agency felt that its limited financial and human resources and infrastructure, at that juncture, would be considerably impacted by the additional burden of human space flight. In the 1990s, the geopolitics changed with the break-up of the USSR, American sanctions on ISRO and the nuclear tests in 1998. All this delayed ISRO's next-generation rocket, GSLV, but it made good progress with launching a range of application satellites using PSLV. Several foreign satellites were also launched from India on a commercial basis. The space programme, thus, had become fully operational but with slow progress for GSLV.

The maturity of the space programme in terms of the indigenous technological capability to design, fabricate, launch and manage a range of satellites using Indian rockets prompted a change in the outlook of ISRO leadership. It thought it was time to go beyond the road map envisaged by Sarabhai and send a mission to the Moon. Encouraged by the generally positive response to the idea, ISRO began developing a plan and gradually worked to develop a political consensus as well as approval of the wider scientific community. Political assent was necessary for a decisive shift from a programme devoted to operational satellites to an esoteric exploratory mission. The whole process took four years, and the mission was finally launched in 2008. Chandrayaan-1 marked a turning point in India's approach to space technology.

While India's lunar mission was on the drawing board, China was preparing to launch its first human space flight. The reports were taken seriously in political, defence and strategic circles in Delhi. Prime Minister Vajpayee inaugurated the ninetieth session of the Indian Science Congress in January 2003 in Bangalore. Its general president was ISRO chief Kasturirangan. While the ceremony was on, the prime minister asked the ISRO chairman if the agency had any plans for manned space missions. Kasturirangan later recalled: 'I explained to him in detail that any such planning would require exhaustive preliminary studies that included the mission scope, requirements of human and infrastructural resources, timelines, investments, and anticipated returns on these investments. He nodded and was briefly lost in thought, seemingly assessing the merits and demerits of such an ambitious effort.'[4]

Vajpayee was aware of the geopolitical significance of manned space missions. As the foreign minister in the Cabinet of Morarji Desai in 1978, he had wanted India to accept the Soviet proposal to fly an Indian into space.

China conducted its first human space flight in October 2003, flying an astronaut (taikonaut, as the Chinese call it) in space for 21 hours. With subtle hints from the political leadership about human space flight and keeping in view developments in China, ISRO initiated some pre-project studies and internal discussions about a future human space flight mission. These studies and internal reviews helped identify critical technologies needed for human flight. Madan Lal, a former scientist at VSSC who prepared the first feasibility report on human space flight in 2006, in an interview with the author: 'Once humans are involved in a flight, reliability and safety take precedence over everything else. First, whatever launch vehicle you choose, it has to be made human-rated. Second, it should have a crew escape system if something goes wrong during the launch or in flight. Third, you need a life support system in the crew module to make it habitable. Fourth, we need ground stations for continuous connectivity with the orbiting module. And most important, the re-entry and landing technologies.'[5]

The report identified and defined technologies needed for human space flight. The findings were presented to a wider group of eminent scientists and engineers from defence research and other scientific institutions in November 2006. The report was received well.

VSSC started working on technologies needed for a human space capsule and a reliable launch vehicle capable of transporting a two-member crew in the capsule to LEO, keeping the module orbiting for a week and bringing it back safely to splash down in the Bay of Bengal or the Arabian Sea. 'When we discussed the crew capsule, we realised that there were many important systems that had to be developed. The environmental control and life support system [ECLSS] and the crew escape system – these were unchartered domains of technology for us,' recalled K. Radhakrishnan, then VSSC director and later chairman of ISRO.[6] The biggest challenge was the launcher. Till 2006, GSLV had flown five times with only two successful launches. The financial outlay projected for human space flight was ₹12,400 crore at 2008 prices.

The project report with details of all the technologies and finances needed for human space flight was ready in 2008. ISRO presented it to the Space Commission in April 2008 while assuring that the initiative would not hamper ongoing operational programmes. The commission approved the plan in August 2008 and recommended that it should be placed before the Union Cabinet for final approval. Before it went to the Cabinet, the Prime Minister's Office (PMO) formed a seven-member national committee to examine both the desirability and feasibility of human space flight. It had Planning Commission deputy chair Montek Singh Ahluwalia, principal scientific adviser Dr R. Chidambaram and eminent scientists Prof. M.G.K. Menon, Prof. Yashpal, Dr M.S. Swaminathan and Prof. Roddam Narasimha, besides VSSC director Radhakrishnan.

After deliberating on different aspects of the plan such as the global scenario, ISRO's technological capability, risk assessment, crew safety and collaboration with other space agencies, the expert panel gave its go-ahead for the human space flight in March 2009. The committee said it 'strongly supports the Indian human spaceflight and recommends that the Project Report submitted by the Department of Space should be processed for further necessary approvals so that the programme, which is a part of the approved 11th plan, could be implemented without delay'.[7] The successful launch of Chandrayaan-1 in October 2008 raised the prospects of the government approving the human space flight plan.

Building Blocks of Human Space Flight

Meanwhile, ISRO started work on two fronts: looking for possible collaborations for certain elements of human space flight and developing and testing critical technologies needed for human flight. The agency looked to its experienced and long-time partner, Roscosmos of Russia. A memorandum of understanding was signed in December 2009 for 'joint activities' for India's human space flight. It was proposed that before India sent its astronauts on a flight from India, it should gain some experience by sending Indian astronauts onboard the Russian Soyuz. It was agreed to send two Indian astronauts on Soyuz on an autonomous mission by 2013.

For the development of the Indian human space flight, Russia agreed to provide expertise for developing the orbital vehicle and its sub-systems, supply the Russian ECLSS for the Indian orbital vehicle, and help in the creation of an astronaut training facility in India. ISRO agreed to supply avionics for the Soyuz spacecraft. In 2015, ISRO signed another agreement with Roscosmos, identifying critical human space flight technologies for which Russia was going to help. The list included technologies for radiation shielding and compatible materials for astronauts; microparticle impact mitigation; personal hygiene management of astronauts; a life support system for the crew module and, besides, development of rendezvous and docking mechanisms for the crew module.

Along with seeking help from other space agencies, ISRO began developing some core technologies. Re-entry of the orbital or crew module into Earth's atmosphere after its mission is over is a critical aspect of any human space flight. To test technologies associated with re-entry, ISRO conducted an important test in January 2007. It was called the Space Capsule Recovery Experiment (SRE). A space capsule was launched as a co-passenger with the Cartosat-2 satellite and placed into an orbit at an altitude of 635 km. It had two scientific payloads for gathering data in micro-gravity. The module was made to revolve around the Earth for ten days, and then it was de-orbited and de-boosted, made to splashdown in the Bay of Bengal and recovered from there. Human space flights work like this, except that the 550-kg module sent was not human-rated and did not weigh the same as the proposed crew module.

The objective was to test a range of technologies: navigation, guidance and control during the re-entry phase; hypersonic aero thermodynamics; development of reusable thermal protection system; recovery through deceleration and flotation using parachutes. Each of them is a critical technology. For example, as the module enters Earth's atmosphere travelling at a speed of 29,000 km per hour, it creates enormous aerodynamic drag and heating. The temperature could go up to 2000 degrees, and the thermal protection system should be such that it does not allow the heat to damage the insides of the module. Hundreds of engineers in different ISRO units worked on SRE for six years. This gives an idea of how much effort goes into developing specific technologies for human space flight.

The second important test relating to technologies needed for human space flight was the Crew Module Atmospheric Re-entry Experiment or CARE launched aboard an LVM3 rocket (Launch Vehicle Mark III) in December 2014. This was the first experimental flight of the heavy-lift rocket as well as a flight-worthy crew module. After its launch from SHAR, the module got separated at an altitude of 126 km and was directed to re-enter the atmosphere. It splashed down 600 km from Port Blair at a location that was just 10 km away from the predicated location from where Indian Coast Guard ships recovered it. This was a crucial test because the weight of CARE (3775 kg) and parameters such as external geometry, parachute system and jettisoning mechanism were the same as they would be in the planned human space flight. With CARE, the space agency validated several technologies needed for the human mission.

The third important technology that ISRO demonstrated for human space flight in July 2018 was the crew escape system called the Pad Abort Test (PAT). The crew capsule is mounted on top of the rocket, and if something goes wrong in the rocket stages during the launch or after it, the crew escape system is designed to quickly pull the crew module, along with the astronauts, to a safe distance from the launch vehicle. To test if it works, scientists launched the crew module with a mass of 12.6 tonnes, and it soared into the sky. After 259 seconds, the module was given a command as if something had gone wrong with the rocket, and it arced out over the Bay of Bengal and floated back to Earth under its parachutes about 2.9 km from SHAR.

SRE, CARE and PAT were only some of the building blocks for the human space flight. There were still many to be tested – human rating of GSLV, technologies related to ECLSS, space suits, astronaut selection and training, experimental flights of human-rated GSLV and so on. For all this, the space agency needed an assured flow of funds and formal approval from the central government. One of the main reasons for the government's reluctance to go ahead with the human space flight was the continued problems with GSLV. The expert panel endorsed the human space flight plan in 2009, but GSLV was not showing signs of readiness. GSLV, along with a precious payload, GSAT-4, crashed minutes after its launch in April 2010, followed by another failure in December 2010. A few months later, another 'explosion' of a different kind occurred. In February 2011, ISRO's commercial arm, Antrix Corporation, was caught in an unsavoury controversy over its 2005 deal with a private company, Devas. The space agency's top brass and the immediate past leadership were caught in a public spat over alleged wrongdoing in the Antrix–Devas spectrum sale. Enquiries followed, and administrative action was taken against a few former top officials.

Amidst all this, human space flight approval took a back seat. ISRO chairman Radhakrishnan ruled out human space flight before 2017 as it did not figure in the Twelfth Plan (2012–2017) of the DoS though he said 'very good progress' was made on developing critical technologies.[8] The development work related to critical technologies continued, but the initial momentum was lost. The public image of ISRO, hit by the Antrix–Devas controversy, somewhat improved in 2012 when Prime Minister Manmohan Singh announced the MOM costing ₹450 crore in his Independence Day speech. ISRO launched a publicity and science communication drive on the mission and engaged with the public, given the positive experience it had with Chandrayaan-1. MOM was launched in November 2013, and it was successfully injected into the orbit around the Red Planet nine months later on 24 September 2014.

By this time, India had a new government headed by Narendra Modi. The National Democratic Alliance government continued with the status quo regarding human space flight. To several questions asked about human space flight between 2014 and 2018, the government kept repeating that human space flight was not on the cards though experiments relating to it continued. The last such reply in the Parliament was given on 2 August 2018.[9]

Human Space Flight Becomes Gaganyaan

The situation changed dramatically in August 2018 when Prime Minister Modi in his Independence Day address committed the nation to achieve a human space flight by the seventy-fifth anniversary of Indian Independence in 2022. He named the mission Gaganyaan. This signalled not only the government's approval for human space flight but put the space agency on a very tight deadline.

Following the announcement, the Union Cabinet approved the project, saying, 'A human-rated GSLV Mk-III will be used to carry the orbital module which will have necessary provisions for sustaining a 3-member crew for the duration of the mission.' The government said ISRO will collaborate with national agencies, laboratories, academia and industry to accomplish the objectives of the mission and build the necessary infrastructure for crew training, the realisation of flight systems and ground infrastructure. 'The mission will be completed within forty months of all the formal sanctions coming in,' the law minister, Ravi Shankar Prasad, told the media after the Cabinet meeting in December 2018.[10]

Media commentators linked the surprise announcement with the upcoming 2019 general elections. 'By approving the project, the Modi government hopes to earn bragging rights during the election campaign. Sending Indians to outer space will address the aspirational class of the country, and portray a New India that Modi has been talking about,' wrote *The Week*.[11] The announcement about Gaganyaan was followed by Mission Shakti, an anti-satellite missile test by DRDO in March 2019. Both the episodes found a mention in the BJP manifesto for the 2019 general elections. The party said, 'After achieving unprecedented success through Mission Shakti, we are committed to ensuring that Gaganyaan successfully demonstrates our scientific capabilities of executing a manned mission in space.'[12] Former ISRO chairman Madhavan Nair, who joined the BJP in October 2018, accused the Congress-led United Progressive Alliance government of pushing the Mars mission by diverting resources meant for Chandrayaan-2 with an eye on the 2014 elections.[13]

ISRO, on its part, got down to business right after the announcement under the new leadership of K Sivan. As the first necessary step, the agency established the Human Space Flight Centre (HSFC) in January 2019 to handle end-to-end mission planning, develop engineering systems for crew survival in space and select and train crew. In addition, the centre was tasked with undertaking R&D in life support systems, human factors engineering, bioastronautics, crew training and human rating and certification of launch vehicles. Dr S. Unnikrishnan Nair, who had worked with Madan Lal in preparing the feasibility report for human space flight, was named the founder and director of the centre. ISRO announced that several precursor missions will be carried out to demonstrate the 'technology preparedness levels' like the Integrated AirDrop Test, PAT and Test Vehicle flights. At least two unmanned missions will precede the human space flight to prove the safety and reliability of all systems. The uncrewed missions will fly Vyommitra, a robot or humanoid developed for the flight.

The LVM3 rocket has been identified as the launch vehicle for the Gaganyaan mission. All systems in the launch vehicle will be reconfigured to meet human-rating requirements, and the rechristened rocket will be called Human Rated LVM3 or HLVM3. On the top end of the rocket will be the orbital module comprising a crew module and a service module. The crew module will have a double-walled construction consisting of a pressurised metallic inner structure and an unpressurised external structure with thermal protection. The service module will provide the necessary support to the crew module while it is orbiting Earth. It is an unpressurised structure containing thermal, propulsion, power and avionics systems and deployment mechanisms. There will be a crew escape system with quick-acting, high-burn-rate solid motors so that it can eject and take the crew module to a safe distance in case of any emergency.

In October 2023, the first test flight related to the project, Test Vehicle Abort mission-1 (TV-D1), was carried out from SHAR. The crew module used in the test was similar to the one that will be used finally, but it was not pressurised. The test demonstrated the emergency escape system of the crew capsule, showing that the vehicle could jettison away from the rocket if there was a problem during the ascent. After separating from the rocket, the escape system propelled the crew module for a distance, and then the two got separated. The crew module then decelerated with the help of three large parachutes (each of 25-m diameter) and splashed down in the sea, from where it was recovered.

Selection and Training of Astronauts

One of the earliest moves of HSFC was to sign an agreement with Glavkosmos in June 2019 for 'selection support, medical examination and space training' of Indian astronauts.[14] The Russian agency agreed to provide consulting services for the selection of astronaut candidates and for conducting medical tests of candidates, besides training selected candidates.

ISRO, in collaboration with IAF, selected four candidates from a pool of experienced test pilots. Gaganyaan being its first space flight, the search was restricted to male combat pilots, much like what the Soviets and Americans did in their early missions. Though IAF threw open combat roles for women pilots in 2016, ISRO Chairman S. Somanath told the media in October 2023 that women pilots could join space flights in future as astronauts or mission specialists.[15] 'Even if the selection committee wanted to limit the first round to IAF pilots, they could easily have allowed the women IAF pilots to compete,' pointed out space entrepreneur Susmita Mohanty in a media interview.[16] Some women scientists had applied to be mission specialists when ISRO wanted to select two scientists for the Shuttle mission in 1985.

The Gaganyaan applicants went through a battery of clinical, aeromedical and psychological tests in Bangalore. IAM conducted preliminary research on the psychological and physiological requirements of the crew, and provided inputs for crew capsule design and control and environmental systems as per psychological and physiological requirements. The shortlisted candidates were interviewed, and the National Crew Selection Board recommended four IAF test pilots for training.[17] As per the agreement with Russia, the four pilots were sent to the Yuri Gagarin Cosmonaut Training Centre for the training spanning thirteen months. Rakesh Sharma and Ravish Malhotra were trained here and so was Sunita Williams before she flew on the Soyuz spacecraft.

The training started in Russia on 10 February 2020 with the mandatory Russian language classes. A few weeks into the training programme, the Covid-19 pandemic struck. After a brief suspension, the training was resumed in May 2020. The Russians informed ISRO that the four pilots were in good health and feeling fine. All infection prevention measures like social distancing, medical masks and gloves and restriction of the entry of outsiders were enforced at the Star City. The health status of the trainees was monitored daily, and once every three months, doctors conducted thorough medical examinations.

Following the language training, the trainees attended classroom lectures on the basics of astrogation (spaceship navigation) and controls of manned spacecraft. The schedule included comprehensive biomedical training combined with regular physical practices. The pilots were trained in the systems of the Soyuz manned spaceship.

Some training modules took place outside the Star City such as the training on crew actions in the event of an abnormal descent module landing in wooded and marshy areas in winter, on the water surface and in the Steppe in summer. These rigorous sessions were conducted between February and July 2020. For weightlessness training, the candidates were flown in the special laboratory aircraft, the Ilyushin-76, which is a four-engine freighter. Another session was about lifting aboard a helicopter while evacuating from the landing point of the descent module. Back at the Star City, astronaut candidates were trained in a centrifuge and a hyperbaric chamber to prepare them for space flight factors like G-force, hypoxia and pressure drops. The instructors praised the effort and high motivation levels of the Indian pilots during the training process.

While the training was on, HSFC signed a contract with Zvezda, another entity under Glavkosmos, for the supply of personal flight equipment, including spacesuits, for the Indian astronauts under training.[18] The four pilots visited Zvezda where their anthropometric parameters were measured for the production of spacesuits, individual seats and custom-made couch liners.

After returning from Russia, the four pilots were trained in the newly established astronaut training facility of ISRO in Bangalore.[19] This included training with simulators, mock-ups and the virtual reality tools. The crew was also trained in various human-centric products and survival scenarios. Physical fitness was maintained through a rigorous training regime. A specialised yoga module was incorporated into the physical training programme for 'the holistic health management' of the astronauts, according to the space agency. Rakesh Sharma was the first astronaut ever to perform a set of yoga asanas in space onboard the Salyut space station. In addition, the pilots attended academic classes in aerospace engineering at IISc.

The Fab Four

While four astronaut candidates were selected in late 2019 and underwent training in Russia in 2020 and 2021, their names were kept a closely guarded secret. Professors and students at IISc where the pilots attended academic classes were also unaware of future astronauts on the campus. The names of the four were revealed on 27 February 2024 when they were presented with the astronaut wings during a special ceremony. The first set of four Indian astronauts formally inducted into ISRO are all IAF test pilots – Group Captain Prasanth Balakrishnan Nair, Group Captain Ajit Krishnan, Group Captain Angad Pratap and Wing Commander Shubhanshu Shukla.

Prasanth Balakrishnan Nair was born on 26 August 1976 in Thiruvazhiyad in Kerala and was raised there. After his schooling, he joined an engineering course but left it mid-way when he was selected for NDA. He opted for a career in the air force where he was commissioned in December 1998 in the fighter stream. Since then, he accumulated 3000 hours of flying experience across a diverse set of aircraft including Su-30 MKI, MiG-21 and MiG-29. He was designated Category A flying instructor and test pilot and commanded the premier Su-30 Squadron.

Ajit Krishnan, born in Chennai on 19 April 1982, is also an alumnus of NDA and was a recipient of the President's Gold Medal and Sword of Honour at the Air Force Academy. He was commissioned in the fighter stream of IAF in June 2003. As a flying instructor and test pilot, he had logged 2900 hours of flying experience and flown a range of aircraft – Su-30 MKI, MiG-21, MiG-29, Jaguar, Dornier, An-32 and so on. He is also an alumnus of the Defence Services Staff College,, Wellington.

Angad Pratap comes from Prayagraj where he was born on 17 July 1982. He had a career trajectory similar to his fellow astronauts: passed out from NDA, was commissioned in the fighter stream of IAF in 2004 and became a flying instructor and a test pilot. He has logged 2000 hours of flying experience on Sukhoi, MiG, Jaguar, Hawk, Dornier, An-32 and so on.

Shubhanshu Shukla was born in Lucknow on 10 October 1985. After NDA, he was commissioned in the fighter stream in 2006. He is a fighter combat leader and a test pilot with about 2000 hours of flying experience, having flown a range of jets.

Soon after the announcement, there was a little storm on Instagram. Malayalam actor Lenaa posted that she was married to the forty-seven-year-old test pilot and astronaut candidate Prasanth Balakrishnan Nair. Though the marriage took place a few weeks earlier, it was kept a secret. Lenaa said she did not want to spill the beans about Nair's selection or their marriage. 'It is a historic moment of pride for our country, our state of Kerala and me personally,' she said about Nair getting the astronaut wings while sharing a picture of the wedding ceremony.

A few months later, it appeared that out of the four candidates, three stood a definite chance of flying in space. ISRO maintained that Gaganyaan could launch a three-member crew to an orbit of 400 km for a three-day mission and bring them back safely to the Earth, but it did not announce if the first crewed mission would include two or three astronauts.

Several scientific institutions, outside ISRO, too, are involved in preparing for the Gaganyaan mission. The Defence Food Research Laboratory (DFRL), which had prepared ready-to-eat food items for Rakesh Sharma's flight in 1984, is doing the same for the Gaganyaan mission. The nutrition plan for the Indian astronauts has been prepared by the Hyderabad-based National Institute of Nutrition, while the actual preparation of the dishes for the space flight has been underway at the Mysuru-based DFRL since 2021. The space worthiness of food is determined by subjecting the food to detailed macro- and micro-nutrient analysis, sensory testing and microbiological safety as per international space food standards.

The food items not only have to remain fresh but also taste good and fulfil the energy and calorie requirements of the astronauts. A range of ready-to-eat dishes would be on the Gaganyaan menu – vegetable pulav, vegetable biryani, sooji halwa, shahi paneer, dal makhani, chicken biryani, chicken kathi rolls, egg kathi rolls, paneer kathi rolls, aloo paratha, dal chawal, kadi chawal and so on. There will be snacks and beverages too. The final menu will be selected before the space flight. All the solid and liquid food items will be packed in specially designed pouches made of space-worthy packaging materials. DFRL scientists were quoted as saying in *Star of Mysore*: 'The idea is to give them [astronauts] balanced meals that are lightweight, low volume and easy to consume. Food kits include special straws for drinking water and instant coffee or tea, food warmers and waste restraining bags. Special containers, sippers, have also been developed to enable the astronauts to have liquids such as fruit juice and water.'[20]

The dark blue–light blue asymmetric ground suits, which the astronaut designates wore during the wing presentation ceremony, were designed by the National Institute of Fashion Technology, Bengaluru. It also designed the 'wing' presented to the astronauts.

While the prime objective of the first human space flight is to demonstrate the capability to launch a manned crew and bring it back safely, the astronauts will also conduct some experiments developed by Indian scientists. These experiments have been designed and developed by the Indian Institute of Space Science and Technology (Thiruvananthapuram), TIFR (Mumbai), Jawaharlal Nehru Centre for Advanced Scientific Research (Bengaluru) and the Indian Institute of Chemical Technology (Hyderabad).

Shubhanshu Shukla's Flight to ISS

Before the likely launch of Gaganyaan in 2026, an Indian astronaut would fly on an American mission to ISS under the Indo-US deal announced in 2023. For this mission,

ISRO decided to send two out of the four astronauts to America. One of them would fly to ISS, while the other one would be a backup candidate. In August 2024, the national space agency announced that Group Captain Shubhanshu Shukla would be the prime astronaut for the ISS journey while Prasanth Balakrishnan would be the backup candidate. He would take over in the case of a contingency.

In November 2024, the Indian space agency revealed that the two astronauts completed the initial phase of training which included familiarisation with the Dragon spacecraft and onboard systems of ISS like photography from space, daily operations routine and communication protocols. The two candidates were also trained for different types of emergencies in space.[21] A successful mission would make Shukla the second Indian citizen to go to space, after Rakesh Sharma. Shukla will be a part of a mission executed by a private company, Axiom Space, in collaboration with NASA. Unlike Rakesh Sharma's space trip in 1984, which was a friendly gesture by the USSR, India is paying for Shukla's fourteen-day trip to ISS. ISRO did not reveal the exact fee being paid to Axiom or NASA, but media reports quoted Pearly Pandya, Director, International Government Business at Axiom Space, as saying 'the cost per seat on a commercial mission like this is in the "mid-$60 million" range'.[22]

Since Shukla is a trained astronaut, he would not be considered a 'space tourist' (just because the flight is paid for) but would be taking part in the operation of the spacecraft as well as scientific experiments onboard ISS. However, both Shukla and Balakrishnan had to undergo fresh training to familiarise them with the SpaceX's Dragon spacecraft and ISS as well as safety protocols, health management and systems operations at multiple training facilities.

The Axiom mission, AX-4, has an international crew. Besides Shukla, astronauts from Poland and Hungary are going to be a part of the mission, which will be commanded by NASA veteran Peggy Whitson. 'As the AX-4 pilot, Shukla will assist me in conducting essential spacecraft operations such as navigation and docking procedures,' Whitson told *Times of India* in September 2024.[23]

After the Dragon spacecraft carrying the four-member crew docks with ISS, the crew would enter the space station. They would stay on ISS for fourteen days, participate in scientific experiments and return to Earth in the Dragon. The experience, according to Somanath, would help ISRO in the Gaganyaan mission.[24]

9

The Way Ahead

SOMETHING INCREDIBLE HAPPENED IN the world of space technology in October 2024 when the private space firm SpaceX launched its spacecraft *Starship* using Super Heavy, its 70-m-tall rocket, made the rocket return to Earth after launching *Starship* and 'caught' the rocket using a giant launch tower named Mechazilla. The company dubbed the giant robotic arms of the tower 'chopsticks' as they grabbed the rocket, which was then manoeuvred to a controlled descent. SpaceX plans to deploy *Starship* to transport astronauts to the Moon and Mars in the future, and its CEO, Elon Musk, envisages Super Heavy to be refuelled and returned to the launch pad within half an hour of its flight, just like an aeroplane.[1]

Reusable rockets have been the holy grail of space technology for decades. Rockets that propel satellites and spaceships to space usually cannot be reused. One of the main reasons for space travel being so costly is because new rockets must be built by national space agencies and commercial operators for every mission. Rockets also take a long time to be fabricated and readied for space travel. If we want to lower the cost of space travel dramatically and increase the frequency of launches, then making rockets partially or fully reusable is one of the primary options.

Space agencies like NASA have been working on developing the necessary technologies for making reusable rockets. ISRO's Reusable Launch Vehicle (RLV) project, too, is aimed at the same. The space agency tested the first RLV prototype in a suborbital flight in 2016 and has been engaged in developing technology components such as autonomous landing, powered cruise flight and hypersonic flight using air-breathing propulsion. The RLV is designed to make a conventional landing on a runway and deploy a booster for parachute landing. A series of landing experiments have been conducted with a winged vehicle, Pushpak. In the test conducted in June 2024, Pushpak was released from an IAF helicopter at an altitude of 4.5 km at a point away from the runway. It autonomously executed cross-range correction manoeuvres and performed a horizontal landing at the Aeronautical Test Range in Chitradurga, Karnataka.[2] The winged RLV is likely to be used in the future to launch small satellites, to begin with.

Coupled with exciting developments in launch technologies, such as the Super Heavy of SpaceX, are important political moves involving space entrepreneurs and business people. In December 2024, President-elect Donald Trump nominated billionaire entrepreneur and SpaceX astronaut Jared Isaacman as the next chief of NASA.[3] SpaceX, heavily supported and funded by NASA, is already taking on space transportation tasks of the federal space agency such as launching commercial satellites and ferrying astronauts to ISS. SpaceX founder Musk is also slated to play a key role in the Trump administration as the co-head of the Department of Government Efficiency. Starlink, another of Musk's ventures, started rolling out satellite internet in many countries in 2024, using a constellation of satellites. All these techno-economic and political developments indicate a definite shift in the American space industry. India has not remained untouched by this decisive shift – the flight of an Indian astronaut to ISS slated in 2025 is being facilitated through a commercial space company.

China, on the other hand, is aggressively moving ahead with its space programme in the State sector with high-visibility missions like crewed missions in LEO, spacewalks and its space station, Tiangong, which became operational in 2022. The station is much smaller than the ISS and can house three astronauts for periods of up to six months. China has successfully delivered several crewed missions and plans to go to the Moon as well. For long, Indian space leaders have maintained that ISRO is not in competition with China, yet the agency has embarked upon ambitious missions like crewed missions to the Moon and its space station, dubbed the Bharatiya Antariksha Station (BAS). All such missions will be primarily State-funded and led by ISRO with the private aerospace industry and space start-ups playing a supportive role. The next twenty-five years would see many ambitious and bold space missions from India.

The successful touchdown of the Chandrayaan-3 lunar lander demonstrated vital space technologies that only a few nations possess. Building on this, ISRO began working on the next lunar mission, Chandrayaan-4, which would not only soft-land and operate a robotic rover on the lunar surface but would also bring back lunar samples to the Earth. Such missions are called 'sample return' missions and involve the development of rovers that can collect lunar samples and spacecraft capable of taking off from the lunar surface with the collected samples and ferrying them back safely to the Earth. The critical building blocks for such a mission include advanced technologies for docking, undocking, landing and returning safely to the Earth. The project will also involve beefing up necessary scientific and academic facilities for the analysis and study of lunar samples. ISRO has said that all critical technologies will be developed indigenously, leading to technological spin-offs for other sectors.[4]

For Chandrayaan-5, however, ISRO is collaborating with Japan and other countries. The mission, named Lunar Polar Exploration (LUPEX), will carry a large rover (weighing about 350 kg, as against the 27-kg Pragyan rover of Chandrayaan-3) built by the Japanese Aerospace Exploration Agency and with instruments from NASA and ESA as well, while ISRO is building the lander. The scientific objective of LUPEX is to 'investigate the quantity and quality of water on the Moon'.[5]

Chandrayaan-4, along with the human space flight Gaganyaan, is supposed to be the vital next step towards a human mission to the Moon, which ISRO has projected to achieve by 2040. Chandrayaan-4, costing ₹2100 crore, is scheduled to be launched within thirty-six months from the time it was approved in late 2024.

Among future scientific missions, Indian scientists are targeting Venus after the successful mission to Mars. An ambitious Venus Orbiter Mission (VOM) would be a major step forward in planetary exploration. Since the start of the space age, there have been several missions to Venus – fly-by, orbiting and landing – but the planet continues to be the subject of scientific enquiry. Venus is the closest planet to the Earth, and scientists believe it was formed under conditions similar to that of the Earth but became inhospitable over time. It has a very dense atmosphere, is covered by layers of thick clouds made mostly of sulphuric acid and has a surface temperature of 464 degrees Celsius.[6] A mission to Venus, therefore, will provide an opportunity to study how planetary environments evolve in dramatically different ways. The objective of VOM would be to place a scientific probe in an orbit around Venus to study its surface, subsurface, atmospheric processes and the Sun's influence on its atmosphere. The mission, costing about ₹1236 crore, is planned for launch in March 2028.[7] It is expected to strengthen capabilities for future planetary missions with larger payloads and advanced orbital insertion techniques. NASA and ESA, too, are readying new missions to the planet.

In addition to VOM, an Indian landing mission to Mars is also on the cards.

Bharatiya Antariksh Station

Perhaps the most ambitious long-term project of the space agency is building an Indian space station, Bharatiya Antariksha Station, by 2035. BAS would be on the lines of space stations Salyut, Mir and ISS, described in Chapters 5 and 6, and the Tiangong space station of China. It has been conceived as a follow-on mission of Gaganyaan because the capability to send humans to space and advanced technologies like docking must be perfected to build a space station. A space station is built on the Earth, module by module, and transported to the LEO and assembled in space piece by piece. The process requires the design, development and fabrication of modules on the ground and a series of missions to send them to LEO.

ISRO envisages that BAS would be of modest size – overall dimensions measuring 27 m by 20 m, and its overall mass would be 52 tonnes.[8] The station will be able to house and support three to four astronauts at a time for a short duration. In comparison, the dimensions of ISS are 108 m by 51 m and it can support eight to ten astronauts at any given time. The Chinese space station, with dimensions of 55 m by 39 m, can support three astronauts at a given time.

In September 2024, the government approved the construction of the first module of BAS as an extension of the Gaganyaan programme. It is expected to be launched in 2028, and the station could take a final shape by

2035. Between 2025 and 2028, the space agency would work on a series of precursor missions for BAS, develop necessary hardware and launch an uncrewed mission. Four missions under the Gaganyaan programme are expected by 2026, followed by four additional missions focused on demonstrating and validating technologies for the space station by December 2028.[9] The key technological building blocks of BAS are docking and berthing systems, roll-out solar array, propellent refuelling and servicing, avionics and communication systems, and inertial and control systems. The first unit of the space station, BAS-1, is slated for launch in 2028. The Indian space station will be used for supporting micro-gravity-based scientific research and technology development.

The Grand Space Vision

While the national space agency of India has unveiled what it calls the 'Grand Space Vision for the Amrit Kal' with bold projects like the space station and moon landing and has obtained the necessary political backing for them, it will not be an easy route. 'We have a dream of making India a space power,' says ISRO chief S. Somanath.[10] To convert this dream into reality, 'the most important thing to do all this is the power of the rocket'. As of 2024, ISRO has the capacity to launch satellites weighing 4 tonnes to GEO and about 10 tonnes to LEO. To launch space station modules or humans to the Moon, it needs higher payload capability, typically 30 to 70 tonnes of mass to be lifted to LEO. This is possible with heavier rockets.

'But we cannot build rockets for this purpose alone. We need to build rockets in a manner which is sustainable and will bring benefits in terms of economic activities. We should be able to launch our satellites regularly and we should do it in a commercial and cost-effective manner,' according to Somanath.[11] Towards this goal, the space agency has begun working on a mega-rocket, the Next Generation Launch Vehicle (NGLV), which will be capable of lifting 30 tonnes of mass to LEO. The 90-m-tall rocket with 5-m diameter will also be partially reusable. NGLV will have three development flights before it is declared operational. The expected time for NGLV development is eight years.[12] The second challenge is to build heavier spacecraft that can transport humans to space. Another key technological building block to achieve the grand vision is the docking capability. ISRO conducted the first Spacecraft Docking Experiment (SpaDex) in January 2025.

Technological challenges apart, the political context of the grand space vision is different from what we have seen with ISRO till recent decades. Since its start, the space programme has benefited from a broad consensus on the goal of deploying space technology for national development. All major scientific milestones were either lauded or endorsed by the Parliament and political parties across the spectrum. When ISRO sought to deviate from the path laid down by its founder Sarabhai with its first lunar mission, Prime Minister Vajpayee made sure that the idea got approval from the multi-party parliamentary standing committee before it was approved by his Cabinet. The idea was also discussed by the Indian scientific community.

In contrast, the grand vision announced in 2023 is seen more as an agenda of the Modi government. The decision to launch a human flight to the Moon and build a space station was announced by the PMO suddenly, without any wider consultation with the scientific community or political forum like the Parliament. In October 2023, the prime minister 'directed that India should now aim for new and ambitious goals, including setting up "Bharatiya Antariksha Station" by 2035 and sending the first Indian to the Moon by 2040'.[13] ISRO chief Somanath has repeatedly said publicly that it was the vision of Prime Minister Modi.[14] After the success of Chandrayaan-3, the National Council of Educational Research and Training released special modules on Chandrayaan-3 for schoolchildren. These teaching modules credited the prime minister personally for prodding ISRO scientists to 'try once more' after Chandrayaan-2 failed to make a soft landing on the lunar surface.[15]

Analysts feel there is little justification for India to go for its space station instead of participating in a collaborative venture like ISS. 'There are no visible military advantages of human space mission or a development of the space station. Also, the years of experimentation carried out by major space players in the zero-gravity atmosphere so far has not yielded any path-breaking results,' notes defence and strategic analyst Ajay Lele in his 2012 book.[16] In his view, the best option for countries like India with limited benefits of undertaking such missions could be to devise a multilateral mechanism for all such activities. If a country has to go solo, it should invest in robotic missions rather than human missions.

'Probably the most troubling aspect of these glamour missions, from Sarabhai's standpoint, would be their unabashed mimicry of what other states are doing,' writes historian Itty Abraham, referring to missions aimed at 'putting a landing craft on the moon and orbiting Mars, spending a reported billion dollars to establish the infrastructure and skills to conduct manned space flights, travelling a million miles to study the physics of the sun'.[17] He feels that while complex missions match well with India's ambition to rank among the world's most important nations and are very popular among the urban middle classes, they 'represent neither major technoscientific advances nor the vision of integrated national development that Sarabhai stood for'.

From being an area of pursuing scientific activities through international cooperation and deployment of technology for national development, space has become an arena of technological supremacy and national pride. 'Space research and technology by its very nature is an international activity,' points out Lele.[18] The notion of dominance in space, according to him, is a Cold War-centric view. India, with its grand space vision, has unwittingly entered the Asian space race with China, though it has not given up the path of international cooperation fully. The ongoing important space missions with America and Japan are prime examples of continued technological dependence and cooperation.

Domestically, space technology has become more a matter of national pride than a tool for evoking scientific curiosity and spreading scientific thinking. The day on which Chandrayaan-3 landed on the lunar surface in 2023, 23 August, has been declared as National Space Day, and the point of Chandrayaan-3 landing has been designated 'Shiv Shakti'. 'National Space Day enhances public awareness of the importance and benefits of space exploration, promoting national pride and unity,' the government said while announcing the day and directing research, academic and educational institutions to hold month-long celebrations.[19]

As India enters a new phase in its long and chequered space journey, one hopes it does not lose the focus with which it began this journey – a scientific pursuit to help ease the lives of millions of Indians and deploy the fruits of technology to address day-to-day needs and problems.

Notes

CHAPTER 1: THE SPACE AGE COMES TO THUMBA

1 Gopal Raj, *Reach for the Stars: The Evolution of India's Rocket Programme* (New Delhi: Viking, 2000).

2 R.S. Anderson, *Nucleus and Nation: Scientists, International Networks, and Power in India* (Chicago: University of Chicago Press, 2019).

3 'Setting Up of National Committee for the International Geophysical Year for 1957–58', Ministry of Education _ SR-2_1953_NA_F-22(1)_53, National Archives of India, New Delhi, 1953.

4 Ibid.

5 'Setting Up of National Committee for the International Geophysical Year for 1957–58'.

6 Colin Burgess and Chris Dubbs, *Animals in Space: From Research Rockets to the Space Shuttle* (Springer Science & Business Media, 2007).

7 R. Kochhar, 'Science as a Symbol of New Nationhood: India and the International Geophysical Year 1957–58', *Current Science*, 94 (6): 813–16.

8 Ibid.

9 A.A. Siddiqi, 'Science, Geography, and Nation: The Global Creation of Thumba', *History and Technology*, 31 (4): 420–51.

10 Ibid.

11 Atomic Energy Commission, *Atomic Energy and Space Research, A Profile for the Decade 1970-1980* (No. BARC/INF--6) (Bombay: Atomic Energy Commission, 1970).

12 'Report of Indian National Committee for Space Research (INCOSPAR) for the Year 1961', Cabinet Secretariat, Nehru Memorial Museum and Library (New Delhi, 1967).

13 E.V. Chitnis, 'Early ISRO – 1961–1971', in P.M. Rao, B.N. Suresh and Balagangadharan (eds), *From Fishing Hamlet to Red*

Planet: India's Space Journey, 20–31 (New Delhi: HarperCollins Publishers India, 2015).

14 K.V. Sarabhai and P. Joshi, 'Vikram Sarabhai', *Current Science*, 118 (8): 1203–06.

15 Jacques Balmont, 'Starting the Indian Space Programme', in P.M. Rao, B.N. Suresh and Balagangadharan (eds), *From Fishing Hamlet to Red Planet: India's Space Journey*, 3–6 (New Delhi: HarperCollins Publishers India, 2015).

16 A.P.J. Kalam, 'India's First Launch Vehicle', in P.M. Rao, B.N. Suresh and Balagangadharan (eds), *From Fishing Hamlet to Red Planet: India's Space Journey,* 100–126 (New Delhi: HarperCollins Publishers India, 2015).

17 R. Aravamudan, ISRO: *A Personal History* (New Delhi: HarperCollins, 2017).

18 A. Parthasarathi, *Technology at the Core: Science & Technology with Indira Gandhi* (New Delhi: Pearson Education India, 2007).

19 Satish Dhawan, 'The Architect', in P.M. Rao, B.N. Suresh and Balagangadharan (eds), *From Fishing Hamlet to Red Planet: India's Space Journey,* 43–52 (New Delhi: HarperCollins Publishers India, 2015).

20 Parthasarathi, *Technology at the Core.*

21 Atomic Energy Commission, *Atomic Energy and Space Research.*

CHAPTER 2: SOARING HIGH WITH DREAM ROCKETS

1 A.P.J. Abdul Kalam and A. Tiwari, *Wings of Fire: An Autobiography* (Hyderabad: Universities Press, 1999).

2 R. Aravamudan, *ISRO: A Personal History* (New Delhi: HarperCollins, 2017).

3 Kalam and Tiwari, *Wings of Fire.*

4 B.R. Janson and E.H. Ritchie, *Astronautics and Aeronautics, 1979-1984: A Chronology* (Vol. 4024) (Washington: National Aeronautics and Space Administration, Office of Management, Scientific and Technical Information Division, 1990).

5 Gopal Raj, *Reach for the Stars: The Evolution of India's Rocket Programme* (New Delhi: Viking, 2000).

6 A.P.J. Kalam, 'India's First Launch Vehicle', in P.M. Rao, B.N. Suresh and Balagangadharan (eds), *From Fishing Hamlet*

to *Red Planet: India's Space Journey*, 100–126 (New Delhi: HarperCollins Publishers India, 2015).

7 P.M. Rao and P. Radhakrishnan, *A Brief History of Rocketry in ISRO* (Hyderabad: Universities Press (India) Private Limited, 2012).

8 'ASLV-D1 Launch', SPACE India (Bangalore: Indian Space Research Organisation, 1987).

9 Press Trust of India, 'ASLV Mission Fails', *Times of India,* 14 July 1988.

10 Raj, *Reach for the Stars.*

11 Abraham E. Muthunayagam, *From Space to Sea: My ISRO Journey and Beyond* (New Delhi: HarperCollins Publishers India, 2022).

12 N. Narayanamoorthy, 'PSLV: The Workhorse of ISRO', in P.M. Rao, B.N. Suresh and Balagangadharan (eds), *From Fishing Hamlet to Red Planet: India's Space Journey*, 137–68 (New Delhi: HarperCollins Publishers India, 2015).

13 Dinesh C. Sharma, 'When India's Space Plans Crashed', *Mail Today*, 18 April 2010.

14 Dinesh C. Sharma, 'Home-made GSLV Fails in the Third Stage', *Mail Today*, 16 April 2010.

15 A.E. Muthunayagam, 'Liquid Propulsion in ISRO', in P.M. Rao, B.N. Suresh and Balagangadharan (eds), *From Fishing Hamlet to Red Planet: India's Space Journey*, 225–41 (New Delhi: HarperCollins Publishers India, 2015).

16 Muthunayagam, *From Space to Sea.*

CHAPTER 3: A REVOLUTION FROM THE SKY

1 Richard B. Marsten, 'A Dream Come True: Satellite Broadcasting', *IEEE Transactions on Aerospace and Electronic Systems*, 33 (1): 361–81.

2 Arnold W. Frutkin, Interview by Rebecca Wright, Washington, DC, 11 January 2002, NASA Headquarters Oral History Project. Available online: https://historycollection.jsc.nasa.gov/JSCHistoryPortal/history/oral_histories/NASA_HQ/Administrators/FrutkinAW/FrutkinAW_1-11-02.htm (accessed 25 April 2024).

3 Frutkin, Interview by Rebecca Wright.

4 A.A. Siddiqi, 'Whose India? SITE and the Origins of Satellite Television in India', *History and Technology*, 36 (3–4): 452–74.

5 Dinesh C. Sharma, 'Yashpal: A People's Scientist', *Down to Earth*, 25 July 2017. Available online: https://www.downtoearth.org.in/science-technology/yashpal-a-people-s-scientist-58341.

6 U.R. Rao, 'Origins of Satellite Technology in ISRO: The Story of Aryabhata', in P.M. Rao, B.N. Suresh and Balagangadharan (eds), *From Fishing Hamlet to Red Planet: India's Space Journey*, 257–63 (New Delhi: HarperCollins Publishers India, 2015).

7 U.R. Rao, *India's Rise as a Space Power* (New Delhi: Foundation Books, 2014).

8 U.R. Rao, 'An Overview of the "Aryabhata" Project', *Proceedings of the Indian Academy of Sciences Section C: Engineering Sciences*, 1: 117–33.

9 R.M. Vasagam, 'APPLE in Retrospect', in P.M. Rao, B.N. Suresh and Balagangadharan (eds), *From Fishing Hamlet to Red Planet: India's Space Journey*, 264–74 (New Delhi: HarperCollins Publishers India, 2015).

10 Satish Dhawan to Krishnaswamy Rao Saheb, Secretary to Prime Minister Morarji Desai, 1979, File no. 17 (1278)/79, PMO, National Archives of India, New Delhi.

11 B.R. Janson and E.H. Ritchie, *Astronautics and Aeronautics, 1979-1984: A Chronology* (Vol. 4024) (Washington: National Aeronautics and Space Administration, Office of Management, Scientific and Technical Information Division, 1990).

12 T.N. Ninan and Rohini Nilekani, 'INSAT – A Damp Squib', *India Today*, 25 May 1982.

13 Guion Bluford, Interview by Jennifer Ross-Nazzal, 2004, NASA Johnson Space Center Oral History Project, Houston, NASA. Available online: https://historycollection.jsc.nasa.gov/JSCHistoryPortal/history/oral_histories/BlufordGS/BlufordGS_8-2-2004.pdf (accessed 17 May 2024).

14 Arvind Singhal and Everett M. Rogers, 'Educating Through Television', *Populi,* 16 (2): 38–47.

15 P.R. Pisharoty, 'Historical Perspective of Remote Sensing: Some Reminiscences', *Current Science* (Bangalore), 61 (3–4): 292–94.

16 George Joseph, *India's Journey towards Excellence in Building Earth Observation Cameras* (Chennai: Notion Press, 2017).

17 Habib Beary, 'India's Spy Satellite Boost', BBC, 27 November 2001. Available online: http://news.bbc.co.uk/2/hi/south_asia/1679321.stm (accessed 1 May 2024).

18 Dinesh Sharma, 'A Spy in the Sky', *Hindustan Times*, 4 November 2001.

19 Shailesh Nayak, 'Potential Fishing Zones: Science to Service', in P.M. Rao, B.N. Suresh and Balagangadharan (eds), *From Fishing Hamlet to Red Planet: India's Space Journey*, 449–52 (New Delhi: HarperCollins Publishers India, 2015).

CHAPTER 4: TO THE MOON, MARS AND VENUS

1 Madan Lal, former VSSC scientist, interview with the author, New Delhi, 2024.

2 Vikram Sarabhai, 'Statement at the Occasion of the Dedication Thumba Equatorial Rocket Launching Station at United Nations, 2nd February 1968', in Kamla Chowdhry (ed.), *India: Science Policy and National Development by Vikram Sarabhai* (New Delhi: Macmillan, 1974).

3 'Chandrayaan-1: How ISRO Got the Backing of the Nation: A Compilation', *Countdown*, 389. VSSC, Thiruvananthapuram.

4 Ibid.

5 M. Annadurai, 'The Chandrayaan-1 Spacecraft', in P.M. Rao, B.N. Suresh and Balagangadharan (eds), *From Fishing Hamlet to Red Planet: India's Space Journey*, 550–54 (New Delhi: HarperCollins Publishers India, 2015).

6 Dinesh C. Sharma, 'ISRO Battles the Truth on Moon Mission', *Mail Today*, 3 September 2009.

7 J.N. Goswami, 'Chandrayaan-1 Mission: The New Face of the Moon', in P.M. Rao, B.N. Suresh and Balagangadharan (eds), *From Fishing Hamlet to Red Planet: India's Space Journey*, 567–84 (New Delhi: HarperCollins Publishers India, 2015).

8 'India's Chandrayaan Missions Redefined Lunar Science for All', *Economic Times*, 10 October 2024.

9 V. Adimurthy, 'Concept Design and Planning of India's First Interplanetary Mission', *Current Science*, 109 (6): 1050–54.

10 'The 6th ICG 2020s Development Dialogue: The Making of India's Rocket Woman with Dr Ritu Karidhal', International Centre Goa, posted 21 May 2021, by Icggoa, YouTube, 1:24:16,

https://www.youtube.com/watch?v=5s9M-psy0Ss (accessed 29 July 2024).

11 'Mars Orbiter Mission (MOM) Is the Most Economical Interplanetary Mission in the World and Paved Way for Cost-Effective Access to Deep Space', Press Information Bureau, 18 March 2015.

12 Dinesh C. Sharma, 'ISRO's Martian Garib Rath', *Mail Today*, 13 November 2013.

13 Ibid.

14 R.V. Ramanan, former VSSC scientist, interview with the author, Chennai, 2024.

15 Ibid.

16 Ibid.

17 Ibid.

18 Dibyendu Nandi, 'Unravelling the Mysteries of the Sun', *Nature*, 31 August 2023. doi:https://doi.org/10.1038/d44151-023-00127-8.

19 'ISRO Synergises National Efforts to Study Planet Venus', ISRO, 22 May 2022, https://www.isro.gov.in/PLANETVENUS.html (accessed 1 July 2024).

CHAPTER 5: RAKESH SHARMA: INDIA'S FIRST COSMONAUT

1 Arkadii Kosmodemyansky, *Konstantin Tsiolkovsky: His Life and Work* (The Minerva Group, Inc., 2000).

2 N. Brady, 'The Geostationary Orbit and Satellite Communications: Concepts Older than Commonly Supposed', *IEEE Transactions on Aerospace and Electronic Systems*, 38 (4): 1408–09. doi: 10.1109/TAES.2002.1145764.

3 Matt Bille, 'The Satellites of Sergei Korolev', paper presented at the 41st Aerospace Sciences Meeting and Exhibit, 2003, 660.

4 Ibid.

5 James S.J. Schwartz and Tony Milligan, eds, *The Ethics of Space Exploration* (Springer International Publishing, 2016), 142–43.

6 C. Burgess and B. Vis, *Interkosmos: The Eastern Bloc's Early Space Program* (Switzerland: Springer, 2015).

7 Madhavan K. Palat, *Selected Works of Jawaharlal Nehru (15 Oct to 30 Nov 1961)*, Second Series Vol. 72 (New Delhi: Oxford University Press, 2018).

8 Research on Lunar Rock by Tata Institute of Fundamental Research, Apollo Samples, Written Answers, Parliament Digital

Library. Available online: https://eparlib.nic.in/bitstream/123456789/942885/1/04_X_15-05-1970_p20_p20_s1660.pdf#search=.

9 Anil Bhardwaj, PRL director, personal communication to the author, September 2024.

10 Welcome to Astronauts Armstrong and Conrad, Lok Sabha Debates, 23 November 1970, Parliament Digital Library. Available online: https://eparlib.nic.in/bitstream/123456789/852398/1/04_XII_23-11-1970_p4_p4_PII.pdf#search=.

11 Death of Soviet Cosmonauts, Resolution on Soyuz 11 Tragedy, Lok Sabha Debates, 1 July 1971, Parliament Digital Library. Available online: https://eparlib.nic.in/bitstream/123456789/844083/1/05_II_01-07-1971_p4_p4_PII.pdf#search=cosmonau.

12 Statement on Skylab Scare, Written Answers, 11 July 1979, Lok Sabha Debates, Sixth series, Vol. XXVIII, No. 3, Parliament Digital Library. Available online: https://eparlib.nic.in/bitstream/123456789/2202/1/lsd_06_08_11-07-1979.pdf#search=Skylab.

13 Burgess and Vis, *Interkosmos*.

14 U.R. Rao, *India's Rise as a Space Power* (New Delhi: Foundation Books, 2014).

15 Sending of Indian Cosmonaut into Space, Written Answers, Lok Sabha Debates, Seventh series, Vol. IV, No. 8, Parliament Digital Library. Available online: https://eparlib.nic.in/bitstream/123456789/2642/1/lsd_07_03_18-06-1980.pdf#search=cosmonaut.

16 Selection of Pilots for Training Abroad in Space Flights, Written Answers, 5 November 1982, Defence Minister's Replies on the Joint Flight, Parliament Digital Library. Available online: https://eparlib.nic.in/bitstream/123456789/2727097/1/07_X_05-11-1982_p125_p126_u4255.pdf#search=.

17 G. Singh, *The Indian Space Programme: India's Incredible Journey from the Third World towards the First* (Astrotalkuk Publications, 2017).

18 Rohan Abraham, 'Only One of the Two of Us Would Go Up into Space', *Economic Times*, 23 July 2019.

19 S.P.K. Gupta, 'Joint Flight', unpublished (Includes despatches and notes of S.P.K. Gupta and Dr K.S. Jayaraman of PTI).

20 Burgess and Vis, *Interkosmos*.
21 Gupta, 'Joint Flight'.
22 Ibid.
23 M.S.N. Menon and V.P. Morozov, 'Indo-Soviet Trade and Economic Ties', The Embassy of the Russian Federation, New Delhi, 1986. Available online: https://india.mid.ru/en/history/articles_and_documents/space_programme_1986/ (accessed 23 July 2024).
24 Dwayne A. Day and Asif Siddiqi, 'Something Goes Boom in the Night: The Explosion of a Cold War Secret', *Space Review*, 13 November 2023. Available online: https://www.thespacereview.com/article/4692/1 (accessed 18 January 2024).
25 Singh, *The Indian Space Programme*.
26 Gupta, 'Joint Flight'.
27 Ibid.
28 Ibid.
29 V.S. Arunachalam, *From Temples to Turbines: An Adventure in Two Worlds* (New Delhi: Defence Research and Development Organisation, 2019).
30 Gupta, 'Joint Flight'.
31 Statement Re: Sqn. Leader Rakesh Sharma Being the First Indian to Go into Space, Parliament Digital Library. Available online: https://eparlib.nic.in/bitstream/123456789/826987/1/07_XIV_04-04-1984_p5_p5_PII.pdf#search=.
32 Gupta, 'Joint Flight'.
33 S.A. Nikitin, *The Space Flight of the Soviet-Indian Crew* (No. NAS 1.15: 77615), Russian summary of the flight via NASA (NASA: Washington, 1985).
34 Gupta, 'Joint Flight'.
35 Rao, *India's Rise as a Space Power*.
36 'Conversation between Indira Gandhi and Rakesh Sharma', posted 9 May 2017, by Indian National Congress, YouTube, 5:47, https://www.youtube.com/watch?v=m4bWUIIo3qg&t=5s (accessed 23 July 2024).
37 Gupta, 'Joint Flight'.
38 'India's First Man in Space – Wing Commander Rakesh Sharma', posted 16 January 2015, by Doordarshan National, YouTube, 25:08, https://www.youtube.com/watch?v=lYU0_-O4KdY&t=1495s (accessed 23 July 2024).

39 Mahendra Ved, *@75 As I Saw It: A Reporter Recounts* (Noida: India Notebooks Pvt. Ltd, 2024).
40 Rakesh Sharma, 'Our First Space Man', *India Today*, 19 November 2018.
41 Gupta, 'Joint Flight'.
42 'Rakesh Sharma – Indian Hero of the Soviet Union', posted 9 October 2014, by AstrotalkUK, You Tube, 35:19, https://www.youtube.com/watch?v=up_ANSNTB-U (accessed 23 July 2024.).
43 Rao, *India's Rise as a Space Power.*

CHAPTER 6: KALPANA CHAWLA: A CITIZEN OF THE MILKY WAY

1 Press Information Bureau, 'President's Address to Parliament', 17 February 2003. Available online: https://archive.pib.gov.in/archive/releases98/lyr2003/rfeb2003/17022003/r170220035.html
2 'Not a Piggy-Back Ride', *Khaleej Times*, 26 January 1986.
3 Ibid.
4 P. Radhakrishnan, personal communication with the author, 2024.
5 Radhakrishnan, personal communication with the author, 2024.
6 Dilip M. Salwi, *Kalpana Chawla: India's First Woman Astronaut* (New Delhi: Rupa Publications, 2016).
7 Ibid.
8 Jean-Pierre Harrison, *The Edge of Time: The Authoritative Biography of Kalpana Chawla* (California: Harrison Publishing, 2011).
9 *Kalpana Chawla: First Indian Woman Fly to Space*, Prasar Bharati Archives, Documentary. Available online: https://www.youtube.com/watch?v=YuAza0WReww (accessed 15 June 2024).
10 Harrison, *The Edge of Time.*
11 John Uri, 'Women's History Month: Celebrating Women Astronauts 2024', NASA, 1 March 2024, https://www.nasa.gov/history/womens-history-month-celebrating-women-astronauts-2024/ (accessed 28 May 2024).
12 *Kalpana Chawla: First Indian Woman Fly to Space.*

13 J.P. Burke, *The Space Above Us*, podcast, episode 174, 'STS-87 – Stranded SPARTAN (USMP-4, SPARTAN mishap)', 2023, https://thespaceabove.us/episodes/ep174_sts-87/#transcript (accessed 15 June 2024).
14 'Kalpana Chawla's Last Conversation with Prime Minister Inder Kumar Gujral', posted 28 November 2022, by KC SPACE, YouTube, 8:45, https://www.youtube.com/watch?v=TD14Wn9Xxd8 (accessed 12 November 2024).
15 S. Mahanti, *Kalpana Chawla* (New Delhi: Publications Division, Ministry of Information & Broadcasting, 2017).
16 STS-107 Shuttle Press Kit, NASA, 2002, https://www.nasa.gov/wp-content/uploads/2023/05/2222main-sts-107-presskit.pdf?emrc=b12820 (accessed 11 June 2024).
17 'Kalpana Chawla's Father Gets Emotional while Talking about His Daughter with Tapsee Pannu', posted 25 October 2019, by Movie Talkies, YouTube, 28:09, https://www.youtube.com/watch?v=3tYx3rm_vbo (accessed 12 November 2024).
18 Anil Padmanabha, *Kalpana Chawla: A Life* (New Delhi: Puffin Books, 2003).
19 Michael Cabbage and William Harwood, 'Comm Check...The Final Flight of Shuttle Columbia', *SpaceFlight Now*, 1 February 2004. Available online: https://spaceflightnow.com/shuttle/sts107/040201commcheck/.
20 Philip Chien, *Columbia: Final Voyage* (Springer Science & Business Media, 2006).
21 'President Bush Attends Memorial Service for Columbia Astronauts', The White House, February 2003, https://georgewbush-whitehouse.archives.gov/news/releases/2003/02/20030204-1.html (accessed 12 November 2024).
22 Rakesh Sharma, 'Kalpana: The Power of Imagination', *Journal of Aerospace Sciences and Technologies*, 56 (1): 85–90.

CHAPTER 7: SUNITA WILLIAMS: MARATHONER IN SPACE

1 'About Sunita Williams Astronaut Space Journey Interview by Devang Bhatt', posted 3 June 2014, by Devang Bhat, YouTube, 24:49, https://www.youtube.com/watch?v=bCkLi9hbc9U (accessed 15 June 2024).

2 J.D. Schmahmann, 'In Memoriam: Deepak N. Pandya (December 6, 1932 to October 4, 2020)', *Journal of Comparative Neurology*, 531: 1870–72. Available online: https://doi.org/10.1002/cne.25447.

3 'About Sunita Williams Astronaut Space Journey Interview by Devang Bhatt'.

4 Ibid.

5 Basant Rawat, 'Sunita Who? Modi Turns a Blind Eye: Price of Haren Pandya Link', *Telegraph*, 21 June 2007. Available online: https://www.telegraphindia.com/india/sunita-who-modi-turns-blind-eye-price-of-haren-pandya-link/cid/972890 (accessed 15 June 2024).

6 Arvinda Anantharaman, *Sunita Williams: A Star in Space* (New Delhi: Puffin Books, 2014).

7 Ibid.

8 J.E. Catchpole, *The International Space Station: Building for the Future* (Chichester: Springer Science & Business Media, 2008).

9 'NEEMO', NASA, https://www.nasa.gov/mission/neemo/ (accessed 12 November 2024).

10 Post from Sunita Williams's blog, https://astrosuni.wordpress.com/, reproduced at 'We're Really Going', *Record Gazette*, 20 July 2007. Available online: https://www.recordgazette.net/news/were-really-going/article_8126c8e8-876e-54fa-88f1-264d76c4e88c.html.

11 Ibid.

12 Anantharaman, *Sunita Williams*.

13 Umberto Cavallaro, *Women Spacefarers: Sixty Different Paths to Space* (Springer, 2017), 298–99.

14 Anantharaman, *Sunita Williams*.

15 Ibid.

16 Post from Sunita Williams's blog, https://astrosuni.wordpress.com/.

17 Sunita Williams, 'Jack of All Trades', *NASA Blogs*, https://blogs.nasa.gov/swilliams/2012/08/01/post_1343677316053/ (accessed on 12 November 2024).

18 Cavallaro, *Women Spacefarers*.

19 Namrata Srivastava, 'NASA's Space Mission Commander Has Telangana Roots', *Telangana Today*, 31 May 2021. Available online: https://telanganatoday.com/

nasas-space-mission-commander-has-telangana-roots (accessed 15 June 2024).

20 'NASA Astronaut Anil Menon', NASA, https://www.nasa.gov/people/nasa-astronaut-anil-menon/ (accessed 15 June 2024).

21 Anil Menon (@astro_anil), X, 1 May 2022, https://x.com/astro_anil/status/1520471496442793984 (accessed 12 November 2024).

22 'Know Anil Menon, NASA's Pick for Future Space Mission', *OnManorama*, 8 December 2021. Available online: https://www.onmanorama.com/news/world/2021/12/08/know-the-malayali-anil-menon-nasa-pick-for-future-space-mission.html (accessed 15 June 2024).

23 Aswin Sekar, 'NASA's First Malayali Astronaut Has a Word for ISRO's First Malayali Astronaut', *OnManorama*, 7 March 2024. Available online: https://www.onmanorama.com/content/mm/en/kerala/top-news/2024/03/07/nasa-isro-malayali-astronaut.html (accessed 15 June 2024).

CHAPTER 8: GAGANYAAN: INDIA'S FIRST HUMAN SPACE FLIGHT

1 Press Information Bureau, 'PM Visits Vikram Sarabhai Space Center (VSSC) in Thiruvananthapuram, Kerala', 27 February 2024. Available online: https://pib.gov.in/PressReleaseIframePage.aspx?PRID=2009320.

2 Vikram Sarabhai, 'Statement at the Occasion of the Dedication Thumba Equatorial Rocket Launching Station at United Nations, 2nd February 1968', in Kamla Chowdhry (ed.), *India: Science Policy and National Development by Vikram Sarabhai* (New Delhi: Macmillan, 1974).

3 U.R. Rao, *India's Rise as a Space Power* (New Delhi: Foundation Books, 2014).

4 B.N. Suresh, ed., *Space and Beyond: Professional Voyage of K. Kasturirangan* (Singapore: Springer, 2021).

5 Madan Lal, former VSSC scientist, interview with the author, New Delhi, 2024.

6 K. Radhakrishnan, *My Odyssey: Memoirs of the Man behind the Mangalyaan Mission* (Penguin UK, 2016).

7 Radhakrishnan, *My Odyssey*.

8 Press Trust of India, 'India Not to Undertake Human Space Flight before 2017: ISRO', NDTV, 17 September 2012. Available online: https://www.ndtv.com/india-news/india-not-to-undertake-human-space-flight-before-2017-isro-499548 (accessed 15 June 2024).

9 'Space in Parliament (July-August 2018)', Department of Space, ISRO, https://www.isro.gov.in/media_isro/pdf/docs/UsefulLinks/ParliamentQuestions/monsoon_session_2018_-_eng.pdf (accessed 15 June 2024).

10 Pratul Sharma, 'Cabinet Approves Rs 10,000 Crore Gaganyaan Project', *Week*, 28 December 2018. Available online: https://www.theweek.in/news/india/2018/12/28/cabinet-approves-rs-10000-crore-gaganyaan-project.html (accessed 15 June 2024).

11 Ibid.

12 BJP Manifesto, 2019. Available online: https://www.bjp.org/files/2019-10/BJP-Election-english-2019.pdf (accessed 15 June 2024).

13 'UPA Govt Delayed Chandrayaan-2, Pushed Mangalyaan to Woo Voters before 2014 Polls: Ex-ISRO Chief', *New Indian Express*, 12 June 2019. Available online: https://www.newindianexpress.com/nation/2019/Jun/12/upa-govt-delayed-chandrayaan-2-pushed-mangalyaan-to-woo-voters-before-2014-polls-ex-isro-chief-1989309.html (accessed 15 June 2024).

14 'Glavkosmos Signed a Contract for Space Training of Indian Astronauts', Press Release, 1 July 2019, Glavkosmos. Available online: https://www.glavkosmos.com/en/glavkosmos-signed-a-contract-for-space-training-of-indian-astronauts/ (accessed 15 June 2024).

15 'Women Can Join Future Indian Human Space Missions as Astronauts, Scientists: ISRO Chief S Somanath', *Outlook India*, 22 October 2023. Available online: https://www.outlookindia.com/national/women-can-join-future-indian-human-space-missions-as-astronauts-scientists-isro-chief-s-somanath-news-326065 (accessed 15 June 2024).

16 Preeti Zachariah, 'Not Considering Women Pilots for First Gaganyaan Flight Huge Missed Opportunity', *The Hindu*, 2 July 2024. Available online: https://www.thehindu.com/

sci-tech/science/women-pilots-first-gaganyaan-flight-missed-opportunity-susmita-mohanty/article68093325.ece (accessed 15 June 2024).

17 'Gaganyaan', ISRO, 23 November 2022, https://www.isro.gov.in/Gaganyaan.html (accessed 15 June 2024).

18 Dipanjan Chaudhury Ray, 'Roscosmos Chief Reveals How Russia Is Assisting India in Gaganyaan Mission', *The Economic Times*, 12 March 2024. Available online: https://economictimes.indiatimes.com/news/india/roscosmos-chief-reveals-how-russia-is-assisting-india-in-gaganyaan-mission/articleshow/108426973.cms?from=mdr (accessed 15 June 2024).

19 'Training Footage of Vyomnauts/Gaganyaan/ISRO', posted 27 February 2024, by ISRO SpaceFlight Now, YouTube, 1:57, https://www.youtube.com/watch?v=3Gl8jYqAIoI&t=117s (accessed 15 June 2024).

20 'Gaganyaan, India's First Manned Space Mission: DFRL's Pouch Technology to Prevent Food Waste in Space', *Star of Mysore,* 9 April 2021. Available online: https://starofmysore.com/gaganyaan-indias-first-manned-space-mission-dfrls-pouch-technology-to-prevent-food-waste-in-space/ (accessed 15 June 2024).

21 'Culmination of Initial Phase of Training for Gaganyatris for Joint ISRO-NASA Mission to International Space Station', ISRO, 28 November 2024, https://www.isro.gov.in/Training_Gaganyatris_ISRO-NASA_Mission.html.

22 Pallava Bagla, 'Indian Astronaut Will Pilot Mission to International Space Station: Axiom Space', NDTV, 10 November 2024, https://www.ndtv.com/india-news/axiom-4-shubhanshu-shukla-axiom-4-indian-astronaut-will-pilot-mission-to-international-space-station-axiom-space-6982303.

23 'How First Indian Astronaut in 40 Years Is Prepping for Space', *Times of India*, 20 September 2024.

24 Vasudevan Mukunth, 'The Joint India–U.S. Mission to Fly Two Gaganyatris to the ISS | Explained', *The Hindu*, 9 August 2024. Available online: https://www.thehindu.com/sci-tech/science/the-joint-isro-nasa-mission-to-fly-two-gaganyatris-to-the-iss-explained/article68484727.ece.

CHAPTER 9: THE WAY AHEAD

1 Marta Musso, 'SpaceX's Dramatic Rocket Catch Brings Interplanetary Travel One Step Closer', *Wired*, 14 October 2024. Available online: https://www.wired.com/story/spacex-starship-super-heavy-mechazilla-catch/.
2 'ISRO Completes Its RLV Technology Demonstrations through LEX Trio', ISRO, 23 June 2024, https://www.isro.gov.in/ISRO_Completes_RLV_Technology_Demonstrations_RLV-LEX3.html.
3 'Trump Picks Billionaire Private SpaceX Astronaut Jared Isaacman to Lead NASA', Space, https://www.space.com/space-exploration/private-spaceflight/trump-picks-billionaire-private-spacex-astronaut-jared-isaacman-to-lead-nasa.
4 'Expanding Horizons in Space Sector: From Lunar Exploration to a National Space Station', Press Information Bureau, 24 September 2024. Available online: https://pib.gov.in/PressNoteDetails.aspx?NoteId=153184&ModuleId=3&reg=3&lang=1.
5 'Lunar Polar Exploration Project (LUPEX) Project Underway', JAXA, https://global.jaxa.jp/activity/pr/jaxas/no092/02.html.
6 'We're Heading for Venus: ESA Approves Envision', European Space Agency, 25 January 2024, https://www.esa.int/Science_Exploration/Space_Science/We_re_heading_for_Venus_ESA_approves_Envision.
7 'Expanding Horizons in Space Sector'.
8 'India's Space Exploration—Presentation by Indian Delegation to 67th Session of UNCOPUOS', Austria, UN Office of Outer Space Affairs. Available online: https://www.unoosa.org/documents/pdf/copuos/2024/Technical_Presentations/26Day/6_item_15_Updated_India_Space_Exploration_Roadmap_21_June_2024-edited_1.pdf.
9 'Bharatiya Anthariksh Station (BAS): Our Own Space Station for Scientific Research to Be Established with the Launch of Its First Module in 2028', Press Information Bureau, 18 September 2024. Available online: https://pib.gov.in/PressNoteDetails.aspx?NoteId=153184&ModuleId=3&reg=3&lang=1.
10 S. Somanath, Sardar Patel Memorial Lecture on Indian Space Odyssey: New Frontiers, Prasar Bharati, 26 October 2024. Available online: https://www.youtube.com/watch?v=4Fy63bgQNGE.
11 Somanath, Sardar Patel Memorial Lecture.

12 'Cabinet Clears Development of Next Generation of Satellite Launch Vehicle', Press Information Bureau, 8 September 2024. Available online: https://pib.gov.in/PressReleasePage.aspx?PRID=2055979.

13 'Prime Minister Reviews Readiness of Gaganyaan Mission', Prime Minister's Office, 23 October 2023. Available online: https://www.pmindia.gov.in/en/news_updates/pm-reviews-readiness-of-gaganyaan-mission/.

14 Ibid.

15 Basant Kumar Mohanty, 'NCERT Module Credits PM Modi for Success of Chandrayaan-3, Ignores ISRO's Track Record', *Telegraph*, 18 October 2023. Available online: https://www.telegraphindia.com/india/ncert-module-credits-pm-modi-for-success-of-chandrayaan-3-ignores-isros-track-record/cid/1974042.

16 Ajey Lele, *Asian Space Race: Rhetoric or Reality?* (Springer Science & Business Media, 2012).

17 Itty Abraham, 'Space, Technology, and Visions of National Progress in India', *Current History*, 123 (852): 123–28.

18 Ajey Lele, *Mission Mars: India's Quest for the Red Planet* (New Delhi: Springer, 2014).

19 'National Space Day 2024: Embracing India's Space Saga with a Month of Inspiring Events', Press Information Bureau, 2 August 2024. Available online: https://pib.gov.in/PressNoteDetails.aspx?NoteId=151986&ModuleId=3&reg=3&lang=1.

Bibliography

Books

Abdul Kalam, A.P.J., and A. Tiwari. *Wings of Fire: An Autobiography*. Hyderabad: Universities Press, 1999.

Anantharaman, Arvinda. *Sunita Williams: A Star in Space*. New Delhi: Puffin Books, 2014.

Anderson, R.S. *Nucleus and Nation: Scientists, International Networks, and Power in India*. Chicago: University of Chicago Press, 2019.

Annadurai, M. 'The Chandrayaan-1 Spacecraft'. In *From Fishing Hamlet to Red Planet: India's Space Journey*, edited by P.M. Rao, B.N. Suresh and Balagangadharan, 550–554. New Delhi: HarperCollins Publishers India, 2015.

Aravamudan, R. *ISRO: A Personal History*. New Delhi: HarperCollins, 2017.

Arunachalam, V.S. *From Temples to Turbines: An Adventure in Two Worlds*. New Delhi: Defence Research and Development Organisation, 2019.

Balmont, Jacques. 2015. 'Starting the Indian Space Programme'. In *From Fishing Hamlet to Red Planet: India's Space Journey*, edited by P.M. Rao, B.N. Suresh and Balagangadharan, 3–6. New Delhi: HarperCollins Publishers India.

Burgess, C., and B. Vis. *Interkosmos: The Eastern Bloc's Early Space Program*. Switzerland: Springer, 2015.

Burgess, Colin, and Chris Dubbs. *Animals in Space: From Research Rockets to the Space Shuttle*. Springer Science & Business Media, 2007.

Catchpole, J.E. *The International Space Station: Building for the Future*. Chichester: Springer Science & Business Media, 2008.

Cavallaro, Umberto. *Women Spacefarers: Sixty Different Paths to Space*. Springer, 2017.

Chien, Philip. *Columbia: Final Voyage*. Springer Science & Business Media, 2006.

Chitnis, E.V. 'Early ISRO-1961-1971'. In *From Fishing Hamlet to Red Planet: India's Space Journey*, edited by P.M. Rao, B.N. Suresh and

Balagangadharan, 20–31. New Delhi: HarperCollins Publishers India, 2015.

Dhawan, Satish. 'The Architect'. In *From Fishing Hamlet to Red Planet: India's Space Journey*, edited by P.M. Rao, B.N. Suresh and Balagangadharan, 43–52. New Delhi: HarperCollins Publishers India, 2015.

Goswami, J.N. 'Chandrayaan-1 Mission: The New Face of the Moon'. In *From Fishing Hamlet to Red Planet: India's Space Journey*, edited by P.M. Rao, B.N. Suresh and Balagangadharan, 567–584. New Delhi: HarperCollins Publishers India, 2015.

Harrison, Jean-Pierre. *The Edge of Time: The Authoritative Biography of Kalpana Chawla*. California: Harrison Publishing, 2011.

Janson, B.R., and E.H. Ritchie. *Astronautics and Aeronautics, 1979–1984: A Chronology* (Vol. 4024). Washington: National Aeronautics and Space Administration, Office of Management, Scientific and Technical Information Division, 1990.

Joseph, George. *India's Journey towards Excellence in Building Earth Observation Cameras*. Chennai: Notion Press, 2017.

Kalam, A.P.J. 'India's First Launch Vehicle'. In *From Fishing Hamlet to Red Planet: India's Space Journey*, edited by P.M. Rao, B.N. Suresh and Balagangadharan, 100–126. New Delhi: HarperCollins Publishers India, 2015.

Kosmodemyansky, Arkadii. *Konstantin Tsiolkovsky: His Life and Work*. The Minerva Group, Inc., 2000.

Mahanti, S. *Kalpana Chawla*. New Delhi: Publications Division, Ministry of Information & Broadcasting, 2017.

Muthunayagam, Abraham E. *From Space to Sea: My ISRO Journey and Beyond*. New Delhi: HarperCollins Publishers India, 2022.

———. 'Liquid Propulsion in ISRO'. In *From Fishing Hamlet to Red Planet: India's Space Journey,* edited by P.M. Rao, B.N. Suresh and Balagangadharan, 225–241. New Delhi: HarperCollins Publishers India, 2015.

Narayanamoorthy, N. 'PSLV: The Workhorse of ISRO'. In *From Fishing Hamlet to Red Planet: India's Space Journey,* edited by P.M. Rao, B.N. Suresh and Balagangadharan, 137–168. New Delhi: HarperCollins Publishers India, 2015.

Nayak, Shailesh. 'Potential Fishing Zones: Science to Service'. In *From Fishing Hamlet to Red Planet: India's Space Journey*, edited by P.M. Rao, B.N. Suresh and Balagangadharan, 449–452. New Delhi: HarperCollins Publishers India, 2015.

Padmanabha, Anil. *Kalpana Chawla: A Life.* New Delhi: Puffin Books, 2003.

Palat, Madhavan K. *Selected Works of Jawaharlal Nehru (15 Oct to 30 Nov 1961).* Second Series Vol. 72. New Delhi: Oxford University Press, 2018.

Parthasarathi, A. *Technology at the Core: Science & Technology with Indira Gandhi.* New Delhi: Pearson Education India, 2017.

Radhakrishnan, K. *My Odyssey: Memoirs of the Man Behind the Mangalyaan Mission.* Penguin UK, 2016.

Raj, Gopal. *Reach for the Stars: The Evolution of India's Rocket Programme.* New Delhi:Viking, 2000.

Rao, P.M., and P. Radhakrishnan. *A Brief History of Rocketry in ISRO.* Hyderabad: Universities Press (India) Private Limited, 2012.

Rao, U.R. *India's Rise as a Space Power.* New Delhi: Foundation Books, 2014.

———. 'Origins of Satellite Technology in ISRO: The Story of Aryabhata'. In *From Fishing Hamlet to Red Planet: India's Space Journey*, edited by P.M. Rao, B.N. Suresh and Balagangadharan, 257–263. New Delhi: HarperCollins Publishers India, 2015.

Salwi, Dilip M. *Kalpana Chawla: India's First Woman Astronaut.* New Delhi: Rupa Publications, 2016.

Sarabhai, Vikram. 'Statement at the Occasion of the Dedication Thumba Equatorial Rocket Launching Station at United Nations, 2nd February 1968'. In *India: Science Policy and National Development by Vikram Sarabhai*, edited by Kamla Chowdhry. New Delhi: Macmillan, 1974.

Schwartz, James S.J., and Tony Milligan, eds. *The Ethics of Space Exploration.* Springer International Publishing, 2016.

Singh, G. *The Indian Space Programme: India's Incredible Journey from the Third World towards the First.* Astrotalkuk Publications, 2017.

Suresh, B.N., ed. *Space and Beyond: Professional Voyage of K. Kasturirangan.* Singapore: Springer, 2021.

Vasagam, R.M. 'APPLE in Retrospect'. In *From Fishing Hamlet to Red Planet: India's Space Journey*, edited by P.M. Rao, B.N. Suresh and Balagangadharan, 264–274. New Delhi: HarperCollins Publishers India, 2015.

Ved, Mahendra. *@75 As I Saw It: A Reporter Recounts.* Noida: India Notebooks Pvt. Ltd, 2024.

Journals

Adimurthy, V. 'Concept Design and Planning of India's First Interplanetary Mission'. *Current Science* 109, no. 6 (2015): 1050–1054.

Brady, N. 'The Geostationary Orbit and Satellite Communications: Concepts Older than Commonly Supposed'. *IEEE Transactions on Aerospace and Electronic Systems* 38, no. 4 (2002): 1408–1409. doi: 10.1109/TAES.2002.1145764.

'Chandrayaan-1: How ISRO Got the Backing of the Nation: A Compilation'. *Countdown*, no. 389, September 2012. VSSC, Thiruvananthapuram.

Kochhar, R. 'Science as a Symbol of New Nationhood: India and the International Geophysical Year 1957–58'. *Current Science* 94, no. 6 (2008): 813–816.

Marsten, Richard B. 'A Dream Come True: Satellite Broadcasting'. *IEEE Transactions on Aerospace and Electronic Systems* 33, no. 1 (1997): 361–381.

Nandi, Dibyendu. 'Unravelling the Mysteries of the Sun'. *Nature*, 2023. *doi: https://doi.org/10.1038/d44151-023-00127-8.*

Pisharoty, P.R. 'Historical Perspective of Remote Sensing: Some Reminiscences'. *Current Science* (Bangalore) 61, no. 3–4 (1991): 292–294.

Sarabhai, K.V., and P. Joshi. 2020. 'Vikram Sarabhai'. *Current Science* 118 (8): 1203–1206.

Schmahmann, J.D. 'In Memoriam: Deepak N. Pandya (December 6, 1932 to October 4, 2020)'. *Journal of Comparative Neurology* 531 (2023): 1870–1872. https://doi.org/10.1002/cne.25447.

Sharma, Rakesh. 'Kalpana: The Power of Imagination'. *Journal of Aerospace Sciences and Technologies* 56, no. 1 (2004): 85–90.

Siddiqi, A.A. 'Science, Geography, and Nation: The Global Creation of Thumba'. *History and Technology* 31, no. 4 (2015): 420–451.

———. 'Whose India? SITE and the Origins of Satellite Television in India'. *History and Technology* 36, no. 3–4 (2020): 452–474.

Singhal, Arvind, and Everett M. Rogers. 'Educating Through Television'. *Populi* 16, no. 2 (1989): 38–47.

Index

About the Author

Dinesh C. Sharma is an award-winning journalist and author based in Delhi. In a career spanning close to four decades, he has written extensively on science and technology, climate change, health, environment and innovation for Indian and global media, including *The Lancet* and *Wired*. He was previously science editor at *Mail Today* and managing editor at India Science Wire. In 2008, he travelled to the Arctic and joined an international scientific expedition there to report on climate change.

He is the author of the national bestseller *Indian Innovation, Not Jugaad*. His book *The Outsourcer: The Story of India's IT Revolution* was awarded the Computer History Museum Book Prize in 2016. His most recent book is *Beyond Biryani: The Making of a Globalised Hyderabad*.

Sharma has been a Jawaharlal Nehru Fellow and also visiting faculty at the Jawaharlal Nehru University, New Delhi and at Ateneo de Manila University, Manila. He tweets on X as @dineshcsharma